THE
CORNCRAKE

AN ECOLOGY OF AN ENIGMA

FRANK RENNIE

Whittles Publishing

Published by
Whittles Publishing Ltd.,
Dunbeath,
Caithness, KW6 6EG,
Scotland, UK

www.whittlespublishing.com

© 2022 Frank Rennie
ISBN 978-184995-502-7

Printed in the UK by Cambrian Printers Ltd.

CONTENTS

FOREWORD

Beguilingly secretive, and widespread across Britain and Ireland in the nineteenth century, the decline of the Corncrake to its seemingly last posts in the Hebrides, Orkney and Ireland is both tantalising and worrying. We may lose it, and with it an embrace with a bird entwined with an agricultural landscape riveted with cultural traditions that many rightly claim are unique.

Across Europe the Corncrake has declined since the late nineteenth century, accelerating from the 1950s and wholescale by the 1970s. Mechanised grass cutting and repeated cuts for silage in spring and summer are the main culprits. The European population currently stands at around 1.3–2.1 million males, far below its pre-1970s level, but promisingly stable since 2002. The largest European population is in Russia, with more than 1 million pairs, followed by Ukraine, Poland, Lithuania and Belarus. Scotland's and Ireland's populations are tiny – but important as the most westerly global outposts.

The last survey of Corncrakes in Scotland was in 2019 and reported 872 calling males in core areas surveyed annually. This was far below the record count of 1,283 birds in 2014. Before then, the Corncrake declined to perilously low numbers in the 1980s, giving rise to a RSPB-led conservation and management programme from 1991 which, with partner and government support, led to agri-environment schemes benefiting Corncrakes. From counts of around 440 males in 1993, the population consistently increased, but now appears to be faltering again.

The backdrop to all this is detailed carefully and lucidly in the pages that follow. For many of us this book is revelatory, not least because the author has kept quiet his deep fascination and expertise on this bird. Like the Corncrake, Frank Rennie is an inhabitant of the *Gàidhealtachd*. His award-winning recent book *The Changing Outer Hebrides – Galson and the Meaning of Place* is a wonderfully intimate and scholarly account of a small village and surrounds in the north-west of the Isle of Lewis, which amongst many assets has nesting Corncrakes. Founding President of the Scottish Crofters Union (now the Scottish Crofting Foundation) and now Professor of Sustainable Rural Development in Lews Castle College in the University of the Highlands and Islands, Frank has specialist research interests in rural and community development and online learning. As we read in the Preface, without the impositions of Covid-19 it is possible this book would not have been written, for Frank has spent considerable time reading, thinking and writing about the importance of nature and culture in trying times. With more than 730 reference works, and fresh insights galore on the bird and its environment, this is a compellingly important work of reference. At its core is a penetrating cultural ecological study, which offers hope for this special bird and its landscape.

For several years in early spring, my family spent short spells on the Isle of Colonsay. Returning in the first week of May on Friday evenings, and eagerly walking on the road north on the western extremity of the island, you pass over a cattle grid, with a cemetery well in view as the road loops down to the right. In the dip, just as a tiny track heads west below Lower Kilchattan, you come to reeds standing tall by the road overlooking the scraggiest of Yellow Iris beds and rough grassland. And here, as you stop amidst the rustling reeds and listen to the sea and its boisterous waterbirds, you hear it for the first time – a rasping 'crex crex'. Just a few utterances if you are lucky. Sometimes we have seen a bird rise and flit sharply before dipping out of sight. And that's it. For days and weeks beyond, you pass this place, and hear the incessant 'crex crex', but not a bird is seen. As the vegetation flourishes into rich meadow as spring takes hold, you rarely see the birds again, but you hear them, sometimes as many as five, intermittently calling, and always further from you than you believe to be the case.

We can enjoy these special birds because some remarkable people have worked tirelessly with crofting and farming communities to snatch the Corncrake from the brink of loss. On Oronsay, reached from Colonsay by the tidal causeway called the 'The Strand', the late Mike Peacock brilliantly crafted habitats perfect for the birds, and worked tirelessly with local people to tweak agri-environment scheme practices in the Hebrides. Exceptional research and ground-breaking conservation management measures have been at the heart of attempts to recover Corncrake populations, with Professor Rhys Green prominent in leading much of it since the early 1990s. Indeed, the detailed research linking a hard-won understanding of the ecology of the Corncrake with measures to support their habitat needs is an exemplar of effective science-based conservation. In the Nene Washes in Cambridgeshire since 2002 and, more recently, the Wensum Valley in Norfolk, the Pensthorpe Conservation Trust and partners have spearheaded a reintroduction 'breed and release' programme with high hopes for a self-sustaining population in England. Yet still we have much to discover about the behavioural ecology of the species, with relatively little known about the highly reclusive females and the complex patterns of migratory movements. In his concluding chapter, Frank poses fresh questions on research and land management issues. His appeal to develop 'Corncrake tourism' as a contributor to rural economies and culture is important and could have wider resonance as we strive to restore nature and communities in rural areas – not as separate entities, but entwined.

I write this on the Isle of Harris in early June, having spent time around Northton Beach, enjoying the rasping '*crex crex*' amid the wonderful soundtrack of breeding Lapwing, Redshank, Oystercatcher, Ringed Plover, Dunlin, gulls and terns. These are sounds enlivened by sea airs, rampant cloud formations and mind-opening landscapes which proclaim a uniquely important place. The Corncrake is quintessentially part of this, and we must not lose it.

Professor Des Thompson FRSE
June 2021 on the Isle of Harris

The Corncrake

LIST OF FIGURES

Colour section

Photos 1–10 are by John A. Love

Photos 11–13 are courtesy of Fiona Rennie @sradagcreative

PREFACE

This book is the product of a long-term gestation, but it would possibly never have seen the light of day without the added stimulus of a full year during the Covid-19 pandemic when travel was restricted, family holidays cancelled, and the luxury made available of simply being at home to think and write.

My fascination with the Corncrake has spanned several decades, and I am one of the lucky people to have been able to open my window, both at home and (separately) at work, and hear the unmistakable *Crex crex* call of summer Corncrakes each year. When I met colleagues at Stornoway airport, they would be delighted to hear a Corncrake call from somewhere in the long grass on the airfield. Their first reaction was often that Corncrakes seemed to be everywhere and, for many years, a long time ago, that was almost true. There are lots of local stories told to me by crofting families of their experiences with *their* Corncrakes, for despite the annoying tendency to call all night outside your bedroom window, a great many people have a special affection for this species. In some inexplicable way, it has become a potent symbol of a previous rural lifestyle, an icon of the crofting communities of the north-west of Scotland, as well as a *cause celebre* for environmental conservation. There was only a slow realisation that this species has a widespread breeding range, covering most of the northern European countries and extending into eastern Russia and western Asia.

In all of these areas, the Corncrake continues to face challenges to its survival as a species. In following the emerging story of its ecology, through personal notebooks, scientific writing and discussions with colleagues, two things in particular surprised me. First, that although so much has been written about the Corncrake, so little is readily accessible to ordinary amateur naturalists. A second surprise is that much of the detailed understanding of this species is only a recent revelation and is a story that many people are still revealing – even as you read this book. Some of the very basic, important and fascinating details of Corncrake ecology have been discovered within the lifetime of our own children, and much still remains to be clarified. In that respect, this book is part of an evolving narrative. In some aspects of its ecology, I have deliberately avoided dogmatism. The exact population figures of the Corncrake within a particular country or location, for instance, although important in terms of the historical record and for future conservation actions, will have changed soon after the publication of this book. Those figures will continue to change in response to local and transnational circumstances, and so we owe it to ourselves to keep abreast of the changing population dynamics and the political and scientific responses, *as they are happening*, rather than simply retrospectively. We also have an imperative to analyse and attempt to understand these trends, and the causes and effects of the ecosystem properties within which the Corncrake lives and breeds – this needs to include a proper understanding of the human relationship with the whole landscape.

Although each of us might regard these birds with a certain amount of geographical and proprietary interest, this is really an international and a transnational story. It is a story of global importance, and it is still developing. I have watched, listened to and read about the ecology of the Corncrake in a dozen different countries. I have tried to relate this information back to what it can tell us about the management of the Hebridean landscape, and what it might mean for the likely future of these intriguing, frustrating and sometimes comical birds.

The Corncrake is essentially a bird of grasslands, but there the generalisation ends. They inhabit the unmown fields of crofts in the Highlands and Islands of Scotland before the climate reluctantly permits the harvest of the hay or silage that will be so valuable for winter fodder. In Alpine meadows or the extensively managed pastureland of Hungary and Central Europe, and in quiet rural corners of Ireland, Sweden, Netherlands, Germany and other countries where traditional agricultural practices are still followed, the Corncrake retains a presence. Most of us do not even think about, let alone observe, the activities of Corncrakes as they pass through Egypt or north-west Africa or as they enjoy their second summer (what we in boreal regions of the north inappropriately term their 'winter quarters', ignoring the fact that it is we who remain for the winter and that the Corncrake flies south to exploit another summer in the southern hemisphere).

The Corncrake lacks the awesome majesty of most raptors in full flight, or the aerial dexterity of Swallows and Swifts. They do not nest in ostentatious numbers in 'seabird cities' covering cliff-faces and offshore islands that leave us staggered by their complexity and the vibrancy of their movements. Sometimes they can make us smile at their apparently self-conscious activities as they peer out cautiously from knee-high sward or waddle jerkily in exposed areas between patches of desirable shelter. Nevertheless, the Corncrake has become a powerful symbol to many people, representing the best of traditional low-input/low-output agricultural management that has not simply sacrificed the long-term ecological health of the landscape for short-term financial gain.

The fact that the Corncrake is such an unobtrusive, retiring species is both its attraction and its potential undoing. Understanding the ecology of this bird from the scientific evidence available to us, including its place in the ecosystem (regional and global) and its significance as an icon representing a certain form of rural lifestyle and human ecology, will be the subject of the rest of this book. The curious thing, as many scientists will quickly tell you, is that the more we seem to discover about a subject, the less we actually know and the more we realise how much we still have to learn. Understanding the ecology of the Corncrake is such a subject.

Chapter 2

The Corncrake in the Rallidae family

Fossil records

The Corncrake has been classified by biologists as part of the family Rallidae – the rails and coots. In a checklist of the birds of the world (Howard and Moore, 1980), a total of 122 species are listed in this family, of which 56 species were further divided into 252 recognised subspecies. Three of those subspecies were noted as already being extinct. By the time this book is published, over 40 years later, it should not surprise anyone if the breakdown of this classification has already altered, as new and more precise genetic data becomes available and as the science of DNA comparison becomes more exact. Nor should it surprise anyone if more of those subspecies listed are now extinct. A few names will possibly be added to the list as new fossil discoveries are made in geological deposits that are not yet fully explored.

To begin to understand the Corncrake and its near relations, we must first understand its history – not just the recent history, but the whole phylogeny. The first birds appeared in the Mesozoic, about 140 million years ago (mya), but really it is not until the Cenozoic (the last 66 million years to the present) that there are reasonably numerous and complete fossils (lightweight, hollow bones are easily susceptible to damage and destruction) that can be linked to extant bird species. Fossil rails fall reasonably neatly into one of two categories: those for which identification has been made on only a few remaining bones or skeletal fragments, and those which have become extinct within relatively recent times and for which there are reasonably whole skeletons.

In an early work that compiled the existing knowledge of fossil Rallidae (Olson, 1977) it was noted that although the earliest known Rallidae were found in geological deposits of the Lower Eocene (around 50 mya), it is not until the Upper Oligocene or Lower Miocene (20–

30 mya) that recognisable rails with similarities to modern Rallids make their appearance. It is possible that rails may have existed earlier than the Eocene, but there is no clear evidence, although DNA studies seems to indicate that the rails diverged from other Gruiform groups as early as 86 mya in the Upper Middle Cretaceous (Sibley and Ahlquist, 1985). Even here, the exact relationship to modern bird species is unclear because the deductions have been made from fragmentary evidence of tibiotarsi (upper leg bones) alone, and so there is no certain way of knowing exactly what the whole bird looked like. Several promising contenders for the earliest Crake have been identified, however, including *Creccoides osbornii* (a 'crake-like bird') from the Upper Cenozoic of Texas (Shufeldt, 1892), *Rallicrex kolozsvarensis* from the Middle Oligocene of Romania (Lambrecht, 1933; said to be intermediate between the *Rallus* and *Crex* genera) and two rails from the Eocene of Colorado and Wyoming (Wetmore, 1931), named *Eocrex primus* (the Crake of the Eocene) and *Palaeorallus troxelli*, which appeared to be slightly larger than the modern Clapper Rail (*Rallus longirostris*). Wetmore (1957) also noted what is probably the earliest large *Rallus* in North America, *Rallus phillipsi*, from the Mid-Pliocene (5.5 mya) of Arizona (Taylor and van Perlo, 1998), which was described as appearing similar to the Clapper Rail, but slightly smaller. Comparing taxonomic data with known fossil and extinct Rallidae (Boev, 2015), a fossil of *Porzana botunensis* was identified from the Early Pleistocene of Bulgaria as possibly a close relative of the Spotted Crake (*Porzana porzana*) and the comparable measurements were tabulated. This discovery added to the already-known Late Pleistocene records of Corncrake remains from cave deposits in western Bulgaria (Boev, 2000). Archaeological excavation in the Liège area of Belgium (also protected in cave deposits) revealed fossils of the Spotted Crake and the Corncrake among Quaternary deposits dated around 30,000 years ago, and again around 9,500 years ago, in what the stratigraphy suggests were open moors and grasslands in a cool, temperate climate (Groessens van Dyck, 1989). Based on available evidence, it seems probable that the ancestral habitat of the Corncrake was in mesotrophic lowland wetlands with a mosaic of vegetational patches, similar to the floodplains currently found in Belarus, Ukraine and Croatia (Flade, 1997).

The earliest well-represented distinct Rallidae are currently *Belgirallus oligocaenus* and *Belgirallus minutus* from the earliest Oligocene deposits of Belgium (Mayr, 2009). The former appears similar to a fossil rail from the early Oligocene of Germany, and this species is similar in size to the modern Water Rail (*Rallus aquaticus*).

The Rallid fossil records from the Quaternary (2.588 mya to the present) are much better represented, partially as a result of their very successful colonisation of oceanic islands (although this was largely accompanied by a loss of flight, which may have helped the birds to conserve energy, but left them more vulnerable to predation and extinction). Of a discovery on the island of New Amsterdam, it was recorded that:

> *'A mummy of a small rail was discovered in a tunnel in a lava flow, under a block that had no doubt protected it from moisture. A sketch was made in situ,*

as well as taking measurements of the beak (22 mm), the tarsus (40) and the middle toe without claw (34), but the mummy fell to dust when an attempt was made to pick it up. In this case one cannot infer the former existence of a rail peculiar to New Amsterdam, although it would be perfectly likely (endemic species of this order exist on most isolated islands), for the measurements cited coincide with those of a skin of a Corncrake (Crex crex Linnaeus) in the British Museum collected 100 miles to the south of Madagascar. Still, this identification is not wholly satisfactory: the mummy did not have the bulk nor the heavy bill of a Corncrake, and it is most regrettable not to have been able to remove it.'

(Olson, 1977)

The wide dispersal of rails across the islands of the tropical Pacific was accompanied by a high rate of extinction, and it has been estimated that possibly 2,000 extinct species of birds previously lived in this region, a majority of which were flightless rails (Steadman, 1995). In Fiji, it has been noted that at least seven sympatric Rails (the same species which evolved differently until they could no longer interbreed) once coexisted in the largest island of Viti Levu, the descendants of which are 'now restricted to the infrequent occurrences of two crakes' (Worthy, 2004). From the Balearic islands of the Spanish Mediterranean, a fossil Corncrake (*Crex crex*) has been recovered from the Upper Pleistocene (around 126,000–11,700 years ago) and also from other Mediterranean deposits (Alcover et al., 2005). A more recent date in the Late Holocene has been attributed to a Water Rail (*Rallus aquaticus*) from Croatia (Sršen et al., 2017), although this bird was possibly a passage migrant, as was a specimen from Israel (Sánchez-Marco et al., 2016). Overall, these are relatively rare and recent fixes on an elusive species. It appears that the phylogeny of this species is as difficult to locate in geological time as the individuals currently in the field, although this has been ascribed (Mayr, 2009) to the low number of specialists studying the subject, rather than a low number of fossils. Just north of Dublin, at a dig at Raytown, County Meath, archaeologists discovered a large amount of Corncrake bones among those of more typical farm animals, suggesting that around AD 500–800, Corncrakes were eaten in early Medieval Ireland (Macconnell, 2008).

What is clear, is that the early fossil record of birds is currently much less commonly understood than that of their contemporary mammals, and the presence of most Rallid fossils tells us little about their evolutionary history other than confirming their geological and palaeogeographical presence. Although a great many fossil rails have been recognised globally, the current evidence is often based on fragmentary remains, and only (at best) provides very tenuous affinities with the rails currently extant (Mayr, 2009).

THE CLASSIFICATION OF THE CORNCRAKE

The classification of the Corncrake in the biological kingdom of fauna is both predictably complex and deceptively simple. To deal with the complexity first, among the class Aves (birds) the Corncrake belongs to the order Gruiformes (crane-like birds including crakes, coots and the gallinules) and the family Rallidae (rails). Part of the initial difficulty is that the order Gruiformes has been used historically as a bit of a 'dumping ground' for families and species of birds that appear to resemble waders but do not seem to fit neatly into any other order. This has resulted in a huge diversity and distribution of bird forms within the order, and a corresponding variety in morphology, habitat and behaviour. As we have seen, the fossil record of rails is patchy and often based upon very fragmentary remains, with the results that the relationships between many of the species in the order remain poorly resolved. There are 10–12 bird families currently recognised within the Gruiformes, depending upon which authority you follow, but most authorities agree that:

> 'The order Gruiformes, for which even familial composition remains contro-
> versial, is perhaps the least well understood avian order from a phylogenetic
> perspective.'

> (Livezey, 1998)

The Rallidae comprise the largest family in the Gruiformes, numbering around 135 species (again the number varies with different authorities and the diversity of the evidence used to support the basis of classification), and have the greatest geographical distribution and taxonomic complexity of all the families in this order. The difficulties of identifying firm relationships within the Rallidae, as well as natural subdivisions within the family, have been repeatedly acknowledged, and several groupings that are currently recognised remain tentative. Most recent classifications of the Rallidae recognise the Nkulengu Rail as probably the most primitive species in the family; thereafter a few assumptions have been made. Representatives of the Rallidae are spread over all major continental regions except Antarctica, and although their choice of habitat may vary (see Chapter 4), they have one of the widest geographical distributions among the families of terrestrial vertebrates (Olson, 1973). A key paper (Livezey, (1998) that comprehensively analyses the comparative morphology of the Rallidae using osteological characters, but incorporates specimen re-investigation as well as an exhaustive literature search, confirmed the conclusion of earlier work that:

> 'one of the difficulties of rallid taxonomy arises from the relative homogeneity
> of the family, rails for the most part being rather generalized birds with few
> groups having morphological modifications that clearly define them.'

> (Olson, 1973)

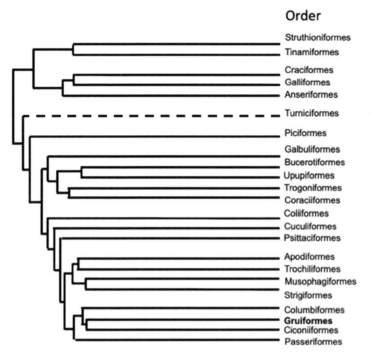

Figure 2.1:
Phylogenetic
relationships of the
23 orders of birds,
reconstructed
from DNA–DNA
hybridization
measurements.
Source: Redrawn
from Brenowitz
(1991) after Sibley
et al. (1988).

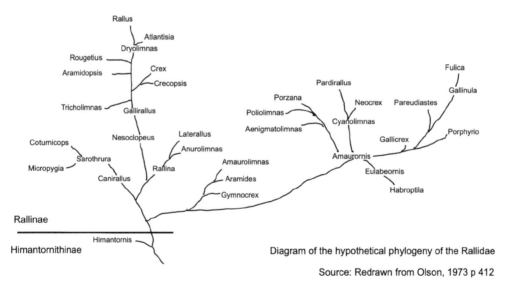

Figure 2.2: Diagram of the hypothetical phylogeny of the Rallidae.
Source: Redrawn from Olson (1973, p. 412).

An early attempt at classification noted that:

'The gradual transition from typical Rails to Crakes... and from Crakes to Gallinules... was so marked that it was impossible to say where the Rails ended and the Crakes began, or where the Crakes ended and the Gallinules began.'

(Sharpe, 1893)

A study using mitochondrial genetics (Ramirez, 2014), estimated that the origin and initial diversification of the Rallidae occurred during the Middle Eocene, about 40.5 mya, and ascribes the apparent conflict between fossil and molecular dates as 'simply explained by the incomplete fossil record'. On the face of it, this is a very reasonable assumption, and will probably stand until a wider and deeper appreciation of the genetic architecture of the whole family is better understood. It is worth noting that Taylor and van Perlo (1998), in their *Rails: A Guide to the Rails, Crakes, Gallinules, and Coots of the World*, recorded that, 'Four new living rail species, all from islands and at least two flightless, have been described in the last 20 years [since the late 1970s]' and added that, 'the chances are good that other species await discovery on poorly known small islands'.

Notwithstanding the complications of its phylogeny, and the controversies in the academic literature over its evolutionary history, the Corncrake can also be viewed as having a relatively straightforward classification. Within the Rallidae, the Corncrake is in the genera *Crex* and the species named *Crex crex*. Until very recently, *Crex crex* was the single species in the genera, and although the African Crake was generally considered to be its closest living relative, the latter had been named *Crecopsis egregia* (or, indeed, *Ortygometra egregia* or *Porzana egregia* at various times) before being reclassified as *Crex egregia* according to modern nomenclature. Now, because lots of documents differ, you might see the genera of this species referred to as either *Crex* or *Crecopsis*. Both the Corncrake and the African Crake are short-billed, with a preference for grassland rather than the wetland habitats of most other rails. From the evidence currently available, it appears that the *Porzana* crakes, especially the Ash-throated Crake, are near relatives of the genus *Crex* (Livezey, 1998).

Initially named *Rallus crex* by Linnaeus (Linnaeus, 1758), and despite a brief flirtation with the name *Crex pratensis* (Bechstein, 1803), the Corncrake has long been identified as the species *Crex crex*, family Rallidae, order Gruiformes. There are no subspecies of *Crex crex*, and no significant variations between individuals in the huge geographical extent of the area in which the species has been recorded (although individuals from the east may appear slightly paler). Unusually, the scientific name of the bird is an onomatopoeic rendition of its territorial call (see Chapter 9).

Despite its obscure origins and disputed pedigree, *Crex crex* is (largely) in a class of its own.

The diagram above, (Figure 2.2) while proposed at a time before the Corncrake and the African Crake were regarded as belonging to the same genera, is still a good schematic representation of the Corncrake 'family tree'.

CONCLUSION

The fossil record of rails extends far back into the geological record, but the current ability to trace the direct lineage of the contemporary Corncrake is indistinct. Along with its close living relative, the African Crake, the Corncrake is included in a very small and distinct genus that has no extant subspecies.

Concluding:

A mystery still to men and boys
Who know not where they lay
And guess it but a summer noise
Among the meadow hay

(Clare, 2004)

An earlier English poet, Andrew Marvell, in a longer poem relating to a country estate in Yorkshire, notes with grim detail in the 50th verse the death of a Corncrake chick by a scythe during the grass harvest, presaging the devastating changes still to unfold (Marvell, 1651). Unsurprisingly, the Corncrake also features in Irish poetry, such as '*Corncrakes*' by Louis MacNeice, in which he compared their 'unmusical' voice to being:

'*Like loud men around the corner*
Whom we never see but whose raucous
Voices can give us confidence.'

(Dodds, 1966)

Another Irish poem, '*The Silly Treun*', rehashes a popular tale that is told in several cultures (often about a Wren) of a small bird that tries to demonstrate its strength by lying on its back and 'holding up the sky' with its feet (Smith and Ó Laoire, 2009). In the nineteenth century and earlier, in common with many migrating bird species, there was often doubt whether the bird migrated at all, or if it simply remained hidden (or other fanciful stories of birds changing shape – or even species!). For instance, the discovery of a vagrant (probably sick) Corncrake hiding in a hole in the stone wall of a farm in Orkney in 1806 prompted speculation on whether it was hibernating or merely a solitary exception to migration (Ręk and Osiejuk, 2011a). Incidentally, this 'folk-tale' pre-empts more modern 'scientific' observations of the same phenomenon (see Chapter 11). In other areas, it was thought that Corncrakes hitched a lift with other birds because of their apparently poor flying skills, and being frequently seen in the company of flocks of Quail, it was nicknamed 'The King of the Quail' (a name still common in mainland Europe; Hull, 2001). The 1716 publication of *A Description of the Western Isles of Scotland* by Martin Martin, who was a remarkable traveller from the Isle of Skye, noted that:

'*The bird Corn-Craker is about the bigness of a Pigeon, having a longer neck, and being of a brown colour, but blacker in harvest than in Summer: the natives say it lives by the water, and under ice in Winter and Spring.*'

(Martin, 1716)

ARCHAEOLOGY AND ART

Although the presence of the Corncrake in archaeology is typically just as elusive as the contemporary Corncrake in tall grass, there is evidence that the Corncrake has been a familiar species to human society for millions of years. Bones of this species have been recovered from the Middle Pleistocene in the Qesem Cave in Israel (Sánchez-Marco et al., 2016), from the Walou Cave in France from the time of the early *Homo sapiens* (Groessens van Dyck, 1989) and from the Late Pleistocene of Bulgaria (Boev, 2000). They have been familiar to humans in the Scottish islands for at least the past 5,000 years, and the bones of ancient Corncrakes have been found, sparingly, throughout these islands from a wide swathe of prehistory. Remains have been recovered from the Neolithic farmhouse at the Knap of Howar – possibly the oldest preserved stone house in northern Europe – in the Orcadian island of Papa Westray (Ritchie, 1983; Mccormick et al., 2003), from several Iron Age sites, and from the Norse farmstead at Bornais in the Isle of South Uist in the Outer Hebrides (Best, 2013). The avian diet of those early settlers consisted mainly of seabirds, waterfowl or waders, but the remains of an uncommon species such as Corncrakes appears to indicate that the human diet was varied. As noted in the previous chapter, Corncrakes appear to have been eaten at a few localities in early Medieval Ireland, and several seventeenth to nineteenth century writers noted that the Corncrake was a favoured culinary item, recording in a ninth century poem that:

> 'The value of the bird as foodstuff is also suggested by the inclusion of two corncrakes as part of a ransom to be paid for Cormac MacAirt.'
>
> (Macconnell, 2008)

There is no firm proof that Corncrakes were harvested in Scotland for human food at this time, but the presence of their bones in several prehistoric kitchen middens would seem to indicate that they were at least an occasional delicacy. The uncle of William MacGillivray was undoubtedly planning to eat the Corncrake that he had trapped, and the inclusion of a recipe for 'Roast Landrail or Corn-Crake' in the famous cookery book by the eponymous Mrs Beeton, published in 1861, would indicate that the Victorians were not averse to its taste (Beeton, 1861). Part of the reason is because until the various iterations of the Parliamentary Acts for the Protection of Wild Birds, the Corncrake was considered to be a gamebird and was frequently shot, often as it flew with flocks of Quail, as it still is in some places.

It might be argued that the Corncrake features at some modest level in the cultural perspectives of the societies in most of the countries that it passes through, from the north of Europe and western Asia, to the south of Africa. Even the custom of hunting and trapping in Iran, Egypt and historically in other countries (see Chapter 11) acknowledges the cultural interconnectedness between humans and Corncrakes. A more conservation-minded celebration of international culture is perhaps suggested by the various representations of the Corncrake on items such as postage stamps. As examples of applied art, some of these postal representations are miniature masterpieces and, up to 2020, there are 16 countries that have produced images of the Corncrake on their national stamps. As might be expected, they are mostly produced by countries where the species is familiar to the public, mainly in Europe, although two countries in Africa (Chad and Zambia) have also celebrated the Corncrake in their postal art.

CONCLUSION

Although the elusive behavioural characteristics of Corncrakes have resulted in only relatively rare observations of individuals, there is ample evidence from folklore, literature and recorded history that their long-term association with humans is well known. Their behaviour, especially their distinctive call, has often added a touch of mystery and romance to the species, and its presence has come to be closely aligned with the rural idyll of small-scale agriculture which is practised in a traditional style.

CHAPTER 4

CORNCRAKES IN THE LANDSCAPE

At its most simple, the Corncrake is a bird that favours grasslands. Considering the fossil evidence, the Eocene/Oligocene transition was accompanied by a drop in mean temperature, a massive extinction event, and global changes in vegetation, which included the spread of open areas of grassland. It seems that many bird species adapted to these new conditions, with the result that wet grasslands seem to be the most likely ancestral habitat of the early Rallidae, and of their modern survivors (Ramirez, 2014). Although the Rallidae as a family have adapted with versatility to inhabit a wide range of habitats from the Arctic Circle to the tip of South America (Ripley, 1976), the Corncrake is rather more specific. The preferred nature and location of the Corncrake grasslands vary within fairly narrow limitations to include slightly drier or more moist landscapes, some altitudinal differences and the predominance of a small range of plant species, but the common factor throughout is grassland. They tend to be found in cool, moist grass, 15–50 cm tall but rarely less than 10 cm in height (Wotton et al., 2015) and usually avoid open ground and rocky areas (Taylor and van Perlo, 1998). Wetland meadows that fringe rivers, marshes and peatland are often considered as acceptable habitat, as are grassy clearances in forests and mountain pastures with low-intensity agricultural management (Green, Rocamora et al., 1997).

Although they might not immediately spring to mind as particularly strong fliers, Corncrakes manage to cover impressive geographical distances in their travels. As we move further west from the oceanic islands of the Outer Hebrides into the enormous grassland habitats of Asia, the local details of Corncrake ecology become less well documented, less observed and, frequently, quite unknown in some areas. The distribution and population status of the Corncrake will be explored in more detail in Chapter 6, but to appreciate the subtleties in this geographical variation, the global spread of habitats, the distribution of the species and the regional population fluctuations will be split into four main regions for descriptive purposes.

These regions are only for the convenience of the narrative here; they are not hard-and-fast boundaries, nor do they have any specific political or land management implications beyond the obvious distinctions of being different topographical and climatic regions. There are sometimes as many significant differences within these broad regions as there are between them, and so the 'divisions' need to be treated carefully.

The four general regions are:

1. Western Europe
2. Eastern Europe and western Asia
3. South-eastern Africa
4. The vast areas between Europe and southern Africa

As might be expected from examining the fossil evidence (see Chapter 2):

'The geographic origins of the Rallidae have been obscured by the antiquity, cosmopolitan distribution, and inadequate taxonomy of the family.'

(Olson, 1973)

This same study was of the opinion that the largest number of species, the greatest number of particular genera and the most primitive members of the Rallidae are to be found in the Old World tropics, and it believed that those ancestral rails were forest dwellers, with the family having only secondarily adapted to aquatic environments (Olson, 1973). Later studies, however, dispute this and suggest that:

'Of modern Rallidae, only a minority of genera… [including the Corncrake]… include members having distributions incorporating (at least seasonally) significant northern-hemisphere components. [It concludes that] A southern-hemisphere origin appears likely for the Rallidae, at least on the basis of distributions of modern representatives.'

(Livezey, 1998)

This ambiguity relating to the first Corncrakes even merited a guest appearance in the classic scientific text of Charles Darwin, *On the Origin of Species*, in which, building his discussion of biological form and function, he drew attention to the fact that:

'What seems plainer than that the long toes, not furnished with membrane, of the Grallatores [an obsolete classification, now replaced, mainly, with the

Ciconiiformes] are formed for walking over swamps and floating plants? The water-hen [Moorhen] and the landrail [Corncrake] are members of this order, yet the first is nearly as aquatic as the coot, and the second nearly as terrestrial as the quail or partridge. In such cases habits have changed without a corresponding change of structure.'

(Darwin, 1994)

Regardless of the phylogeny, more recent studies have concluded from the accumulated evidence provided by extant taxa, that wetland and grassland appear to be the predominant ancestral habitat rather than forest (Ramirez, 2014). Let us begin our look at Corncrake habitats from that perspective.

WESTERN EUROPE

There are minor variations in habitat type across the countries of western Europe but due to the human population density and general accessibility of the landscape, this diversity is relatively well documented. The mention of Corncrakes has become closely associated with the discussion of hay meadows and, in more recent years, with the production of silage and haylage, and this relationship with land management will be discussed more fully in Chapter 12. To take a contemporary overview, Corncrakes in the UK are almost entirely confined to the north-western islands of the Outer Hebrides and some of the Inner Hebrides of Scotland. This is the landscape that I know best, and it is as good a place as any to begin looking at the detailed complexity of Corncrake habitats.

A seminal study in 1978–79 recorded that from a total of 730–750 calling Corncrakes:

All but 12 of these birds were north of the Scottish border, with the Outer and Inner Hebrides accounting for 37% and 34% of the total, respectively, and Orkney 15%.'

(Cadbury, 1980a)

By 1988, the population had declined to 551–596 males, with only four calling Corncrakes recorded in England, and 88–98% of these males in the Inner and Outer Hebrides (54% in the Outer Hebrides alone; Newton, 1991). Land use in the Hebrides is traditionally dominated by extensive low-intensity crofting agriculture that has an emphasis on small units of individually-tenanted land called crofts. Within each of these crofts there has traditionally been an even smaller-scale mosaic of vegetational variety that creates a patchwork of biodiversity (Rennie, 1991). In the north of the Isle of Lewis in the Outer Hebrides, entire crofts are often only 1–2 hectares (3–5 acres), and although other crofting areas such as the islands of South Uist or Tiree in the Inner Hebrides may have slightly larger field sizes, these are never the huge areas of intensive industrialised monoculture that is now the norm for agriculture on the UK mainland. Although the summer months of the north-west have short nights with almost continuous daylight, the growing season is short. The position of the islands at the junction of the European landmass and the oceanic influence of the Atlantic mean warm, but not hot, summers and mild winters, with frequent high winds in any month. This has important ramifications for land management and will be addressed later.

In this landscape, when Corncrakes first appear from their African migration they tend to prefer to shelter in stands of Yellow Iris or Meadow-sweet (Harvie-Brown and Buckley, 1888), or among clusters of Soft Rush or Compact Rush, or indeed among almost any other tall herbaceous vegetation (Newton, 1991). That these plants frequently demarcate the lines of fences and ditches that link suitable foraging habitat can be as important as the height of the vegetation and afford potential lines of escape when birds are disturbed (Brown, 1938). As soon as other vegetation is tall enough to provide cover, the birds move out to forage in adjacent hay fields, (silage is more common now). After cutting, they seek shelter among plots of cereals and the unfenced sandy grassland known as machair (Angus, 2001) along the western oceanic edge of the islands (Stowe and Hudson, 1988). In the 1978–79 Corncrake survey, around 61% of all calling birds were recorded from areas of grass that were intended to be cut for hay or silage, but in the Outer Hebrides almost half of the birds were in marshy areas that included Yellow Iris, and/or Common Reed (Cadbury, 1980a). In some areas, such as the Inner Hebrides, this might also include rough vegetation containing Common Nettle, Butterbur, Reed Canary-grass, Compact Rush and/or Hogweed (Green and Stowe, 1993). Again, the fact that these plant species are relatively tall (and taller than the early-season grassland) is the most likely reason that Corncrakes exploit them for shelter in the first few weeks after their arrival. Hayfields and marshy areas seem to be the nesting territories of choice, rather than unimproved grassland or ungrazed permanent pastures (Swann, 1986). By July, the Iris is hardly used at all, and most birds occupy the taller grass of the hay fields until these are harvested, or the adjacent cereal crops that provide cover from taller vegetation (Green, 1996). Almost all second clutches are established in the hay fields (Stowe and Hudson, 1988).

More than three-quarters of recorded Corncrakes in the Hebrides and Orkney were in 'improved' grassland rather than 'natural' meadows, but this should come as no surprise since the climate and soils of the region have long required reseeding and liming with sand to promote the growth of grass suitable for grazing or harvesting. A small number of Corncrakes have been recorded calling from cereal crops, particularly Oats, and from patches of Marram Grass or Heather, but these are probably only temporary territories. In most areas of improved grasslands, White Clover, Perennial Rye-grass, Cock's-foot and Common Cat's-tail are commonly the dominant species locally. Although there may be a great deal of regional variation, the areas of grassland that have not been specifically improved for agriculture frequently contain Sorrel, Meadow Buttercup, Bird

Vetch, Yellow-rattle and/or Yorkshire-fog as the dominant vegetation (Cadbury, 1980a). Unmown or ungrazed grass that is dense and difficult to navigate is generally avoided (Niemann, 1995).

Outwith the Hebrides, swampy grassland was a common habitat frequented by Corncrake, but possibly only because the majority of other fields seemed unattractive to birds as the grass was kept too short, for example with close grazing, to provide safe cover. This was almost certainly the case in England (Norris, 1947) where it was noted that after the hay had been cut Corncrakes would move out of the marshy areas into cereal crops of Barley, Oats and sometimes Wheat. Although Corncrakes have been extremely scarce in England for many years, if not completely extinct, the population in Ireland, though reduced, has remained in landscape not dissimilar to the western Highlands and Islands of Scotland. In addition to frequenting lush river meadows, calling males in Ireland have been recorded in spring from areas of Reed Canary-grass and other marshy patches (Cadbury, 1980a), before following their familiar behavioural pattern of moving into adjacent hay meadows (Stowe et al., 1993). Localities such as the Shannon Callows may be preferred because flooding often delays the time of grass cutting due to the inability of the ground to support tractors (Green, 1996). The Shannon Callows is historically one of the three core areas where Corncrakes have been common in Ireland, along with Mayo/West Connacht and North Donegal. Their presence has been encouraged by the fact that hay is still the most common crop in the Callows, and the regular flooding of the ground frequently ensures that the grass is cut late in the season (McDevitt and Casey, 1999).

Elsewhere in western European countries, Corncrakes select similar habitats to occupy, essentially cool, damp grasslands, including Alpine meadows and the fringes of moorland or marshy areas (Taylor and van Perlo, 1998). In Central Europe, birds arriving in Germany, Poland and Croatia select areas of Iris, as well as rough stands of fescues and sedges, and may immediately take up territories there to start breeding (Flade, 1991a). In some areas, abandoned land, as well as fields of cereals, Rape and fodder plants may also be occupied, and this is documented to be similar in Scandinavia. The changing structure of abandoned agricultural land usually provides an increased density for at least 5–10 years (BirdLife International, 2015) of ground-level vegetation which is favoured as a breeding habitat for Corncrakes, but there are indications that this abandonment also attracts mammalian predators (see Chapter 11), and so increased breeding might not lead to increased survival rates of the young (Arbeiter and Franke, 2018). In Finland, Corncrakes have been recorded in wet meadows near lakes (Asikainen, 1999), in the vicinity of cultivated meadows associated with arable cultivation and, to a lesser extent, in fields of Rye (Haartman, 1958). In this northern region, the species population has had a dramatic decline during the twentieth century and, as birds become less numerous and more difficult to locate, the subtleties of the habitat selection of the remaining population are problematic to establish in detail (Asikainen, 1999).

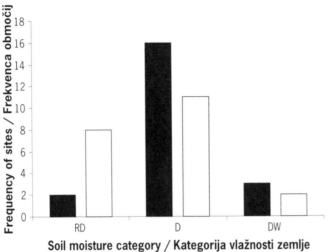

Figure 4.3: *Soil moisture characteristic of 21 habitats in north-east Italy. Corncrakes were either present (black) or absent (white). RD = rather dry, D = damp, DW = damp with waterlogging.* Source: Redrawn from Rassati and Tout (2002).

occasional vagrant to north-east Italy and is a sparse breeder; the majority of calling birds are normally found between 500 m and 999 m on regularly-cut grassy fields that have good vegetational cover and either flat ground or only moderately sloping land (Rassati and Tout, 2002). The most important regional habitat is provided by areas of late-cut meadow grass with no spring grazing, it is moist (rather than either dry or waterlogged, see Figure 4.3) and typically dominated by False Oat-grass, with Cock's-foot, Meadow Fescue and White Bedstraw. This combination of plant cover would seem to provide a good structure that enables birds to have a low density of vegetation at ground level to permit easy movement, but with some cover higher up to hide them from potential predators (Rassati and Rodaro, 2007). As the abandonment of land increases, the habitat change may initially benefit Corncrakes because of a patchy mosaic of unmanaged grass, but this is a subclimax vegetation and over time, the succession of bushes and shrubs such as Common Beech, European Hop-Hornbeam and Black Pine eventually renders the habitat less suitable for successful breeding. In years of low population density, it appears that the optimal habitats are claimed first as calling sites, and in years of high density, the suboptimal habitats are gradually established, possibly in clusters around already-established territories (Borgo and Zoologia Botanica, 2010). A common feature of Corncrake studies in the Italian Alps is that lower elevations are favoured earlier in the breeding season, with movements to higher elevations later in the year, which may be as a result of the combination of variations in weather, food availability, disturbance by land management, or patterns of competition and predation, as well as the later availability of suitable habitat at higher altitudes (Brambilla and Pedrini, 2011). For these reasons, the population of Corncrakes in Italy seems to be increasingly dependent on schemes to manage grassland for environmental purposes.

EASTERN EUROPE AND WESTERN ASIA

Further east, in the countries of the former Soviet Bloc, the irony is that although there is a greater population of Corncrakes (see Chapter 6), less is known about their ecological details. In part, this is due to the huge geographical area compared to the number of ornithologists, and also due to a lack of historical emphasis on the biology of this species. The broad characteristics of the preferred habitats continue to be similar to those in Western Europe, with several significant differences, mainly relating to the scale of the suitable landscape and the legacy (and continuing management) of agricultural areas. Slovakia is a good example: in the past half-century there have been substantial changes to the landscape as fields were amalgamated and agriculture became more intensive, but following the late twentieth century political changes, large sections have been abandoned to management (Demko, 1999). Important areas are the floodplain meadows in western Slovakia and the foothills of the more mountainous regions. Poland is the exception, and considerable studies have been made of Corncrake behaviour in the country over a lengthy period (Budka and Osiejuk, 2013a). A sizeable population of Corncrakes, particularly in the meadows and marshlands of eastern Poland, inhabit semi-natural communities of damp meadows, abandoned fields, and grasslands that are not intensively grazed. Arable fields are rarely occupied, although worked pastures and some forest plantations may provide territories (Budka et al., 2012), and even small, uncultivated areas around shrubs or ditches can prove attractive to calling males early in the breeding season (Budka and Osiejuk, 2013a). Clearly, in central and northern Europe, abandoned fields can provide a landscape mosaic that is attractive to the Corncrake, although some level of ongoing management will be required to prevent shrub succession reducing this suitability (Orlowski, 2010; see Chapter 12). In central Poland, in a landscape mosaic of dry and wet meadows which provides a marshy environment with areas of open water and clumps of Alder, the Corncrake may cohabit with the Spotted Crake and the Water Rail. This illustrates a nice example of the importance of habitat diversification because Corncrakes apparently prefer the drier grasslands, while Spotted Crakes like the swampier ground or shallow water, and Water Rails prefer wetlands with reed beds, even permanently submerged areas (Ręk and Kwiatkowska, 2016).

A significant discovery is that in the habitats that Corncrakes prefer, it is not simply the assemblage of specific species of vegetation that is important (though this is fundamental) but also the associated level of soil moisture and, crucially, the vegetational structure (Wettstein et al., 2001). The ideal habitat has vegetation that is fairly open about 20–30 cm above ground level to allow easy movement of the birds, but tall and more closed at higher levels to give cover from aerial predators. A study in southern Hungary found that the vegetation was 90–100% closed at the height of 1 m (Kiss, 2004). In eastern Hungary, large areas of natural grassland are dominated by species such as Meadow Foxtail, and fields that have been abandoned for agriculture or set-aside, often dotted with single trees, hedges and damp hollows, provide areas of strong local Corncrake populations that extend eastwards into Russia. Corncrake territories in this kind of habitat were found to be more diverse in a range of plants, butterflies, birds such as Cuckoo, Tree Pipit, River Warbler and Grasshopper Warbler, and invertebrates than neighbouring areas which were not selected by Corncrakes. This would seem to suggest that the presence of Corncrakes can be a good indicator of local biodiversity (Wettstein and Szép, 2003).

The situation is similar in south-eastern Europe, although for various reasons the numbers, distribution and habitat preferences of Corncrakes are not well documented in the historical literature of the region, and in many areas are still largely unknown in any detail. In Slovenia, Corncrakes have been recorded in damp meadows that contain fescues, Common Wild-oat and sedges (Ferlan et al., 1998). In fact, in central Slovenia there is a positive association between Corncrakes and regularly flooded meadows, with over 90% of calling (male) Corncrakes being present on land that is occasionally or regularly flooded (Tome, 2002a). Similar to elsewhere in Europe, there is a close association between recording a high density of Corncrake and the patterns of land management where physical constraints such as flooding or mountainous and rough terrain favour the persistence of extensive agriculture and late mowing of grass. Further south in Croatia (Radovic and Dumbovic, 1999), Bosnia-Herzegovina (Obratil, 1999) and North Macedonia (Micevski, 1999), the ecological recording of Corncrakes is even less clear. Historically, birds were abundant in the floodplain meadows of lowland Croatia. Calling males are still heard, although in reduced numbers (see Chapter 6), in the periodically flooded meadows of the Turopolje region between the Sava and Odra rivers, areas unsuitable for intensive agriculture (Radovic and Dumbovic, 1999). Little is known of the potential for breeding in the mountain habitats. A similar tale is found in Moldova (Zubcov, 1999), where the known breeding population is concentrated on the floodplain meadows and in woodland clearings; however, changing land use continues to provide numerous threats to Corncrake survival in this region. The numbers appear to be healthier in Romania, where the birds breed in a mosaic landscape of grassy meadows, woodland pastures and agricultural fields. Small-scale farms (less than 5 hectares) are more common in eastern Europe than in western Europe, for example in 2011 Romania had over 50 times more small farms than the UK, and Poland had 20 times more than Germany (Tryjanowski et al., 2011). On the hillside meadows, the habitat is broken up with various trees and bushes, including Hawthorn, European Spindle, Dogwood, Elder, Common Hazel and Wild Privet. The damper areas commonly have sedges, Common Reed and cottongrasses such as Common Cottongrass and Broad-leaved Cottongrass (Moga et al., 2010).

The 'surprise' discovery was the comparative abundance of breeding Corncrakes in Russia, both in the European geographical zone and in the vast areas stretching eastwards into Asia. This is partly because, as one study expressed, the Corncrake was considered:

'as a quite common species with favourable conservation status, and thus as not deserving special surveys.'

(Mischenko and Sukhanova, 1999a)

As in other areas of eastern Europe, information on the numbers and habitat distribution of Corncrakes throughout Russia is scant; however, after the implementation of systematic studies in the 1990s, more precise data is becoming available and a similar pattern of habitat preference is now being recognised. Although the steppe zone contains huge areas of grassland, this is generally too arid to suit Corncrakes, and the choice of optimum habitat quality remains wet meadows, partially flooded meadows on floodplains, and extensive or recently abandoned farmland in river valleys (Mischenko and Sukhanova, 1999a). The regional variation in weather patterns, and hence the soil moisture content, is probably a key factor in the characteristically erratic fluctuations of Corncrake numbers from year to year, with population levels dropping when the substrate is too dry or too wet for their liking – floodplains are very susceptible to this type of change (Mischenko, 2008).

In Russia, and extending to Georgia and into northern Iran, the Corncrake is regarded (legally or illegally) as a gamebird and is often killed during Quail hunts (Javakhishvili, 1999). Although comparative data is scarce, the species is seen on migration and takes a brief refuge among the cover of dense vegetation, such as rice stubble, as they pass through towards Africa (Ashoori and Zolfinejad, 2008). There are thought to be large numbers of breeding Corncrakes throughout the Asian part of Russia, and, in Siberia, Corncrakes are frequently found in damp meadows and river valleys within the taiga zone, the great coniferous forests of the northern hemisphere (Rogacheva, 1992). In this broad geographical region almost nothing is known of their detailed ecology and much remains to be documented (Mischenko and Sukhanova, 1999a). The large uninhabited areas and the few experienced observers – even fewer with the resources to investigate systematically – mean that there are undoubtedly new Corncrake localities waiting to be discovered. Reports of several thousand Corncrakes have been recorded from oases, river valleys and subalpine grasslands, and also in cultivated fields of Sesame, Alfalfa or Barley in the western borderlands of China (Ma Ming and Wang Qishan, 2002). In this region of western China (Xinjiang), a riverside scrubland of Birch and Poplar trees with an undergrowth of Hawthorn, Honeysuckle and Barberry gives way to rolling grassland that is ideally suited for Corncrakes. The species has also been recorded in fields of Flax at 750–1,200 m in the lower reaches of the Künes River valley in Xinjiang (Braunlich and Rank, 1999).

SOUTH-EASTERN AFRICA

If knowledge of the locations, habitat preferences and behavioural patterns of the Corncrake is sparse in most of Asia, it is even more so for almost the whole of Africa.

Figure 4.4: *Summary of the principal habitats of Corncrakes in Europe in 1997. (0 = not used; 3 = most birds in this habitat).* Source: redrawn from Green, Rocamora et al. (1997).

	Dry meadows	Floodplain meadows	Alpine meadows	Marshes	Crops
Austria	1	1	3	1	1
Belarus	2	2	0	2	1
Belgium	2	2	0	1	1
Bulgaria	1	3	3	2	1
Czech Republic	0	0	2	0	1
Denmark	0	3	0	0	2–3
Estonia	2	2	0	1	1
Finland	2	0	0	1	2
France	0	3	1	1	0
Germany	1	2	0	1	1
Great Britain	2	2	0	2	0
Hungary	1	2	0	1	1
Ireland	2	2	0	0	0
Italy	1	0	3	0	0
Latvia	2	3	0	0	2
Liechtenstein	0	1	0	3	0
Lithuania	3	2	0	1	1
Luxembourg	0	1	0	1	1
Moldova	2	1	0	1	1
Netherlands	1	3	0	1	1
Norway	2	1	0	1	2
Poland	2	2	1	1–2	0–1
Romania	3	0	0	0	1
Russia	1	3	0	1	1
Slovakia	0	2	3	0	1
Slovenia	1	3	2	1–2	0–1
Spain	0	1	0	2	3
Sweden	2	0	0	2	0–1
Switzerland	1	0	2	2	0
Ukraine	2	3	0	2	0
Number of habitats with top score	12	17	6	7	4

It is known that the majority of European and Asian Corncrakes migrate to spend their non-breeding period of the year mainly in the savanna grasslands of south-central and south-eastern Africa, from southern Tanzania to South Africa, but beyond that, regular, reliable details are hard to come by (Walther et al., 2013a). In general, their habitat choice is superficially similar to the environment of their breeding habitats, that is, moist grasslands that are tall enough to provide cover but comparatively open near the ground level to permit easy movement. This grassland, perhaps slightly drier than is normally expected in the breeding areas or edged with permanent swampland, is frequently studded with thickets of Acacia trees or Verbena, or with clumps of Weeping Fig or Miombo (Taylor, 1984). As elsewhere, this diverse vegetational mosaic seems to be preferred by the species. The ground may remain dry throughout the year or may become inundated with regional floodwater, in which case Corncrakes seem to relocate within Africa to accommodate the changes in local conditions. The habitat is often shared with its distant relation, the African Crake, and while these birds prefer the wetter patches of grassland for foraging and breeding, the Corncrakes coexist peaceably and feed separately in the drier grass.

By far the most common habitat in which to observe Corncrakes during their visitation to south-eastern Africa is the drier natural grassland. Of course, these are not the grass species of the temperate northern hemisphere, but growths of tussocky tropical grasses such as Thatching Grass, Seed-thrower Grass, Lovegrass, Hair Grass, Beard-grass, Lemongrass and Signal Grass, or grasses of the genus *Panicum*, *Andropogon* or *Themeda* that have no common name in English (Walther et al., 2013b). In their non-breeding period, Corncrakes are frequently solitary and may often take advantage of cover in a large variety of grassy locations, such as the tall verges of sports fields, airfields, golf courses, planted pastures or woodland edges. Lacking the imperative of breeding and the need to attract a mate to an established territory of land, the Corncrake appears quietly content to forage widely and seek cover opportunistically, but much more research is required in this area.

THE VAST AREA BETWEEN EUROPE AND SOUTHERN AFRICA

Of the huge continental expanses between the breeding areas of Corncrakes in Europe or Asia, and their non-breeding refuges, little is known but the sporadic reports of individual birds being observed from various geographical locations. It is known, for instance, that Corncrakes have been recorded in at least 35 African countries, but very large areas of the continent remain under-sampled or unsurveyed (see Chapter 6; Walther et al., 2013a). The records of visibility are further frustrated by the lack of knowledge about whether the sighting is that of a migrating bird simply passing through, or if the individual bird has decided to interrupt its migration and remain in the locality until stimulated to fly north again to the breeding areas. Rarely is the sighting of a Corncrake in a new locality documented, and even more rarely does that report contain any additional detail on their behaviour or the nature of the habitat where the sighting was noticed. Some interesting discoveries have recently been made through recording Corncrake calls during their nocturnal migrations (so-called 'nocmig'), which have noted their passing during the hours of darkness, even when their visible presence has remained undetected. This research is still in its infancy, but already it is evident that Corncrake flight calls are more noticeable in the spring, rather than autumn, presumably because of the influence of breeding hormones at that time of the year. There are isolated sightings of Corncrakes during the winter months of the northern hemisphere in the countries bordering the Mediterranean, but little systematic recording. There are also tantalising accounts of passage migrants in the rice paddy fields of Iran (Ashoori and Zolfinejad, 2008), or in the arid scrublands of northern Egypt and Sinai (Baha el Din et al., 1996), and even a rare reward of a geolocation tag that placed a Corncrake ringed in Scotland in forest-clearings in the western part of the Congo Basin (Horton, 2013). But between its northern hemisphere breeding areas and its sojourn in south-east Africa, the Corncrake maintains its enigmatic and reclusive reputation.

CONCLUSION

Throughout its range, the Corncrake is a bird of grasslands, but not just any grassland for it prefers cool, damp meadows where the grass is tall enough to provide cover, protection from predators and a variety of invertebrate prey. Wetland meadows, especially those that are subjected to regular flooding, are attractive as these often combine cover but at the same time are not too dense at ground level to inhibit the easy movement of the birds. Their close association with human agricultural communities, particularly hay meadows and the tall vegetation along field boundaries, means that their preferred habitats are subject to threat both from agricultural intensification and from field abandonment.

CHAPTER 5

DESCRIPTION AND MORPHOLOGY

In one way, this should be the easiest chapter (to write and to read), but simple descriptions tend to mix subjective assessments (for example, of colours or behaviours) with highly specific objective details (for example, of anatomical measurements) and this can make rather dry reading. Throughout the ornithological literature, many authors appear simply to quote an earlier author, but the basic description of a Corncrake is uncontroversial.

APPEARANCE

In various accounts (Snow and Perrins, 1998; Cramp and Simmons, 1980), the adult Corncrake has been described as a medium-sized rail, a little larger in body size than a Water Rail and approaching the bulk of a Partridge. Other than in small groups during migration, there are seldom more than two adult birds seen together. Normally the upper parts are brown-black with ashy-coloured streaks, giving a grey-brown impression, with the feathers on the back having a dark central area, giving a black barring effect, but there can be subtle variations in individual colouring. There are no subspecies but, generally speaking, birds tend to become paler and greyer towards the eastern extents of the species range. The Corncrakes in Kazakhstan tend to be paler than those in western Europe, with more grey and less brown above and less buff below, and in the Ural Basin the colouration appears intermediate between these end-types (Taylor and van Perlo, 1998). The sexes are similar in colouring, with no real seasonal variation, although outwith the breeding season, the upper parts of both sexes may become darker and the underparts less grey. The most distinguishing feature is that the wing-coverts and inner flight feathers are tawny or a bright chestnut colour. It has been noted that no other rail shows such bright colours

of using bodyweight (as above) to estimating the age. In practice, using body weight is recommended for chicks younger than about 22 days, while using the primary feathers is more effective for chicks 22–45 days old, with substantial errors in the area of overlap (Green and Tyler, 2005). The recovery of ringed Corncrakes is generally low (Green, 2004a), but in general the results reveal a low survival rate of adult birds (Anderson and Green, 2009).

MOULT

Immediately after the fledging of the second brood, usually around mid-August in Scotland, the adults begin a complete moult lasting 3–4 weeks. The birds are unable to fly during this period, and usually walk only short distances within the breeding area (Green, Rocamora et al., 1997). Soon after this late-summer moult is complete, they normally depart on their autumn migration. All of their wing and tail feathers are shed simultaneously, starting with the flanks and hind-parts of the body, with the head last (Cramp and Simmons, 1980). Not all birds necessarily moult at the same time, and some may postpone their moult until after post-breeding dispersal, or even post-migration (Cramp and Simmons, 1980). Fat reserves are accumulated during the moult, and birds may become 30–60% heavier than what they weighed in midsummer (Green, 2007). These reserves will stand them in good stead for their long migration. A pre-breeding adult may have a partial moult of head and body while in its non-breeding habitats (Cramp and Simmons, 1980). For the second brood of the season, (to avoid undue disturbance after the first brood), the onset of the moult of the flight feathers during or just after the period of chick care can be a useful indicator of the end of the breeding period (Green, 2010). The worn plumage often appears to be more ashy-grey in the upper parts, with the black barring more prominent.

GENETICS

Corncrakes in France, Ireland and Scotland are on average heavier and larger than Corncrakes in other countries, and they have other subtle structural differences across Europe (Koffijberg et al., 2016). Studies have noted that individual Corncrakes from Scotland are significantly larger in mean dimensions and weight than those from the nearest neighbouring populations, which suggests the maintenance of some relatively discrete regional populations.

Three distinct genetic clusters have been recognised across the entire breeding range, namely Scotland, western France and Italy, and all populations further east, with weakly differentiated western European groups, such as in the German/Polish border region (Fourcade et al., 2016). Recent analysis indicates a:

'low genetic structure across the entire range, with high levels of genetic diversity in all sites…[although there was] some evidence that the westernmost populations were, to a very limited extent, differentiated from the rest of the European population.'

(Fourcade et al., 2016)

In general, all regional populations of Corncrakes are apparently similar in terms of genetic diversity, and considerable gene flow is present between the regional populations. The fact that all European Corncrake populations appear (now and recently) to be interconnected has important ramifications for the migration links between geographical localities, and on the local population dynamics of sustainable populations versus the dependency on in-migration of breeding individuals. This will consequently have an influence on the potential management techniques for Corncrake conservation (see Chapter 12), as it is important to understand if population numbers are the result of improved local management, or simply due to the arrival of birds from elsewhere. For example:

'despite a strong and continuous demographic decline, the Corncrake population of western France did not undergo a reduction in its genetic diversity… [and] …the most likely scenario is that genetic diversity was maintained by gene flow from distant populations that have not suffered from the same demographic decline.'

(Fourcade et al., 2019)

In general, low genetic diversity can lead to inbreeding and a loss of the ability to adapt to a changing local environment. With our current information, there is no evidence for a decline in the genetic diversity of Corncrakes across their breeding range, but it remains unclear if fragmented and isolated regional populations outwith the core area in Russia may be at risk in future (Fourcade et al., 2019).

Studies in avian DNA are not only useful for classifying species and establishing genetic connections (Sibley et al., 1988). The difficulty of quickly identifying the gender of an individual Corncrake in the field, in addition to other perplexing issues, could possibly be resolved soon by the adoption of rapid genetic analysis. This involves the isolation of microsatellite markers, sets of short DNA sequences taken from a specific part of a chromosome which vary between individuals and therefore function as a sort of genetic fingerprinting (Trontelj, 1999). Where this has been done for Corncrakes, it enables a close comparison of individuals between different geographical populations (Gautschi et al., 2002). In addition to comparisons between the structure (for example, size) and appearance (for example, plumage colouration) of different regional populations of Corncrakes, this biotechnology might be used to differentiate between different geographical populations (Kempe, 2008), and help determine the source of individual birds (for example, locally bred as a result of improved habitat management or immigrants from displaced breeding populations in another country; Gautschi et al., 2002). Genetic markers may also be useful in understanding certain aspects of Corncrake behaviour such as the female choice of male for breeding purposes – is it the larger males that receive the most attention, or the most vocal, or even the most exotic migrant (Thom and Dytham, 2012)? The technique can also be used to provide information on the prevalence of the genetic susceptibility to disease, for example Corncrakes in the eastern parts of its range have a disposition towards haemosporidian infection, whereas western populations appear to be almost free of these parasites (Fourcade et al., 2019). There is a strong correlation with the dominant forms of agricultural practices in these respective regions, and although pathogens can spread rapidly between well-connected patches of habitat and the within-season migration of birds can lead to a mixing of populations, genetic markers can be used to identify the historical biotope of individual birds.

Conclusion

The Corncrake is a medium-size rail with no subspecies, but there is a subtle gene flow throughout the huge range of its breeding area. Males are slightly larger, but the plumage is similar between the genders, with only minor differences in juvenile birds. There are various anatomic measurements and comparisons that can be used to distinguish the age and sex of individual birds, and, in combination with genetic markers, between the individuals of different geographical populations.

CHAPTER 6

POPULATION AND DISTRIBUTION

It seems strange to start a chapter this way, when gathering together the scientific evidence of the global Corncrake presence, but it is almost certain that by the time you have finished reading this chapter, the information will already be out of date. The enigma of the Corncrake is that as more information about its ecology is accumulated, the more we seem to understand about specific issues, but the greater the number of questions arise about the totality of our understanding. Although passing mention needs to be made here to the recorded numbers of Corncrakes in various localities at various times in recent history, these numbers, as we will see, are often very vague and always transitory. Survey estimates frequently have huge error-bars in their calculations. That is, possibly, the story of the Corncrake. Many observers in different countries have commented that it was apparently common everywhere until, suddenly, it was not. Although this chapter discusses some of the historical data for the regional populations and geographical distribution of Corncrakes across the globe, it is not intended to be a comprehensive listing of numbers, some of which are often partial surveys, disputed counts or, at best guess, approximations. Rather than make a definitive statement about the current numbers of 'national' populations, which by definition will constantly need updating, it is best to check the figures that are maintained by the International Union for the Conservation of Nature in the Red List of Threatened Species and listed on the Internet (BirdLife International, 2016). For those reasons, I have avoided giving 'current' population estimates, which could be misleading as the population of Corncrakes at any one time is likely always to have a high degree of uncertainty. This account is *not* an exhaustive litany of the gains and losses in regional population figures, however important that may be. The distribution of Corncrakes across the vast area of their potential breeding range is important and summarised in this chapter, although this requires a lengthy description, and some readers may wish to jump to their own specific area of geographical interest. For brevity, I have tried as far as possible to give the main sources of the historical basis for the population dynamics of Corncrakes across their breeding areas, and to summarise some of the regional trends.

To avoid getting bogged down with the Corncrake (if you will pardon the pun), it is probably better to look at the overall geographical trends and what they can inform us about its population dynamics. For convenience, the northern hemisphere distribution of the Corncrake will be summarised in four broad geographical areas: (1) Scotland, including the UK, (2) western Europe, (3) eastern Europe, mainly the countries formerly under the influence of Soviet agricultural economics (Green and Rayment, 1996), extending to Asia, and (4) Africa and other non-breeding areas. A considerable amount of significant research has been carried out in Scotland for almost half a century, and so let us start there first, and then widen our studies.

Figure 6.1: *Global distribution of the Corncrake.* Source: From the compilation of Koffijberg and Schäffer (2006).

SCOTLAND AND THE UK

The classic book *The Birds of the West of Scotland including the Outer Hebrides*, published in 1871, opens the account of the Corncrake with the following seemingly all-embracing sentence:

> *'There is, perhaps, no Scottish bird more generally distributed than the familiar Corncrake; it is found in every district, cultivated and uncultivated, on the western mainland, from the Mull of Galloway to Cape Wrath, and also over the whole extent of both groups of islands, and all the rocky islets of the west coast, extending to Heisker rocks, the Monach islands, and St. Kilda.*
>
> Gray, 1871

In 1888, Harvie-Brown and Buckley, in their milestone volume on *A Vertebrate Fauna of the Outer Hebrides,* noted the huge variation in the presence of the Corncrake in the islands throughout the year, from late March until late November in some years, and Harvie-Brown even suggested that some birds may remain all winter (Harvie-Brown, 1903). By the 1953 publication of *The Birds of Scotland*, Baxter and Rintoul had documented, in great detail, the earliest and the latest recordings of Corncrakes in every parish throughout Scotland. This list includes the records by Sibbald (Sibbald, 1684) in 1684 and from St Kilda in 1697 by Martin (Martin, 1698). It was apparent by the early 1900s that for several decades the Corncrake had suffered a catastrophic decline in numbers throughout most of its previous breeding territory. In 1840 John Macgillivray had heard it call on St Kilda (Macgillivray, 1842), in 1915 it was reported to Eagle Clarke (Eagle Clarke, 1915); and it was noted intermittently by visiting naturalists, even after the human inhabitants had evacuated the archipelago (Love, 2009). Baxter and Rintoul recorded sightings of Corncrakes from many of the small islands, including in the lighthouse garden in the Pentland Skerries (Baxter and Rintoul, 1953), and almost incredibly, in 1904 and 1906 it was noted by the lighthouse keeper on the wave-lashed rock of Skerryvore (Tomison, 1907).

The earliest record from the British Isles is in 1544, where it was noted that, *'I have not heard it anywhere in England, save in Northumbria alone'* (Norris, 1945). That, together with other early records:

> *'suggest that in the sixteenth and seventeenth centuries the Corn-Crake was very uncommon in the greater part of England south of Yorkshire, Derbyshire and Cheshire, but was much commoner in the north (and perhaps also in Wales) and very plentiful in Ireland.'*
>
> (Norris, 1945)

The decline in the Corncrake population was first reported (Hudson et al., 1990) between 1850 and 1875, and the decline seemed to accelerate in the early 1900s. The former county of Cumberland was the last English county where four calling Corncrakes were recorded in 1978 (Cadbury, 1980a).

In the early years of the twentieth century, it was noticed that the Corncrake was becoming scarce in the eastern and south-eastern counties of England, and that:

> *'it would seem as though the distribution of the species was gradually shifting towards the north-west.'*
>
> (Ticehurst, 1913)

There were voices of scepticism raised, but this focused the proposal in 1913 for 'a united and carefully organized inquiry' and emphasised that the information sought should be:

> *'limited to the presence or absence, past or present – and the relative numbers and changes in numbers – of <u>breeding birds</u> in each district.'*
>
> (Ticehurst, 1913; emphasis in original paper)

By the following year (1914) reports had been received from local informants, mainly in the counties of England, and a few from Scotland and Ireland, as the patterns of the decreasing Corncrake population were being summarised in greater detail (Alexander, 1914). It is noticeable at this early stage that 'ornithological ecology' was still in its infancy and that there was still some considerable confusion about the reasons for the decline. Several suggestions were made, although by now it was proposed that:

> *'by far the most popular view is that the machines now in general use for cutting the hay destroy many nests which were formerly spared, and that this is responsible for the decrease... [which] ... does not kill chance individuals, some old, some young, but it kills whole families of young.'*
>
> (Alexander, 1914)

The connection was also being made that the areas where machine harvesting was most prevalent were also the areas with the earliest and greatest decrease in Corncrake numbers, and the timing of decline was being documented county-by-county for England and Wales (Shrubb, 2003). More recent analysis of museum specimens provides information that is consistent with the population decline being largely due to the loss of young birds and the subsequent lack of replacement breeders (Green, 2008).

The discussion limped along until in 1938 it was decided to instigate a comprehensive study under the auspices of the British Trust for Ornithology. A short talk on the radio news bulletin and appeals for information produced nearly 3,000 responses over the next 2 years and, for the first time, the documentation was extended to explore the status of the Corncrake in western Europe (Norris, 1945). Few data from those early surveys survive, and the local reporters generally made no attempt to estimate the actual numbers of birds, only their distribution; however, the surveys proved conclusively that the progressive decline had begun in the east and south-east of England and was working towards the north and west. Details were published for most of the counties throughout the UK and Ireland, with short notes on some other European countries. This survey recorded that southwards of a line roughly from Hartlepool on the east coast to Swansea on the west coast, Corncrakes were regarded as, 'still found in isolated instances'. Most of the mainland of north Wales, northern England and virtually all of Scotland and Ireland showed a distribution of 'varying intensity, considerable decrease'. Only in the islands of Scotland and the north-western counties of Ireland was the species regarded as numerous, with 'little or no change of status beyond local fluctuations' (Norris, 1945). Significantly, it was noted that in the western European mainland, the Corncrake decline exhibited much the same pattern, although the decrease appeared to be more recent than in the UK and Ireland.

By 1939 the Corncrakes were:

> 'considered to be numerous only in Shetland, Orkney, the Outer and Inner Hebrides of Scotland and western Ireland.'
>
> (Green and Williams, 1992)

In 1883 it was reported that the district of Dunrossness, in the south end of the Shetland mainland,

> '... in early summer simply swarms with Corn-Crakes, and walking to and from Sumburgh, on a fine evening, you hear the "craik, craik" on every side of you.'
>
> (Venables and Venables, 1950)

However, by the mid-1900s, the species was virtually extinct in Shetland, and some observers linked this to a reduction in the arable land due to depopulation and the post-war scarcity of young men (Venables and Venables, 1950). Nine years after the Corncrake Inquiry had begun, the analysis in 1947 of the accumulating evidence had encouraged a broader investigation of the ecology of the species and a clearer understanding that the links with grassland mowing and habitat management were not just idle speculations (Norris, 1947). In addition to the style of mowing, the timing of the harvest was also attracting attention. By the 1960s, the main causes of the decline were no longer just supposition (Norris, 1963). Comparing the early studies (Norris, 1945) with later studies on species distribution (Parslow, 1973), including the work published in 1976 for the *Atlas of Breeding Birds in Britain and Ireland* (Sharrock, 1976) and in 1996 for the *Historical Atlas* (Holloway, 1996), the decline in range is self-evident. Full censuses have since been conducted in 1978–79, 1988, 1993, 1998 and 2003, and surveys have been conducted annually in its core range in NW Scotland since 1993. The story that unfolds is outlined below.

A large-scale survey in 1978–79 indicated that the population decline and range contraction was continuing, and this was confirmed over the following decade (Green and Williams, 1992). A comprehensive survey in 1988 recorded 551–596 calling Corncrakes, 88–98% of which were in the Inner or the Outer Hebridean islands, with 24–29 in the Scottish mainland, 4 in England and 1 in the Isle of Man (Newton, 1991). In contrast to an estimate of 3,250 in the early 1970s, a full survey of the UK in 1993 recorded just 488 calling males, 90% of which were in the combined area of the Inner and Outer Hebrides (Beaumont and England, 2016). There was a small rise in the local populations in Tiree and in North Uist, and half-a-dozen scattered birds recorded in set-aside fields in the east of Scotland and north of England, but an 82% decline over five years in Orkney (Green, 1995a). A small population of Corncrakes was reintroduced to England in Cambridgeshire in 2002 (Graham, 2009), and since 2004 these have been closely monitored (Carter and Newberry, 2004), recording 23 calling males in 2009 and a further 11 noted from other parts of England (Wotton et al., 2015).

A census in 1993 showed a decline of 17% in the Corncrake population in Britain since the 1988 survey, and a dramatic decline of 81% in Ireland (Green, 1996). When dealing with small numbers, percentages can be misleading, but the tabulated census numbers of recorded males area by area and island by island show a continued decline of the Corncrake population in Britain and Ireland. Between 1993 and 2004, the total UK population had more than doubled (see Appendix 3), but its territorial range had not increased (see Figure 6.2). Although the population in Orkney had decreased, the core areas of the Outer and Inner Hebrides had increased, partially due to demographic changes, for example through the enhanced survival rates of adults and chicks. These changes had been influenced by agri-environmental schemes in the region to modify mowing practices and to provide greater cover during the breeding season, although, significantly, about 64% of calling Corncrakes were on land with no schemes of assistance (O'Brien et al., 2006; see Chapter 12 on management and conservation).

The national Corncrake population in Ireland was estimated to be around 4,000 calling males in the 1970s, but by 2018 only 151 calling males were recorded (O'Donoghue, 2019). There was a slight UK increase between 2003 and 2007, but very little expansion of the range, and then there was another decline in 2013 and 2015, probably due to cold springs and limited vegetational cover. However, despite a predicted fall in 2014, there was a rapid population rise to give the highest numbers since counts began, recording 1,289 calling males in Scotland and 396 in the Isle of Tiree alone (Anonymous, 2014). An atlas survey in 1968–72 found breeding Corncrakes in 528 10-km grid squares in Britain, but by 1978–79 this had fallen to 160 grid squares, then to 91 in 1988, and to 83 by 1993 (Green, 1999b). The changes were most marked in the east of Scotland (88 grid squares reduced to 10) and in the south-west (67 grid squares reduced to 20; Cadbury, 1980b). In those 160 grid squares in 1978–79, a total of 700–712 calling Corncrakes were estimated, and all but 12 of those birds were in Scotland (Cadbury, 1980a). However, another source quoted 700–746 birds (Hudson et al., 1990). Figure 6.2 shows the census methods. The distribution on the Scottish mainland was sparse, with only two grid squares holding more than five calling birds (both areas in Sutherland). No fewer than 71 Corncrakes were heard in a single grid square in Tiree in 1977, twice the next highest population, which was 35 calling birds in a grid square in North Uist (Cadbury, 1980a).

Simply by scanning these numbers, it can be seen that the managed habitat of the Outer and Inner Hebrides seems particularly favourable for the attraction and maintenance of breeding Corncrakes (see Appendix 3). As a result, these islands have been the focus for recurring studies over the past several decades. In the Outer Hebrides, a variety of detailed ecological studies have been pursued, including feeding and breeding behaviours (Stowe and Hudson, 1988), habitat preferences (Booth and Milne, 1999) and habitat management techniques (Aberdeen Centre for Land Use, 1991), especially in the Corncrake population hotspots of North Uist and South Uist (Newton, 1991). Meanwhile, the focus on the Inner Hebrides has been largely in the neighbouring islands of Tiree and Coll (Cadbury, 1989). By the mid-1980s, although a lot of the detailed ecology still remained unknown, there was sufficient evidence of the strong links between grassland management and Corncrake conservation to support the initiation of a range of specific agri-environmental measures and species conservation schemes (Williams et al., 1997; see Chapter 12). At the time of writing this chapter, the survival of the Corncrake in the UK is still in the balance, and though there has been a slight increase in the population over the past decade, there is no sign of any extension to its range outwith the core areas of the Scottish islands (Wotton et al., 2015). A bird reserve for Corncrakes in Coll is a tourist attraction (Hume, 2010) and has helped to further our knowledge of the population dynamics of the species, but not without contention (Mitchell, 2006). The importance of these local populations of Corncrakes is of such national and international significance that both Tiree (Leitch, 1999) and Coll (Grant, 2002) have been surveyed as Special Protection Areas specifically dedicated for Corncrake conservation. In Ireland, however, although Special Protection Areas for the Corncrake have been designated, in 2018 more than half of calling males were located outwith these protected areas (O'Donoghue, 2019). This is a reminder that protected areas alone are not sufficient to ensure the conservation of the targeted species, and this will be discussed further in Chapter 12. The decline in numbers and range contraction in Northern Ireland has mirrored the trend on the UK mainland, and by

Figure 6.2: Number of 10-km grid squares historically occupied by calling Corncrakes in the UK (confirmed and probable for 1968–72). Sources: Green (1995a); Green and Gibbons (2000); O'Brien et al. (2006).

	Number of 10-km grid squares occupied					
	1968–72	1978–79	1988	1993	1998	203
Shetland	9	2	1	3	4	3
Orkney	30	27	12	4	10	15
Outer Hebrides	32	31	29	29	30	29
Inner Hebrides	54	36	31	20	21	26
Rest of Scotland	216	54	14	18	15	5
England	133	9	3	7	11	2
Wales	42	1	0	1	2	0
Isle of Man	12	0	1	1	0	1
Total	**528**	**160**	**91**	**83**	**93**	**81**

Figure 6.3: Map of Corncrake distribution in Scotland by 10-km grid squares 1988–2009 (a = 1988; b= 1993; c = 1998; d = 2003; e = 2009. Source: Wotton et al. (2015).

1990 only 45 Corncrakes were recorded; by 1993 there were only nine calling males; and by 1994 none were noted, although a calling male was heard in 1995 and 1996 on Rathlin Island (Williams et al., 1997).

WESTERN EUROPE

In the rest of Ireland, 'conservative estimates put the population at the turn of the century in tens of thousands' (Hynes et al., 2007); by 1968–72 it was estimated at 4,000 males, but this estimate had fallen to around 1,500 males by 1978 and to 903–930 males by 1988 (McDevitt and Casey, 1999). A national census in 1998 recorded only 151–155 calling males, of which 69–71 were in the Shannon Callows and 63–65 in north Donegal (Casey, 1999). By this time, the Corncrakes range had contracted drastically, and they were only being noted in three core areas: the Shannon Callows (Donaghy, 2007a), Mayo/West Connacht and north Donegal. Despite several Corncrake conservation initiatives (Copland, 2001), by 2015 the species was considered to be locally extinct in the Shannon Callows. Numbers were rising and falling in other areas, but there were only 151 calling males confirmed in the whole of Ireland in 2018, with the stronghold remaining in Donegal (Duffy, 2018).

Across western Europe, the geographical movements of individual Corncrakes within a single breeding season seem to be very common (Michalska-Hejduk et al., 2017),

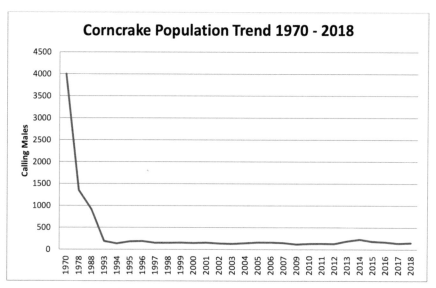

Figure 6.4: *The Corncrake population (estimate) in Ireland 1970–2018.*
Source: O'Donoghue (2019).

sometimes relocating over very long distances, with varying arrival dates and durations of stay in each locality (Mikkelsen et al., 2013). These movements may be explained by a number of different causal factors, including habitat disturbance, local weather conditions, movements to seek a second mate or relocation because the first breeding attempt had failed. Annual fluctuations in Corncrake numbers, and the population trends between and within countries, are constantly changing, sometimes dramatically, from year to year, but the general trend is declining numbers (Green and Stowe, 1993). Interestingly, these fluctuating population levels are much less pronounced in France, the UK and Ireland, and those birds tend to show a different dispersal behaviour, perhaps indicating subtle genetic gradations (Koffijberg et al., 2016). In the early 1990s, habitat changes in the breeding area were considered to be a major cause of decline, but this was hard to prove conclusively (Stowe et al., 1993), and other factors such as losses during migration and in their African habitats were largely unknown – and still lack substantial details.

In the late 1980s, France was thought to be the single most important country for Corncrakes in western Europe, with around one-third of the European population – Britain and Ireland together accounted for around another 24% of the total (Hudson et al., 1990). Over the three decades since the early 1990s, there was a staggering 90% reduction in the Corncrake population recorded in France (Hennique et al., 2013), from around 500 calling males in 1983 to about 60 in the 2016 count (Fourcade et al., 2019). This was accompanied by a massive contraction of the range and fragmentation of habitat (Broyer and Renaud, 1998). In the 1930s, Corncrakes were recorded in 74 out of 95 French départements; by the end of the 1990s, almost 82% of the national population of around 1,200 calling males was recorded from just 12 regional locations (Deceuninck, 1999). In several of these areas, despite the pervasive agricultural changes, the presence of adjacent cover and uncut refuge strips provided a continuing attraction, particularly for juvenile birds (Broyer, 2003). Despite fragmented initiatives to encourage agri-environmental management (Broyer et al., 2014), the downward trend in the population has continued. This pattern was also mirrored in neighbouring Belgium (Ryelandt, 1995), where numbers at most localities have been recorded in single figures, with only 14 calling males between 1973 and 1977, mainly calling from arable crops or refuge areas (Jacob, 1988), suggesting perhaps the lack of optimal habitat. At the start of the 1990s, up to 200 calling males were recorded (Lippens and Wille, 1972), but by 1998 only 60–72 were found, with a minimum of 1 in 2014 and a maximum of 31 calling males in 2012 (Verbelen et al., 2016), and only 20% in nature reserves (Ryelandt, 1999). A small and fluctuating population is now largely restricted to the Fagne-Famenne area (Vassen and Ryelandt, 1997), and there is a strong suggestion that the population in Belgium only remains due to the intermittent relocation of birds from other countries, casting doubts about the long-term stability (Verbelen et al., 2016). Surveys in Luxembourg revealed a maximum of five calling males per year in the 1900s, sometimes none at all (Lorge,1999), and in Liechtenstein, a few birds were breeding in the late 1960s, but then nothing was recorded again until 1977, and then only in single figures during the 1980s and 1990s (Willi, 1999).

Corncrakes were thought to be common throughout Norway, but by the 1960s they had virtually disappeared, with an estimated 20 calling males in the 1970s, dropping to 2–5 during 1995–97, before stabilising at 50–70 over the past few decades, mainly in the south-western parts (Folvik and Øien, 1999). Similarly, in Finland, where the species was common below roughly 60 degrees north, there was a well-documented decline during the 1900s (Haartman, 1958), to an estimated 600 calling males in the mid-1990s. Since then, a small and scattered, but reasonably stable, population remains (Asikainen, 1999), with the Corncrake population in Finland in 2003–2008 averaging around five times that recorded in the 1990s (BirdLife International, 2020). Most of the remaining Corncrakes in Scandinavia are to be found in Sweden, where some significant studies have been conducted (Berg and Hiron, 2012). Corncrakes in Sweden extended to about the same degree north (roughly the Arctic Circle) and although very little population data is known before 1958, they suffered a strong decline from the early 1990s onwards with the progressive mechanisation of agriculture and are now mainly found in eastern central parts of the country (Ottvall, 1999b). There has been a significant loss of potential habitat throughout Sweden, from around 2 million hectares of semi-natural grassland in 1870 to less than 400,000 hectares in 1990, including the loss of wet meadows during this same period from 1,200,000 to around 24,000 hectares (Berg and Gustafson, 2007). Since then, there have been increased management efforts for the conservation of wet meadow avifauna (Berg and Gustafson, 2006). Despite a dramatic historical decline, the number of calling Corncrakes in Sweden has increased slightly since the 1980s (Berg and Hiron, 2012). Although the population of Corncrakes in Sweden exhibits quite large annual fluctuations (Ottvall and Pettersson, 1998b) and a low breeding density (Alnås, 1974), it is almost certain that the national records depend upon incoming birds from central European countries to maintain the numbers (Enemar, 1969). In Denmark, the situation is more severe and, with the last two permanently occupied sites abandoned in 1972 and 1984, the Corncrake was considered to be functionally extinct as a breeding species in Denmark by 1998 (Thorup, 1999a).

By contrast, there is a long history of research into Corncrakes in the Netherlands (Van den Bergh, 1991), including the early suggestion that fluctuations are due to incoming birds from Central Europe due to regional weather patterns (Braaksma, 1962). Surveys in 1968 and 1969 gave the first national estimate of around 875 calling males (Koffijberg, 1999a), and although numbers have followed the decrease experienced by other western European populations, the birds are still heard in the great river valleys that run through the centre of the country (Schoppers and Koffijberg, 2008). From a dip to 50–60 calling males in 1993 and 1994, numbers rose again in 1998 to about 525 calling males (Koffijberg, 1999a). The valleys of the River Waal (Van der Straaten and Van den Bergh, 1970), with their floodplains and tributaries, have traditionally been a stronghold of the Corncrake in this country, although successive studies have documented the steady decline in numbers (Van der Straaten and Meijer, 1969) to the point of disappearance in some areas, such as in the Biesboch wetland towards the river mouth (Meijer, 2007). A small number of floodplains in the Rhine valleys may also be important (Leuven et al., 2006), and although there has been a lot of habitat loss, these areas may hold about a third of all territories in the Netherlands (Atsma, 2006). About half of all territories have been recorded from managed grasslands, and about 10–20% from areas intentionally managed to encourage breeding birds to return. A particular novelty, however, is the presence in the Oldambt area in the north-east of the country (Voslamber, 1989) of a reasonably large population (around 35% of the national population in 1990; Koffijberg and Nienhuis, 2003) as these birds appear to prefer residing in crops on arable land, such as Alfalfa and winter Wheat (Koffijberg and van Dijk, 2001). Unlike most other regions, in which the early-cut Alfalfa attracts Corncrakes but provides poor breeding success, the Oldambt area seems to prove a local exception, perhaps due to the easy access to the relatively open landscape and the cover provided in surrounding fields (Koffijberg and Nienhuis, 2003).

A similar phenomenon is observed in the Hellwegbörde area in the North-Rhine Westphalia region, which is among the larger Corncrake breeding sites in Germany (Joest and Koffijberg, 2016). In both areas, the comparatively open landscape with a combination of crop varieties and the unmanaged field margins of set-aside may provide higher densities of invertebrate food, as well as refuge sites that enable successful breeding, even in these dry, intensively managed farmlands. Most recently, although Corncrakes are found scattered throughout Germany (Götte, 2009), there are small and fluctuating local populations, such as in Baden-Württemberg (Kramer and Armbruster, 1997), in the Rhön area (Kolb, 1997), in Upper Bavaria (Mandl and Sandner, 1997), and even in the green belt around some cities such as Bremen (Pfützke, 1999). The species is especially common in the north-east (Bellebaum, Grüneberg et al., 2016) and the floodplains of the Lower Oder Valley (Helmecke, 1999), which hold the largest Corncrake population in the country (Arbeiter, Franke et al., 2017). Although showing a declining trend in the earlier part of the century, the presence of Corncrakes in Germany has shown an increase in site occupancy since the mid-1990s, and nearly doubled breeding occupancy in the North German Plains between 1982–1995 and 2005–2009 (Bellebaum, Grüneberg et al., 2016).

Across the whole of the western European breeding range of Corncrakes, annual population fluctuations occur frequently, perhaps caused by changes in large-scale weather conditions, particularly flooding of the breeding sites or the arrival of particularly dry weather (Frühauf, 1999). In the Netherlands, as in other areas of western Europe, it seems likely that the peak occurrences followed by steep declines, which are noted simultaneously in several countries, are highly dependent on influxes from further east,

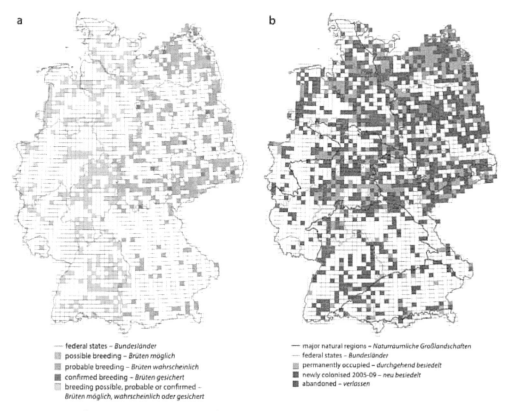

a

b

federal states – *Bundesländer*
possible breeding – *Brüten möglich*
probable breeding – *Brüten wahrscheinlich*
confirmed breeding – *Brüten gesichert*
breeding possible, probable or confirmed –
Brüten möglich, wahrscheinlich oder gesichert

major natural regions – *Naturräumliche Großlandschaften*
federal states – *Bundesländer*
permanently occupied – *durchgehend besiedelt*
newly colonised 2005-09 – *neu besiedelt*
abandoned – *verlassen*

Figure 6.5: *Changing site occupancy of Corncrakes in Germany between 1974–1995 and 2005–2009.* Source: Bellebaum, Grüneberg et al. (2016).

probably stimulated by weather-related events (Koffijberg, 1999a). The Rhine valleys have suffered a strong decline in the Corncrake population, and in the floodplains, the years when nests have been destroyed by summer flooding generally results in exceptionally low numbers of Corncrakes in the following year (Frühauf, 1999). Across Switzerland, the within-season movements are generally from the lowlands to the higher Alpine pastures as birds relocate to seek better habitat conditions at higher altitudes, (see Chapter 4). Although widespread during the nineteenth century, the later years and the early 1900s saw the commonly observed drastic decline noted in most other countries, and by 1970 the Corncrake had virtually disappeared from the Swiss lowlands (Inderwildi, 2016). A low point in 1998 recorded just seven singing males (Maumary, 1999), and Corncrakes were no longer breeding regularly (Inderwildi and Müller, 2015), with between only 12 and 87 calling males found each year over the past two decades (Inderwildi, 2016). A Corncrake conservation programme initiated in 1996 has resulted in a slight recovery (Inderwildi and Müller, 2015), but confirmed breeding numbers are still very small.

Despite the initiation of a Corncrake conservation scheme (Brambilla and Pedrini, 2013), the species is not faring well in Italy and breeding success will require continued effort, including a focus on between-season shifts of habitat (Brambilla and Pedrini, 2011). Historical data on numbers and distribution are scanty, but there has been a large decline in both, with currently 95% of the population being found in the north-east of the country (Pedrini et al., 2016), and in particular the Eastern Alps (Borgo and Zoologia Botanica, 2010). During the first two decades of the twenty-first century, when other European populations saw a trend towards stabilisation or even a slight increase, the numbers in Italy continued their drastic decline, with a reduction from a high point of 325 calling males in 2000 to a low count of 61 in 2013 and a slight rise the following year (Florit and Rassati, 2016). The main areas in which to find the birds are in the regions of Trentino (Pedrini et al., 2012), Veneto and in particular Friuli-Venezia Giulia (Rassati and Tout, 2002) where the landscape mosaic currently provides suitable habitat (Rassati and Rodaro, 2007) and encourages a monitoring programme (Florit and Rassati, 2013). Unfortunately the common twin threats of grassland intensification or abandonment continue to provide unsuitable habitat over most of the region and the long-term distribution is uncertain (Pedrini et al., 2016).

Over the border, in Austria, little was known about Corncrake numbers and distribution until the surveys for the *Austrian Bird Atlas* between 1981 and 1985, with the first national census in 1994 and 1995 (Frühauf, 1999). Although solitary birds are found through the country, the largest regional population is along the eastern border of the Alps and in the uplands bordering Slovakia. Other parts of the country have suffered strong historical decline (Frühauf, 1997), and in the Rhine delta, the population dropped from 170 males in 1964 and disappeared only 6 years later following land-use changes (Frühauf, 1999). The total Austrian population in 1995–2015 was estimated at 150–500 calling males, a slight increase over 1989–1995, although it is thought that the maintenance of the numbers nationally is due to frequent incoming birds from Central and eastern Europe (Frühauf, 2016). Several local western European Corncrake populations have seen a partial recovery since 1997, but there have been large fluctuations, and the future stability remains uncertain (Koffijberg et al., 2016).

This roll-call of declining numbers and range distribution all across western Europe was ringing a constant alarm bell before the turn of the millennium, and two important publications on the conservation status of birds in Europe (Tucker and Heath, 1994) and globally (Collar and Andrew, 1988) highlighted the plight of the Corncrake. The species was classed as 'most endangered' in the Red Data Book, and some authors, rather precipitously, began writing about the 'global extinction' of the Corncrake (Green, 1996; Green and Gibbons, 2000). The growing coordination of international knowledge and further research led to several ornithological conferences in the 1990s focusing specifically on the Corncrake and, by the start of new millennium, to the production of an *Action Plan for the Corncrake* (Crockford et al., 1996), which was intended to be the basis for a conservation plan covering the whole of western Europe (Schäffer and Green, 2001). This initiated a succession of regional, national and transnational action plans that attempted to document the current ecological knowledge relating to Corncrake management and conservation, and to propose numerous points for action (for example, Koffijberg and Schäffer, 2006).

EASTERN EUROPE

In the mid-1990s, thriving Corncrake populations were discovered in Russia and several other countries in Central and Eastern Europe, and this has necessitated a reconsideration of the global dynamics of the Corncrake population (Koffijberg et al., 2016). Survey work in European Russia in 1995–96 estimated between 1 million and 1.5 million calling Corncrakes, which is 10 to 15 times greater than the 'educated guess' prior to this point. The relatively modest monitoring in Russia indicates that numbers have remained stable since 2002 or are even increasing, and the predicted declines of around 30% have not taken place (BirdLife International, 2020). As a result of these discoveries, the Corncrake has been reclassified from Vulnerable to Near Threatened in 2004, to Least Concern in 2010, and currently to Secure (BirdLife International, 2015). The global population is now thought to include between 3.6 to 6.7 million mature individuals, including 1–1.5 million pairs in European Russia and a further 515,000–1,240,000 pairs in Asiatic Russia (BirdLife International, 2020), and although counts over much of that vast country remain few-to-non-existent, the limited information available indicates that Eastern Russia and Central Asia is the core of the Corncrake range (Fourcade et al., 2013). Based upon the known rates of its population decline, the Corncrake is now regarded as Least Concern among the categories of vulnerable bird species, which means that it is judged to have at least a 10% likelihood of extinction within 100 years (Schäffer and Green, 2001). Although current data for the eastern regions are patchy, the numbers may actually be underestimated in its Asian range, but first we should summarise recent knowledge.

Almost nothing is known about the population in Lithuania before the 1980s, but it was estimated that there were around 25,000–30,000 pairs in the 1996–97 census (Adomatitis et al., 1998), and although no systematic surveys were carried out (reports were based upon personal observations) the trend in the 1990s was positive (Preiksa, 1999). A similar situation existed in Estonia where a 1995 estimate gave 10,000–18,000 calling pairs in the country, and though it was felt that river floodplains were probably undercounted, a downward trend had been noticed for the previous three decades (Elts, 1997). Only a few reviews have been conducted in Estonia (Elts and Marja, 2007) and even fewer surveys have been published (Elts, 1997), but more recent work has identified high densities of calling males throughout the country, especially, for example, in the Lahemaa National Park, with 11.7 calling males per km^2 recorded (Marja et al., 2015). In contrast, although there is no reliable population figure before 1990, studies in Latvia from 1989 to 2000 reported increases in the average breeding densities from 0.84 to 1.36 calling males per km^2 (Keišs et al., 2007). A survey in 1996 on 20 randomly selected plots (each 100 km^2) estimated the total population in Latvia around 26,000–38,000 calling males, 43% of which were found in hay meadows and a further 23% in fallow grasslands (Keišs, 1997). A comprehensive study of ringing data in Latvia and other eastern European countries, however, shows an overall decline in the number of Corncrakes ringed (Keišs et al., 2007). Numbers had decreased markedly since the beginning of the twentieth century, although there was a slight population rise during the 1990s (Keišs, 2003; Keišs and Kemlers, 2000). The highest breeding density of around three males per km^2 was observed in abandoned grasslands due to an increase in favourable habitats caused by changes in agriculture throughout all the Baltic states (Keišs, (2005). The increased numbers around the turn of the millennium are likely to be due to in-migration from populations further east, rather than as a result of any specific conservation efforts (Keišs, 2003). In all of these regions, the continually changing agricultural situation, together with the long-term unsuitability of abandoned farmland as suitable habitat, combine to make the long-term stability of the Baltic population uncertain (Keišs and Mednis, 2006).

Moving southwards, the first detailed estimate for the Corncrake population in Poland was made only in 1997 (Chylarecki et al., 1998), and proposed around 30,000 calling males across the whole country, although the actual census covered only 3.22% of Poland (Gromadzki, 1999). In the first half of the 1990s, numbers fell (Tomialojc, 1990) in common with regions further west, but Corncrakes were still numerous in the eastern regions (Dyrcz et al., 1984) and, more recently, high densities (up to 12 males per km^2) were recorded in the Kampinowski National Park in Central Poland (Juszczak and Olech, 1997). Earlier studies have made significant contributions to the behaviour and breeding biology of the species (Schäffer and Zub, 1994), as well as pioneering work on Corncrake vocalisation (Ręk and Kwiatkowska, 2016). By the end of the 1990s there were an estimated 2 million hectares of abandoned farmland in Poland (around 11% of all farmland; Orlowski, 2010), and although these areas have been favoured by many Corncrakes, the changing vegetational structure as abandonment continues is likely to produce ongoing changes in both numbers and geographical distribution.

Continuing to the south, the history of the Corncrake in both the Czech and Slovak Republics presages the story that will be repeated again and again as we consider the breeding regions further to the east. Until the middle of the twentieth century, the species was quite common across both countries, with around 200–400 calling males in the Czech Republic estimated for 1985–1989 (Pykal et al., 1999), and there was a slight increase during the 1990s, with a count of 483 in the 1995 season (Bürger et al., 1997), rising to 1,500 to 1,700 by the end of the decade (Pykal and Flousek, 2016). Most calling birds were distributed around the country's border areas, in the north, east and south (Bürger et al., 1998), where there is also some movement into northern Austria. Stronghold areas are in the wet meadows of the Šumava Mountain zone (Skliba and Fuchs, 2002) and around the confluence of the Morava and Dyje Rivers. The increase in the Corncrake population during the 1990s coincided with the reduction and abandonment of intensive State-directed agriculture, and also with a large decrease in the farmland application of chemical pesticides and fertilisers. In Šumava, 32 calling males were recorded in 1993 and 34 in 2015, with a peak of 59 in 2000 and 2003, while in the Krkonoše region 60 were recorded in 1998 and 59 in 2015, with a peak of 105 in 2002 (Pykal and Flousek, 2016). A similar habitat management situation exists in the Slovak Republic, with Corncrake numbers decreasing as agriculture became more intensive and many meadows were amalgamated or converted into arable land. In both countries the initial increases due to land abandonment are unlikely to continue due to the constantly changing agricultural situation. Little interest in the species was taken until relatively recently, with an estimated 600–900 pairs in the 1973–1994 period (Murin et al., 1994) and a slight increase to 1,400– 1,700 pairs by the end of the 1990s, although this figure probably results from better counting rather than a real population increase (Demko, 1999).

Maintaining our drift to the south-east, Hungary has historically had a reasonably stable Corncrake population (Boldogh, 1999), mainly located in the floodplains in the north-east of the country (Boldogh et al., 2009). Although annual details are often lacking, the species was previously common, but became rare by the 1970s (Szép, 1991), and there can be a considerable fluctuation in numbers, often due to local flooding (Boldogh, Visnyovszky et al., 2016). The Szatmár-Bereg area (Wettstein et al., 2001), the Zemplén Mountains, the floodplains of the Bodrog and Tisza Rivers, and the region of the Aggtelek National Park (all located in the north-east) are key areas of Corncrake distribution. In 2007–2015, the size of the national breeding population was estimated at 400–1,600 calling males, with around 45–50% of the breeding population located in protected areas (Boldogh, Szentirmai et al., 2016). An estimated 500–2,000 pairs bred in Hungary in 2016, although the population had declined by about 55% during the previous 20 years and has recently been in a steep decline outwith protected areas, with the main threats being environmental damage by either drying or flooding of habitats (Szentirmai et al., 2016).

Throughout the area formerly known as Yugoslavia, the story is similar, with apparently little historical interest in the numbers or distribution of Corncrakes, other than random observations (Grobelnik and Trontelj, 1999), not even as approximate estimates (Tadic, 1999). The threats are similar throughout the region – local intensification or abandonment of agriculture, flooding (Tome, 2002a) or drainage of wet meadows, or game hunting. In Slovenia, the first national survey took place in 1992–93 and estimated 510 calling males, mainly in the wet meadows and marshes in the Ljubljanica river system (Grobelnik and Trontelj, 1999). This locality constituted 84% of all known Corncrakes in the country (Trontelj, 1995), but the population continued to decrease drastically (Tome, 2002b) between 1999 and 2002. There have been small remnant populations recorded in the western Julian Alps, but overall the population has decreased considerably over the past 50 years. In central Slovenia, the total numbers of calling Corncrakes heard (Božič, 2005a) were 170 in 2002 and 137 in 2003, with a decrease in range as well as numbers, and although 391 calling males were detected in 2004, that was a 30% reduction from the 1999 estimate of 590 calling males (Trontelj, 2001). In the previous stronghold of the Ljubljansko marshes in central Slovenia, a 56% decrease was recorded over this period (Božič, 2005b). In another key area, around Lake Cernica (Polak et al., 2004), there was a low count of 42 calling males in 1997 compared with the highest count of 101 in 1993. The main breeding areas in Croatia have historically been in the floodplains of the Sava, Kupa and Drava rivers, and numbers were estimated in 1990–1999 as 460–1,000 calling males, although the baseline knowledge is so poor that the real population may be slightly larger (Radovic and Dumbovic, 1999). Despite agricultural changes throughout the country, an estimate in 2010 gave 500–1,000 calling males, but it is difficult to say if this indicates a level of stability, regional fluctuation or simply a reflection of the counting methods (Tutiš, 2010).

Detailed records of calling male Corncrakes in Bosnia-Herzegovina have been re-viewed from the earliest bird heard in 1847 to the estimates of a total of 500–800 in 2013, but these were mainly geographically distributed in small numbers or individual birds (Sackl et al., 2013). Habitat destruction is also a major problem in Bosnia-Herzegovina, and despite very little historical interest in the species (Obratil, 1999), about 1–3 singing individual males per site were recorded in 13 scattered locations in more mountainous areas during 2014–2016 (Dervović and Kotrošan, 2016). Little current or historical in-formation is available from Serbia (Radišić et al., 2019), and almost nothing from North Macedonia (Micevski, 1999), but the ongoing agricultural changes in both countries make future numbers precarious. The majority of Corncrakes in Moldova were located in the floodplains of the Prut, Reut and Jalpug rivers, with an estimated 700–1,100 nesting pairs at the end of the 1990s, although there was a sharp decline between the 1980s and 1990s, both in range and total population (Zubcov, 1999).

A pilot study in 1995 covering about 8% of Bulgaria, but 70% of the potential Corncrake habitat, found 323 calling males and estimated that this was around one-third of the total population for the country (Delov and Iankov, 1997). In contrast, there have been several studies on Corncrakes undertaken in Romania, although little of this has been published, and many areas lack surveys, with little attention to the general ecology of the species (Moga et al., 2010). A survey in 1997 estimated 10,000–22,000 calling males (Gache, 1999), the largest number being in the floodplains of the Jijia River (Gache and Trelea, 2004). There is no reliable information available before this date. Studies in the Ciuc Basin and Gheorgheni Basin (Demeter and Szabo, 2005) in the Eastern Carpathian Mountains in 2001–2004 found Corncrake densities of 2.4–4.6 individuals per km^2 and estimated 50–100 calling males. More recent surveys have found the majority of the Romanian Corncrake population in Transylvania, in the central northern part of the country, and have estimated 8,000–30,000 calling males (Todorova, 2016). These are wide margins of counting error, but the figure may represent between 5% and 8% of the EU population, making Transylvania a hotspot for Corncrakes. Despite these large survey uncertainties, there has been no observed decrease in the regional population in recent years (Page and Popa, 2016).

Along the eastern edges of Europe, in Armenia (Adamian and Klem, 1999), Georgia (Javakhishvili, 1999) and Turkey (Eken et al., 1999), there is almost no detailed information on the population numbers of the distribution of Corncrakes, or even if they are regularly breeding or only passage migrants. Not until we move northwards into Ukraine does this situation improve. The Corncrake was considered to be one of the most numerous bird species in the river valleys of Ukraine until the mid-twentieth century, with a rapid decline thereafter. The floodplains of the Dnieper and Desna rivers saw an 80% decrease during this period (Atemasov et al., 2016). Early surveys were probably incomplete, giving countrywide estimates of 2,500 males in 1988, 55,000 in 1995, 127,000 in 2000 and 102,000 in 2001 (Atemasov et al., 2016). Breeding pairs are scattered throughout the river valleys of the country, but the key populations are historically in the northern and north-western parts of Ukraine. A similar lack of historical data, but an apparently reasonably healthy Corncrake population, has been recorded for Belarus, particularly in the meadows of the wide river floodplains (Nikiforov and Vintchevski, 1999). Although there was a five-fold decrease during the 1990s, by the end of that decade calling males were estimated at 25,000–40,000.

The real surprise, however, is that Russia provides breeding territories for around 80–95% of the global Corncrake population (Grishchenko and Prins, 2016). The breeding range is large throughout Russia, although the distribution is uneven and the vastness of the country means that in many (most?) areas, population estimates are little more than educated guesses. Even in areas where a census has taken place, the usual internationally agreed threshold of significance of 20 breeding pairs for the recognition of an 'important birds area' is insufficient and requires a threshold of 100 calling males in Russia (Mischenko and Sukhanova, 1999a). In previous decades, it had been assumed by Russian naturalists that the Corncrake was so ubiquitous (apart from in the northern regions above 60 degrees north) that it was not regarded as requiring special monitoring (Sukhanova and Mischenko, 2003), and that although numbers had declined in some regions in the late 1990s, by the end of the century 'there was no tendency for Corncrake numbers to reduce'. There were reports that in some areas the air was 'literally filled with Corncrake calls', although regional increases and decreases in populations have been noted throughout the twentieth century, which is unsurprising given the scale of Russian geography (Sukhanova and Mischenko, 2003).

In the mid-1990s, surveys and new information obtained in countries formerly under Soviet influence revealed thriving populations of Corncrakes across the eastern zone of their potential breeding area (Koffijberg et al., 2016). From the Baltic states to the far east of Russia and into western China, a combination of better international communications, new surveys and changing agricultural environments produced an entirely new perspective on the global population ecology of the Corncrake. There was no systematic monitoring of Corncrakes in Russia before 2000, and any local surveys frequently demonstrated considerable fluctuations in numbers, but a large-scale count in 1995–96, based upon 22 sample sites in 13 regions, estimated between 1 million and 1.54 million Corncrake males, with the highest density in the Sverdlovsk and Vologda regions (up to 72.2 calling males per km^2; Mischenko, 2008). The extrapolation from these random counting plots (each 1,034 km^2) gave a more precise estimation based on better data, rather than the discovery of a population increase in the country (Mischenko et al., 1997).

Surprisingly, the species is not rare, even in cities like Moscow (Mischenko, 2016), and there are records from across the country from the boundaries of western Europe, across the northern taiga and tundra of the Siberian Plain (Ravkin, 1999), and into Asia. As a result of new information, and the discovery of the huge, previously unrealised potential of Corncrake numbers throughout Russia and the western reaches of China, it is worth repeating that the Corncrake, which was considered to be globally threatened has been reclassified by the International Union for the Conservation of Nature to be a species of Least Concern, but the matter is still a highly-contested issue. Although the dramatic rise in population estimates now recognises millions of birds, this is undoubtedly a result of better sampling techniques and better geographical coverage by surveys, and the figure remains only an estimate. There are very large areas of the country that remain without regular, adequate surveys and the continuing changes in agriculture mean that farmland that is currently providing good habitats is likely to become less suitable as farm abandonment intensifies (Grishchenko and Prins, 2016). Several western European countries have regularly reported the arrival of Corncrakes from the east to boost local/regional populations, but there is little accurate information available to indicate if these are the characteristic fluctuations of Corncrake numbers caused, for instance, by regional weather disruptions, or if it is a result of displacement due to deteriorating habitat in other regions (Grishchenko and Prins, 2016).

The future for the Corncrake is certainly much more optimistic than it was in the 1990s when global extinction was being predicted, but the long-term future is still in the balance. Continuing landscape changes throughout its huge breeding range, particularly in terms of agricultural intensification, land abandonment, drainage and other disruptions, are potentially threatening, and habitats will undoubtedly need to be monitored, maintained and managed to ensure the future of healthy Corncrake populations.

AFRICA

Despite a general knowledge of the presence of Corncrakes during their migration throughout most of eastern Africa, from Egypt to South Africa, a study in Zambia published in 1984 stated that, 'almost nothing has been recorded of its habits in Africa'

(Taylor, 1984). Sporadic sightings have been recorded throughout the continent (Walther, 2008), but although local occurrences throughout this vast region have been known and documented (Walther et al., 2013b) for many years, there is still much unknown. The timing of local movements seems to be related to the rains, but the numbers and distribution of the populations, and the relative importance of different areas are little known in any detail, apart from the sporadic records of sightings (Stowe and Becker, 1992). Of course, the success of the migration (see Chapter 8) depends not only on finding a suitable habitat at the final destination, but also at the stops along the route (Ashoori and Zolfinejad, 2008), as well as the successful evasion of predators in these stopover sites (Eason et al., 2010; see also Chapter 11).

The threats from traditional hunting and trapping along the Mediterranean coast of Egypt are well known (Baha el Din et al., 1996), and although regular monitoring is weak, there is enough detail to justify concern that the rate of bird capture is not sustainable, although Quails are often the main target species (Eason et al., 2016). More recent accounts have suggested that Corncrakes are not under immediate threat in their sub-Saharan quarters, but have also confirmed that much of their detailed ecology in that environmentally-diverse continent remains little understood (Walther, 2008). There are few ringing recoveries from most of the core areas of their known migration routes, and this will probably remain the case until more sophisticated systems are readily available to monitor avian mobility and travel destinations. Taken overall, the number of records and their distribution indicate that the majority of Corncrakes migrate from their home breeding areas to eastern Africa, but reports from throughout the continent are likely to be a result of the combination of the availability of suitable habitat, as well as local weather and climatic conditions (Walther et al., 2013a).

OUTLIER RECORDS

Although the great majority of the recorded sightings of Corncrakes have been from their European breeding areas and along the length of the two great migration fly-paths into central and south-eastern Africa (see Chapter 8), there are many ornithological records from a remarkably wide swathe of global locations. Most of these sightings are due to the intermittent identification of vagrant birds, but the records are incredibly persistent, including from the 1870s in Nova Scotia (Mckinlay, 1899), and in 1889 from Maine (Brock, 1896) and Long Island (Latham, 1964), to the first record in 2012 for South America (Burgos and Olmos, 2013) on the island of Fernando de Noronha, Brazil. From Greenland (Gray, 1871), south along the entire eastern coast of North America, there are many records (Decandido and Allen, 2018), but few can have caused the intense flurry of interest (Feustel, 2018; Trezza, 2017), that was produced by the Corncrake that turned up in New York State in 2017.

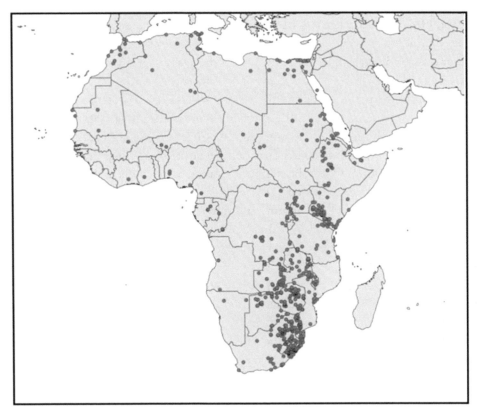

Figure 6.6: *An example of the recorded distribution of Corncrakes in Africa in 2012.* Source: Walther et al. (2013a).

As if the wanderings of Corncrakes along the Atlantic shores of the Americas are not surprising enough, their ability to appear in the widely-scattered reaches of the Pacific is still more amazing. In 1996 a Corncrake was spotted in the snake market of a Vietnamese town in the Mekong Delta (Meek, 1996). Other records or vagrants have been made from Pakistan, Sri Lanka, Tibet, India, Ladakh and western China, while records from Xinjiang (Ma Ming and Wang Qishan, 2002) and other Chinese localities (Braunlich and Rank, 1999) seem to indicate that a sizeable breeding population may have been previously overlooked. Occasional Corncrakes have been noted as passage migrants in Iran and Afghanistan and, at what must surely be the edge of its range, in Mongolia and Australia; a single report from New Zealand has not been accepted (Braunlich and Rank, 1999). From this extreme scatter of recorded global sightings, it is difficult to know what to conclude, apart from the fact that the enigmatic Corncrake continues to provide surprises for observant ornithologists.

CENSUS METHODS

In a masterclass of understatement, it has been said that:

'Monitoring rare species often fails to account for imperfect detection.'

(Arbeiter, Roth et al., 2017)

One of the great problems in counting the population of this reclusive bird is that, in most circumstances, the watcher does not know that the Corncrake is there until the male advertises his presence by calling. Unfortunately, there is currently no known large-scale method of live capture that is not biased towards the selective sampling of male birds (Fourcade et al., 2016). Of course the great scientific maxim, 'absence of evidence is not evidence of absence' means that silent males and females may remain largely uncounted, but it does not necessarily mean that they are not present in the locality. There is an account of a farmer in north Wales calling an engineer to investigate a pylon 'shorting' in his field, merely to discover the only breeding Corncrake in Wales that year (Cocker and Mabey, 2005). For this reason, despite attempts to set international standards for censuses (Schäffer and Mammen, 2003), many of the census counts give widely varying figures, coupled with the fact that different observers in the same location may hear (or not hear) different calling birds. This produces imprecise numbers and locations and gives rise to gaps and duplications in biological recording data (Hudson et al., 1990). In addition, the surveyors often have a potential emotional investment and even a possible personal unintended bias in conducting a census (Lorimer, 2008), which observers frequently undertake only on fleeting visits to the core breeding areas.

During the 1988 UK census, conversations with local people in the Isle of Lewis and in Ireland, showed that local populations of Corncrakes had been present during the earlier 1978–79 survey, but had not been counted (Stowe et al., 1993). Many birds also relocate during the breeding season and may be duplicated or missed in any count, however systematic. The most common survey method is for observers to walk around areas of potentially suitable habitat, generally between 23:00 and 03:00 in the morning when the Corncrake calls almost continuously from their (normally stationary) territorial calling site. Even this apparently simple method of counting has been shown to be subject to variation, depending on the method of locating the apparent site of the calling male. It may overestimate the population size when the density of calling birds is low and underestimate it when birds are more numerous (Budka and Kokocinski, 2015). This combination of varied arrival dates, departure times and territorial movements within a single breeding season must also be carefully considered to ensure that counting the site occupancy within any particular area is assessed reasonably accurately (Arbeiter et al., 2018).

More recent studies (Peake and Mcgregor, 2001) have indicated that traditional census techniques in North Uist were later thought to underestimate the actual number of

Corncrakes by 20–30%. The tendency of Corncrakes to cluster in favourable habitats and to respond to each other's call may mean that single birds might sing less frequently and are overlooked (Hudson et al., 1990). Using mathematical modelling in much the same way that the breeding success has been estimated (Green, Tyler et al., 1997) can improve counting techniques in the field. With a highly mobile species such as Corncrakes, low detection rates due to the irregular departure and arrival of birds, their calling frequency and the ability of the surveyor to hear an individual on any one night, means that there is considerable scope for miscounting. Based on an average detection probability, taking all these various factors into account, it has been calculated that standard counts in the field may underestimate by up to 50% the number of birds present (Arbeiter, Roth et al., 2017).

Colour ringing of Corncrakes to assist individual identification is not really feasible due to the rarity of individual sightings, and mark-and-recapture monitoring is not practical for both logistical and welfare reasons (Peake et al., 1998). On the whole, recovery of ringed birds is relatively uncommon (see Chapter 8 on migration), and by itself is of little use in following the local and regional movements of birds, not least because Corncrakes are rarely seen out in the open field. Some pioneering work in the Outer Hebrides used radio telemetry to track the local movements of birds (Stowe and Hudson, 1988), but this is obviously only of use for tracking known birds that have been trapped and then fitted with a small transmitter, rather than for establishing the unknown number of birds in an area. This work has been followed in other areas to investigate the habitat use of Corncrakes (Faragó and Szentirmai, 2014) as well as their habitat range and site fidelity (Ottvall and Pettersson, 1998a), but there are limitations to its application. Radio-tracking cannot easily follow birds from one season to the next, and although radio transmitters are small and becoming more powerful, the handling process of telemetry is a non-trivial intrusion that can disturb birds, which may also have unintended effects (Cuthill, 1991). New techniques in microsatellite tracking may better inform us about Corncrake dispersal in the future (Wettstein et al., 2003), and may even be used for very localised young birds (Green et al., 2019), but it may not be cost-effective for short-lived species compared to birds with a longer lifespan.

In some localities (Swann, 1986; Wotton et al., 2015) it has been shown possible to attract Corncrakes to land by playing a recording of the Corncrake call (Ottvall and Pettersson, 1998b). It has been suggested that this might be a future management tool to encourage males to establish a territory (Toivanen, 2009). The technique of vocal individuality has also been attempted as a tool for counting the local population, but with limited success (Winkler et al., 2014). It has further been suggested that recordings of a Corncrake's distress call might be employed to encourage birds to leave a particular area, for example prior to mowing activities, but there are no published reports on the efficacy of this (Aberdeen Centre for Land Use, 1991). This vocal profile of an individual Corncrake (see Chapter 9) has been used to assist greater counting accuracy during a census. The basis of this method is that calling males frequently move to call from areas other than their own calling site (later returning to their main site), so that some birds may appear to call less than others (for example, after finding a mate). This means that a census of an area may undercount or double count the population when it is based only on noting the birds that are calling. It was found that the individual distinctiveness of a Corncrake call can help to reduce counting error by identifying individual calling birds. In fact, a major source of any bias would appear to be the systematic undercounting due to some males calling only intermittently. Using vocal identification in combination with other techniques (Peake and Mcgregor, 2001) has been shown to increase census estimates by 20–30%. Other innovations undoubtedly await discovery (Fiedler, 2009), and while this book was being written, exciting research is being planned in the Republic of Ireland to use passive acoustic monitoring and thermal imaging techniques to detect and conserve Corncrakes. All of these techniques, and more, will certainly help in any future census to identify more accurately the actual numbers and distribution of this particularly elusive species.

CONCLUSION

The Corncrake has a huge breeding range, from the Hebridean islands of Scotland in the west, throughout the north of western Europe north of the Alps, stretching eastwards through Russia and into western Asia. Across most of its range in western Europe, the Corncrake population has been steadily declining for more than a century, largely in response to the intensification of agriculture and to habitat loss. Since the turn of the millennium, a much larger population has been identified in Russia than was previously estimated and this has, to some extent, reduced the level of global threat, although most areas of potential habitat in the northern hemisphere are subject to relatively rapid incremental change and species loss. Estimating the total numbers and distribution is difficult in most regions due partly to the in-season mobility of birds, which gives the characteristic population fluctuations observed in many areas from year to year. Outwith the breeding season, most birds migrate to African locations, although vagrant individuals have been recorded from a very wide range of settings.

CHAPTER 7

BREEDING BIOLOGY

RETURN TO THE BREEDING TERRITORIES

Corncrakes tend to leave Africa between mid-March and early April (Taylor, 1984), with males arriving in the northern hemisphere breeding localities from late April onwards, and female birds arriving only slightly later (Green, Rocamora et al., 1997). The later arrivals of birds in suitable European habitats (in June, July and even August) and their attempts to establish territories are likely to be birds relocating for a second breeding attempt (see later). A study in Sweden (Alnås, 1974), found that the homing rate of ringed Corncrakes varied considerably from year to year, with 20–25% in years of high population density and a much lower percentage in other years. The return of birds to the same territories after two years has also been observed in several other areas (Budka and Osiejuk, 2013b). Key features of potentially suitable habitat are that the grass should be tall enough to provide cover for this reclusive bird – at least 15–30 cm high (Forrester et al., 2007) – and that the vegetation at ground level should not be too dense for the birds to walk though (Tyler, 1996; Green, Rocamora et al., 1997). In some countries, such as Germany (Schäffer and Münch, 1993) and Russia (Grabovsky, 1993), singing males are frequently heard from the herbage at the forest edge, which provides cover early in the season.

Corncrakes breed from 1 year old and within a few days of their return from migration. If they are able to settle within a potential breeding habitat, the male birds begin their nocturnal calling. This generally peaks from around 22:00 until 04:00 (approximately dusk until dawn) after which time the male birds move away from singing sites and become less vocal (Stowe and Hudson, 1988). Not all male birds call every night, and females appear to play no active role in defending the territory. Several studies have shown that males rarely move more than 250 m between calling sites within one territory

(Peake and Mcgregor, 2001), but this can vary widely. It has been suggested that male Corncrakes move greater distances throughout the breeding season in localities where suitable habitat is scarce, rather than in places where there is more homogeneous vegetational cover (Peake and Mcgregor, 2001). In optimal habitat in Poland, the distance between a territorial male and its nearest neighbour ranged from 50 m to 340 m (Budka and Osiejuk, 2013b), while radio-tracking of birds in the Outer Hebrides of Scotland indicated that the home ranges of males varied considerably, from 3 hectares to over 50 hectares, and although one female wandered over 100 hectares, the home range of most females was less than 30 hectares (Stowe and Hudson, 1988). The home ranges of Corncrakes in the Netherlands were found to be overlapping and considerably smaller than those in Scotland and Ireland, possibly due to food availability or to the conformation of the available territory on the narrow Dutch floodplains (Koffijberg et al., 2007). In Germany, the overlapping of several home ranges is striking, with an average home range of 6.3 hectares (0.4–16.1 hectares) (Helmecke, 1999), while female birds in Hungary used around 2–3 hectares during their breeding attempts (Boldogh, Szentirmai et al., 2016). In part, this is due to the demands of the incubation and brood-raising roles of the female, and also the fact that some males may use more than one home range during a single breeding season (Tyler, 1996).

The abundance and density of Corncrake territories can vary greatly among different localities in the same area within the same year, and local effects such as the height of the grass in response to seasonal growth can make an appreciable difference. In Poland, the clustering of males can be pronounced, with local densities from 10–25 per km^2 depending on local habitat conditions, and with a territorial male having on average six calling neighbours (Budka et al., 2012). Singing males are generally not dispersed evenly within any suitable habitat but, at least at the start of the breeding season, they are likely to be loosely clustered, with groups of 3–10 being common, although isolated calling birds are also known (Green, Rocamora et al., 1997). This tendency for calling males to cluster in relatively close proximity has been noted from a number of geographical localities. It has been suggested that birds gather in suitable habitats around the first individual(s) to arrive (Rassati and Tout, 2002), and that the evolutionary importance of clustering is that, among visually constraining vegetation, the combined calling of the cluster amplifies the opportunities to attract females from a greater distance (Atsma, 2006).

A study in Romania found four to five calling males per km^2, and defined 'high-density Corncrake areas' as those localities with more than 10 males on a site, with a maximum distance of 1,000 m from the closest neighbour (Demeter and Szabo, 2005). Other areas of western Europe have recorded similar densities of territory occupation, at around three to four calling males per km^2 in the Netherlands (Koffijberg and Nienhuis, 2003), Latvia (Keišs, 2004) and Ukraine (Dudkin, 2001), and up to 10 males per km^2 have been recorded in the UK and Ireland (Green, 1996). The extent of clustering of the males appears to vary mostly in response to the local composition and suitability of the vegetation (its species composition and structure; Corbett and Hudson, 2010), as well as variations in the use of pesticides, agricultural practices and/or predation rates (Pedrini et al., 2012), and can reach quite high densities in optimal habitat conditions (Budka et al., 2012). A study in the marshland of Karelian Russia (Marja et al., 2015) reported up to 22 calling males per km² in the late 1960s. Depending on different local situations, there may also be slight discrepancies in the recorded number of occupied territories depending on the method of census used for counting (Budka and Kokocinski, 2015; see also Chapter 6).

Spatial behaviour in a local Russian population (Grabovsky, 1993) suggests that in years of relatively high population density the spacing of the Corncrakes was random in the first half of the year and contagious (clustered) in the second half. In years of low population density, the spacing was contagious during the whole season, and irrespective of population density, the distance between neighbouring birds was usually around 300–400 m, with an individual home range of 1–10 hectares. It has been suggested that there is a social attraction implicit in this clustering, and that the social attraction of males is reflected in the call-and-response behaviour of males seeking mates (see Chapters 7 and 9). This system of dispersal of male Corncrakes, in loose clusters within hearing of each other, appears to be an example of a form of 'exploded lek' (Alonso et al., 2012) in which 'information exchange among males is almost restricted to the auditory channel' (Ręk, 2014).

Courtship and pair formation

The male bird calls repetitively and continuously for several hours each night with the intention of attracting the attention of a female. This initial rasping call is broadcast loudly and contains mixed signals that are meaningful to recipient birds, such as advertising the presence of the male and also perhaps providing information on the male's breeding quality and body condition (Thom and Dytham, 2012). The fact that most male birds cease to call quite so repetitively after they have found a mate indicates that this signalling is at least partially a female-seeking behaviour (see Chapter 9). Several nests may be prepared for the female to select from and

> *'a short sound of medium pitch, appears to be used initially to attract the female to the prepared nests so that she can select a nest for laying.'*
>
> (Graham, 2009)

In an early series of experiments with a stuffed decoy and accompanying simulated calls using notched bones, the initial approaches of wild birds were observed and fully documented, and this detail is worth quoting in the original text:

'Usually the bird answers our call and then approaches without craking, but uttering an occasional "growling-mew" note... [described in Chapter 9] ... They then make a courtship display and finally attempt... [copulation]. In a full display the head is held low with the neck outstretched. The wings are fully spread and directed slightly backwards, with the tips touching the ground. The flank and neck feathers are puffed out and the tail coverts erected vertically like a fan. Not all displays observed were as complete as this. The neck and flank feathers were not always puffed out, but the wings were in all cases fully extended and the tail coverts, whenever they could be seen, were erected.'

(Mason, 1945)

In at least one recorded observation, the male interrupted its attempts at copulation to go away and return with a green caterpillar, which it offered to the decoy ... and then resumed its display and attempted to mate (Mason, 1945). Normally the male tries to approach the female from behind and leaps on her back to attempt copulation. Food may be offered to the female by the male during courtship (Forrester et al., 2007) to encourage the pair bond. This behaviour is in contrast to that of the Spotted Crake and the Water Rail who do not appear to do this (Salzer, 1999).

Although the approaching male indicated an aggressive motivation when the decoy bird did not respond, it then resumed a more silent and passive reaction and appeared to treat it as a female. This courtship display is distinct from the combat display which, although similar to the sexual display in most initial aspects, then develops into lunging attacks and may occasionally lead to fights, with contact being made with the feet and/or the beak (Mason, 1951). In the aggressive mode, the head and neck of the approaching male is held at an angle of about 45 degrees, possibly to enable the attacker to maintain eye contact with the other bird. As the male lunges to attack, its feathers are erect (especially on the breast) and has 'wings forward and twisted them so that the leading edge was down and the surface of the wing almost vertical' (Mason, 1944).

THE NEST AREA AND NEST BUILDING

Although it had always been assumed that nest building is 'probably by the female only' (Cramp and Simmons, 1980), it has been noted in captive birds that 'this activity is undertaken solely by the male' (Graham, 2009) and this behaviour is now regarded as widespread in the wild. Depending on the local habitat diversity, nests are usually well-concealed in tall grassland or dense vegetation, such as sedge-meadows (Fitter and Richardson, 1968), and occasionally in the shelter of field margins near hedges or bushy areas (Taylor and van Perlo, 1998). Early in the season, nests can be concealed among Yellow Iris, Cow Parsley or clumps of Common Nettles often within 200 m of the male's singing place (Green and Riley, 1999). The nest itself is sometimes just a scrape in the ground (Taylor and van Perlo, 1998) but, usually, it is a small cup of grass, roughly 15–20 cm in external diameter and 3–4 cm deep, among the taller grass. The nest is woven carefully with coarse, dry grass and other local vegetation, including possibly a few leaves swirled loosely to form a cup, which is lined with fine grass (Seebohm, 1896). Occasionally the surrounding tall grass may be pulled over the nest to form a loose dome-shape. Although some 'males [may] build their nests before a female is introduced, some wait until a female joins them' (Graham, 2009).

EGGS, LAYING AND INCUBATION

The first clutch can vary hugely between 6 and 19 eggs, but usually 8–13 eggs are laid, about 33–41 × 24–29 mm and 13–16 g in weight (Taylor and van Perlo, 1998). The eggs are various shades of white or cream, each spotted or blotched with reddish-brown, green, blue and/or grey (Fitter and Richardson, 1968). From around late-May or early June, the eggs are laid at daily intervals (sometimes more frequently) and the incubation is by the female only, usually lasting around 18–20 days, after which the eggs hatch synchronously. Incubation starts immediately upon completion of the clutch (Cramp and Simmons, 1980), and during the incubation period the female normally leaves the nest for only 10–15 minutes every hour to search near the nest site for food (Green and Riley, 1999). The usual date for the start of incubation is around the first week in June in Scotland, but it may be mid-May in France, with proportionate variation in other climates and different latitudes and altitudes (Green, Tyler et al., 1997; see also Figure 7.1). As early as 1871 it was noted that there may be a second clutch laid around the middle of July (Gray, 1871). If the first clutch is destroyed, Corncrakes may lay again, as a 'first clutch', and may also produce a second clutch if the first brood is reared early in the season (Stowe and Hudson, 1988). The duration of the male–female pair bond formation is relatively short, around 7–10 days (Tyler and Green, 1996), with the males generally stopping their nocturnal calling once the pair bond is established, and subsequently leaving their females 3–7 days before the start of egg incubation (Tyler and Green, 1996). As Corncrakes are sequentially polygamous (Green, Rocamora et al., 1997), the pair separate before half of the first clutch is laid, with the male (and sometimes also the female) moving to occupy another territory, which can be close by or some considerable distance away. The males resume their nocturnal singing in their new territory in an attempt to attract a second mate (Tyler, 1996). It has been reported that some males may perhaps sequentially breed with up to three females during a single season (Forrester et al., 2007). This differs from the Spotted Crake and the Water Rail, which are monogamous and provide biparental care (Salzer, 1999). Incubation on the second clutch begins around 42 days after the start of incubation of the first clutch, and about 12 days after the abandonment of the first brood (Taylor and van Perlo, 1998).

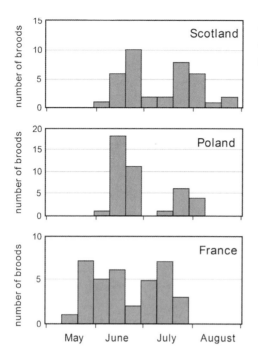

Figure 7.1: Approximate breeding times of first and second clutches. Source: Green, Rocamora et al. (1997).

NESTING SUCCESS AND CHICK DEVELOPMENT

Corncrake chicks are described as precocial, that is to say they are relatively mature and mobile from the moment of hatching, although unlike the young of many other precocial species, they do receive maternal attention from hatching until independence (Tyler and Green, 2004). The chicks are normally 9–14 g at hatching (Taylor and van Perlo, 1998) and leave the nest for good soon after hatching, but they continue to be fed and kept warm by the female until they begin to live independently and feed for themselves around 12 days old, which correlates with the start of wing growth (Salzer, 1999), at which point they are abandoned by the female (Tyler, 1996). Feeding is bill-to-bill at first, but the chicks begin to feed for themselves around 3 or 4 days old (Taylor and van Perlo, 1998). In fact, Corncrakes become independent from their mother at an earlier age than most other rails (Taylor, 1984), and they are independent of their mother for more than half the period between hatching and fledging (Green, Tyler et al., 1997). During this early period, they learn to forage by day within 100–200 m of the nest site (Green, Rocamora et al., 1997) and, as they usually become silent after they become independent of the mother, it is very difficult to locate and count them (Green, Tyler et al., 1997). A female was observed to eat the empty eggshells as soon as the young had hatched (Stowe and Hudson, 1988), but the density of the habitat and the relative reclusiveness of Corncrakes means that an opportunity to observe this behaviour is rarely available.

Figure 7.2: *Timing of breeding Corncrakes across Europe. x: occurrence during each half-month; + where only a few known examples were found.*
Source: Redrawn after Green, Rocamora et al. (1997).

	Nest with eggs								Flightless chicks							
	May		June		July		August		May		June		July		August	
	1	2	1	2	1	2	1	2	1	2	1	2	1	2	1	2
Belarus		x	x	x	x	x					x	x	x	x	x	
Belgium	No data								x							
Bulgaria		x	x	x	x						x	x	x	x	x	
Czech Republic		x	x	x	x				No data							
Denmark			x	x								x	x	x	x	
Estonia			x	x	x							x	x	x		
France	x	x	x	x	x						x	x	x	x		
Germany		x									x	x				
Ireland	x	x	x	x	x	x	+			+	x	x	x	x	x	+
Italy			x										x	x	x	x
Latvia		x	x	x					No data							
Liechtenstein	No data				x											
Lithuania		x	x	x	x	x			No data							
Luxembourg					x							x				
Moldova				x								x				
Netherlands		x	x	x	x							x	x	x		
Poland			x	x	x	x						x	x	x	x	x
Romania	x	x	x	x	x				No data							
Russia			x	x	x									x	x	
Scotland	x	x	x	x	x	x	+			+	x	x	x	x	x	+
Slovakia		x	x		x	x							x	x		
Slovenia		x	x										x			
Spain		x								x	x	x				
Sweden			x	x	x								x	x	x	+
Switzerland	x	x	x	x	x	x	x		No data							
Ukraine			+									+				

Although Corncrakes usually lay 8–13 eggs, it appears that broods of more than six or seven chicks are uncommon (Stowe and Hudson, 1988); however, in Scotland, apart from the destruction of the nests by mowing (see Chapter 12), nesting success can be relatively high, with around 93% surviving from laying to hatching (Tyler, 1996). Another study, of Corncrakes in Ireland, recorded that 72% of first-clutch chicks survived from independence to departure and 76% of the second broods (Donaghy et al., 2011). Adult survival rate is generally low, and the population dynamics are very sensitive to changes in the number of chicks that a female can successfully raise to independence (Green, 1999a). Studies in Scotland have suggested that at least 1.3 breeding attempts per female each season are needed to secure a self-sustaining population (Green, Tyler et al., 1997), so there is a biological imperative for a second breeding attempt. Studies in Scotland, Sweden, Poland and France have shown that females are frequently able to successfully produce two broods in areas where mowing is later in the season, and this is often imperative to compensate for the high mortality of both chicks and adults (Ottvall and Pettersson, 1998b). In the absence of mowing, research has recorded that the survival rates for the chicks of first and second broods are broadly similar (Duffy, 2018). Interestingly, in Poland unrelated males have been observed to associate with females accompanying broods of chicks near to independence (Green, Rocamora et al., 1997).

When the chicks hatch, they are covered in jet-black down, tinged rufous-brown on the upper parts, with black legs and feet, and a pink bill which becomes darker after a few days (Taylor and van Perlo, 1998). As this plumage is gradually replaced, the juvenile assumes a similar colouration to the adult birds. This is a difficult period, however, and in Scotland 10–20% of whole broods have been lost between hatching and independence, as well as partial losses which mainly occur in the first 5–6 days after hatching (Green, Rocamora et al., 1997). The young chicks move slowly in response to any disturbance (Tyler et al., 1998), and when human intruders approach an adult with chicks at this time, the adult may perform a distraction display, consisting of short flights (Bannerman, 1963) and a gentle summoning noise to the chicks (Schäffer et al., 1997). An early observer noted that:

> 'At the end of two days she led her chicks into a neighbouring field. When the hen was approached she ran away from her chicks for a few feet, then turned and faced the intruder, usually making a clicking noise with her mandibles, and at times a high-pitched creaking note'.

> (Brown, 1938)

The surviving chicks begin to live more independently from maternal care after around 16–20 days (Green, 2010). The mother gradually moves them further from the nest (Stowe and Hudson, 1991), and although they are unable to fly until they are about 35–45 days old, they gather together each night to roost, frequently in a temporary nest built by the female (Green and Riley, 1999). Little is known of the movement of chicks between independence and fledging at about 45 days old (Green et al., 2019). In a study of a reintroduced population of Corncrakes in England, it was noted that chicks up to 20 days old (mostly still dependent on the mother) tended to remain close (median distance 78 m) to the singing location of the father, whereas older, more independent chicks wandered further away (range 149–601 m, median 261 m; Green et al., 2019). This tendency for broods to remain closer to the singing location of the father, rather than that of other unrelated males, was regarded as statistically significant.

Multiple partners and second clutches

Corncrakes are sequentially polygamous, and both males and females change partners during the breeding season (Budka and Osiejuk, 2013b). Before the first full clutch is laid and incubation started, the male Corncrake leaves his partner and relocates to attempt to establish another territory, which may be relatively close (within hundreds of metres) or may be greater than 10 km away (Budka and Osiejuk, 2013b), perhaps even greater than 100 km away (Schäffer and Koffijberg, 2006). One individual bird was noted to relocate 132 km away within a single breeding season (Mikkelsen, 2010). Data collected in several regions suggests that, in addition to the seasonal change in vegetative cover, the exposure to mowing is the most important single variable to encourage the relocation and/or departure of both male and female individuals, but especially the male movements (Bellebaum, Arbeiter et al., 2016). On average, the incubation on the second nest begins around 42 days after incubation started on the first nest, and around 12 days after the female has left her first brood (Tyler, 1996). Males usually start to call again in their new territory on the first night after the termination of the first pair bond in order to attract a new female (Tyler and Green, 1996).

When Corncrakes move into a second territory later in the season, they may select a slightly different habitat due to the different seasonal states of vegetation and/or the changes in agricultural management. This may mean that the optimal habitat at the start

	EL	INC	CC	IC	First clutch		
Second clutch			EL	INC	CC	IC	
May		June		July		August	

Figure 7.3: *Breeding schedule of a typical female in Scotland. EL= egg-laying; INC= incubation; CC= chick care; IC= independent chicks (not fledged).* Source: Redrawn after Green, Tyler et al. (1997).

of the breeding season might not be the optimal by the end. In Poland there is evidence that Corncrakes may shift their territories as a response to intensified agricultural activity, such as grass mowing, in their first breeding territory and also due to changes in water levels during the year, for example, from flooding of lower-lying fields (Michalska-Hejduk et al., 2017).

This second clutch may be laid more rapidly, sometimes two eggs per day, and incubated over 16–18 days (Taylor and van Perlo, 1998). The changing availability of optimal habitat throughout the season can affect breeding success in other ways. In Switzerland, for instance, birds are now arriving later (in June), and successful nests tend to be formed at a higher altitude than in previous years. This is at least partially because when the birds arrive from Africa the vegetation in lowland meadows is too dense or is mowed too early to provide suitable habitat, whereas later in the season, higher altitude, less intensively managed meadows are in an optimal condition (Inderwildi, 2016). In previous decades, Corncrakes arrived earlier and bred mostly in lowland areas, which are now more intensively managed (Inderwildi and Müller, 2015). More recently, most of the breeding individuals have been found at altitudes above 1,000 m or even above 1,400 m, with the highest confirmed brood in the Alps in 2005 at 1,940 m (Inderwildi, 2016). Corncrakes have also been found at 3,000m above sea level in Russia (Green, Rocamora et al., 1997). It has been suggested that:

> 'first broods are presently rare in Switzerland. Most of the birds registered in this country are probably trying to perform second broods or lay replacement clutches after having been forced to leave their breeding territories in other parts of Europe due to mowing or vegetation becoming unsuitable due to seasonal succession.'
>
> (Inderwildi, 2016)

In a reintroduced population of birds, it has been observed that, 'both broods of one female were sired by the same male, with first-egg dates 34 dates apart [between first and second clutches]' (Green et al., 2019).

This shift in the altitudinal distribution of breeding has also been observed in Austria (Frühauf, 1997), Slovenia (Trontelj, 1997b), and Italy (Pedrini et al., 2012). In addition to changes in agricultural intensification, there may be an underlying relationship with climate changes that are now permitting a more intensive form of agriculture at lower levels and also encouraging new areas of suitable vegetational growth at higher altitudes (Inderwildi, 2016). In Sweden, however, there was no noticeable difference in the habitat preferences between early and late-season nesting attempts (Berg and Hiron, 2012). Using voice-recognition analysis (see Chapter 9) in Norway, Corncrakes were found mainly in hayfields (Mikkelsen et al., 2013), but in eastern areas they were also in grain fields, and the regional difference in vegetation growth during the breeding season produced a significant movement of calling birds. Late arrivals of calling males in some areas suggest that many birds may move long distances to relocate breeding territories within Norway, perhaps due to habitat disturbance in the initial territory or to exploit regional differences of vegetational growth, or perhaps simply in search of (relatively few) females (Mikkelsen et al., 2013). A similar situation has been reported from Italy (Pedrini et al., 2012), where the number of calling Corncrakes was higher in the early season for low-elevation areas, and more numerous in the late season for the high-elevation sites. This may be a common occurrence within many regions across western and eastern Europe in areas of potentially suitable habitat. The female usually remains for a longer duration (around 15–20 days) with her second brood of chicks as there is no further biological pressure to lay another brood, and she will stay with them until they all leave on migration to Africa.

THE END OF THE BREEDING SEASON

The adult birds start their annual moult after nesting and towards the end of the breeding season, (see Chapter 5), and most complete this moult in the nesting areas, although some birds may postpone until after post-breeding dispersal or until they reach their wintering areas (Taylor and van Perlo, 1998). A study of radio-tracked chicks in Ireland found that the juveniles fledged and departed on migration to Africa between early August and mid-September. The chicks were between 36 and 55 days old, with a mean age of 44 days and a mean weight of 155 g and they had fully-grown primary feathers (Donaghy et al., 2011). There was little appreciable difference between years in the timing of departure. Chicks from the first clutch departed from the natal area from mid-July until early August, while chicks from later broods departed from late August to mid-September. Ringing studies have shown that second-clutch chicks have as good a chance as first broods of surviving to the following year. Significantly, compared to the Water Rail and the Spotted Crake, the Corncrake spends less time in the breeding areas before migrating, possibly because it has the longest distance to travel, and this is reflected in it having the shortest laying interval, shortest incubation times and fastest growth rate of chicks of the three species (Salzer, 1999).

CONCLUSION

Corncrakes are sequentially polygamous, with the males (and frequently also the females) relocating geographically during the breeding season in an attempt to produce a second brood of chicks with another mate. A second brood may be raised in a nearby territory, but frequent long-distance relocations also occur. The males call loudly and consistently, usually at night, during the period when they are attracting a mate, and are generally more silent after pairing. The female incubates the eggs alone and raises the chicks to independence, while the male often separates from the female after egg-laying and attempts to find a new mate. The female remains with the young of the second brood until they can fly and depart on the migration southwards.

CHAPTER 8

MIGRATION

WHEN? (TIMINGS)

Recognising that the Corncrake is such a reclusive species in the relatively populous areas where it is well known and identifiable, it should come as no surprise to discover that detailed information on its long-distance transnational movements is even more sparse. Saying this, however, is not to disparage the many reliable records and geographical anecdotes that have noted the presence of a Corncrake in this or that country or region. It is simply that given the combination of ambiguous details on regular passage migrants, and/or proof of breeding, and/or occasional vagrant birds blown astray by contrary winds, in addition to the considerations of isolated reports based on a small number of observations, the reality is often difficult to disentangle.

The basic information, however, is relatively well documented. Corncrakes start to leave their breeding areas in the northern latitudes in August, and this behaviour continues into October or November, with a peak of departures in September (Green, Rocamora et al., 1997). At this point, individuals begin their movement towards the southern hemisphere. This is often described as the birds moving towards their wintering area, but that is very anthropogenic and western European terminology, as it is only the humans near the breeding territories who remain for the winter, while the Corncrakes fly to spend the following few months in the summer of the southern hemisphere. It is probably more accurate to refer to those regions simply as 'breeding' and non-breeding' areas of residence. There is no significant evidence of any substantial Corncrake population spending the non-wintering part of their year outwith the continent of Africa (Stowe and Green, 1997b).

The young generally depart if/when they reach an age of between 36 and 55 days. The fledged young of the first brood generally leaving earlier – from around mid-July until the end of the first week of August – and the young of the second brood depart around late August to mid-September, generally at the same time as the adult birds (Donaghy et al., 2011).

The main passage of Corncrakes across the Mediterranean usually lasts from early September to mid-November, and few birds have been recorded south of the equator before this date (Taylor and van Perlo, 1998). Large flocks have been observed in southern Russia and along the Crimean coast during this southward migration (Dement'ev et al., 1969), but generally the birds fly between stopover locations during the night. Pairs of birds may fly together, and groups of 20–40 may form during migration, clustering during the daytime at key stopping-off sites where flocks of several hundred birds may be seen resting together (Taylor and van Perlo, 1998). Records of sightings as the birds move southwards through eastern Africa (Walther et al., 2013a) clearly illustrate this wave of Corncrake movements (Figure 8.1). Survival, of course, is dependent on the birds evading the trapping and shooting activities in northern Egypt (Baha el Din et al., 1996) and Libya, as it does for the millions of other birds that are hunted in this region during this period of the year (Eason et al., 2016; see also Chapter 11). These hunting and trapping activities continue to be monitored in North Africa but are not intensively controlled (Emile et al., 2014). Apart from hunting during the post-breeding migration (by design or as a 'by-product' of hunting other bird species), there appear to be few specific threats to the Corncrake in Africa, and suitable habitat seems abundant (Taylor and van Perlo, 1998). Some studies (Swann, 1986), although on small numbers of birds, have suggested that as both the breeding and non-breeding habitat was recorded as substantially unchanged, the population decline may be at least partly related to the additional stress of migrating birds crossing an enlarged Sahara and a drought-stricken Sahel region. Localised habitat changes due to flooding, unusual rainfall patterns, scrub clearance or other landscape disturbances seem, however, to have minor effects and result in itinerant movements within the region (Walther et al., 2013a). This makes it difficult to precisely determine the extent of the geographical distribution of Corncrakes during their non-breeding period (Walther and Schäffer, 2014).

Most reports claim that during their non-breeding residence in southern and eastern Africa Corncrakes are normally solitary and silent, but comparatively little of their behavioural ecology can be easily confirmed (Taylor, 1984). Their preferred habitat seems to be dry grassland, but to a lesser extent they may also frequent moist grasslands, where they coexist with their nearest relative, the African Crake. Unlike their nocturnal activity in their breeding areas, they appear to be encountered mainly during daylight during the non-breeding period of their lives (Taylor, 1984). Although studies are few on the distribution of the Corncrake in suitable habitats in sub-Saharan Africa, the localised clustering of birds at a density of around 20–30 individuals per km^2 seems likely (Walther et al., 2013a).

A small number of birds may spend the northern hemisphere summer in Africa, and it has been suggested that these are largely sickly birds or first-year birds that

Male Corncrake in classic calling pose © John A. Love

*Clumps of Iris are favourite spots to shelter, especially
early in the breeding season © John A. Love*

*Opposite page, upper: An open structure to vegetation at
ground level allows easy movement for birds © John A. Love*

*Lower: A well-grown chick explores the tall
vegetation at the field edge © John A. Love*

*This page: Adults may come close to a car and the
barring on the back is clearly visible © John A. Love*

*Above: Males and females look very alike, but the male
is the source of the crekking call © John A. Love*

*Opposite page, upper: Often only a glimpse
of a bird is available, peering from the
cover of knee-high grass © John A. Love*

*Lower: Another favourite place to take cover is
among the stands of tall Nettles © John A. Love*

They can be quite fast when breaking cover, holding the body horizontally © John A. Love

Low summer light can really accentuate plumage colours © John A. Love

Corncrake country - Habitat management on the community-owned
Local Nature Reserve at Loch Stiapabhat, in the north of the Isle of Lewis.
Courtesy of Fiona Rennie @sradagcreative

are not ready for the long journey northwards and subsequent breeding (Walther et al., 2013a). It has been noted (Walther et al., 2013b) that the biological record of an individual Corncrake in KwaZulu-Natal in June 2005 is probably the first confirmed sighting of this species in South Africa during the breeding season. Otherwise, most Corncrakes make their northward migration to their potential breeding areas in late February to April, and so spend only a relatively short time in their non-breeding areas (for example, in Zambia from late November/early December to late March/early April; Taylor, 1984). The return migration to the breeding areas may take place more rapidly than the southward migration, with birds crossing the Mediterranean from late March to mid-May, and with a peak in the second half of April (Taylor and van Perlo, 1998). The actual arrival of birds on the breeding grounds varies considerably, depending only loosely on geography and on whether their arrival is straight from Africa, or from a relocation following a first breeding attempt in another location (see Chapter 7). In Central Siberia, birds normally arrive from a 10,000 km journey in June (Rogacheva, 1992), whereas in the Outer Hebrides of Scotland, most birds arrive in late April and early May (Stowe and Hudson, 1988), and perhaps a week or two earlier in Ireland (Burkitt, 1921). In Switzerland, most Corncrakes arrive in the second half of the breeding season (June and July). This may be a relocation attempt to establish a second territory because, in previous years, they have arrived in May in the lowland areas (Inderwildi, 2016). The female birds usually arrive slightly later than the males in the prospective breeding localities (Niemann, 1995).

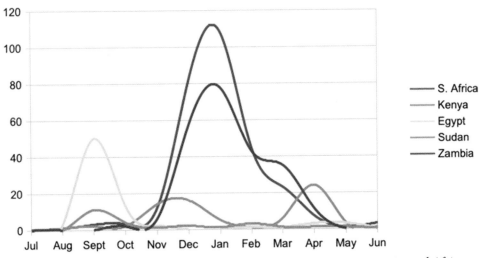

Figure 8.1: Selected records documenting Corncrake migration across continental Africa. The peak sightings move left to right as birds fly north to south towards southern Africa. Source: Drawn from the data in Walther et al. (2013a).

WHERE? (DESTINATIONS AND LOCALITIES)

Part of the difficulty in gaining a detailed understanding of Corncrake migration is because some birds often make their individual journeys to highly-dispersed destinations. This is possibly due to the fickle influence of contrary winds blowing birds off-course and, at least partially, because some birds do not make the full migratory journey to South Africa, but rather stop off at various localities en route, and more or less remain there until it is time to make the return migration back to the breeding areas. Another reason for our patchy understanding is that the recovery and/or recapture of ringed birds is very poor. In a study designed to compare methods of establishing the age of unknown adult Corncrakes (Green, 2004a), the ringing of 900 birds produced only 40 recaptures in subsequent years. The same study estimated that the overall rate of recapture of Corncrakes was about 5% of ringed birds, and a mere 1% of recovered (injured and dead) birds.

The nuggets of information that are discovered, however, can be very interesting, such as the study that found that 'about half of young males ringed as chicks and recaptured as adults in Scotland returned to within about 10 km of the natal site, but nothing is known about the movements of females' (Forrester et al., 2007). Among those few recoveries was an adult Corncrake ringed in Scotland in the Isle of Coll who was shown to have visited the Democratic Republic of the Congo in Central Africa (Horton, 2013). In a review of ringing recoveries from Africa (Walther, 2008), several records were noted for Corncrakes ringed in western Europe that were subsequently found in the Congo and Angola. This, it was suggested, may be a result of Corncrakes that breed in western areas of Europe and migrate to spend their breeding part of the year in the more western regions of Africa, while birds breeding further to the east in the northern hemisphere may largely move to eastern and south-eastern Africa. Some individual birds, however, were noted to fly from west to east across southern Europe and to cross the Mediterranean by the eastern route to Sinai and Egypt – and so the picture is neither uniform nor simple. It appears that most birds migrate north again when the rains cease and their habitat becomes less suitable, and it is probable that most birds return north by the route they used to travel south, although our knowledge of the movements of Corncrakes within the African continent itself is poor.

In the northern hemisphere, there are numerous brief reports of Corncrake sightings during the winter months, such as in Ireland, for example, in County Galway at the end of November (Congreve, 1904), or killed by a dog in Country Down in January (Patterson, 1901), or the unfortunate vagrants shot in January in Donegal (Campbell, 1903) and County Antrim in February (Turtle, 1935). These records are mainly from the late nineteenth and early twentieth centuries when the breeding population was much larger. The agglomeration of other reports documents the migration of Corncrakes like a geographical scatter diagram (see Figure 6.6). There are also records in the ornithological literature from the Congo, Egypt, Zaire and Central Africa (Swann, 1986) and isolated reports scattered across Africa like dust (see Chapter 6 for geographical distribution). Elsewhere, vagrant birds have turned up in Maine, USA (Brock, 1896) or as the star attraction on a New York beach (only to be found dead beside a highway a few days later) (Decandido and Allen, 2018).

The main flyways, however, appear to be along two specific routes (Taylor and van Perlo, 1998). The majority of migrants apparently follow an eastern route, travelling from both western and eastern Europe, as well as an unquantified number of Asian Corncrakes passing through Egypt, Sudan and East Africa to settle in the eastern regions of southern Africa (Walther, 2008). The earliest Corncrake record from Egypt is a fossil collected by the 1964–65 Yale University expedition (Yale University, 1965) from Catfish Cave in the El Dirr region (Walther et al., 2013b), indicating that this is a migration route with a long historical pedigree.

A second, though less frequented route, seemingly mainly for birds breeding in the western areas of Europe, is to fly through the Azores and Canaries (Glutz von Blotzheim et al., 1973), or Morocco, Algeria and across the Sahara to a common area in central or south-eastern Africa. In a comprehensive review of Corncrake records and ringing reports from across Africa (Stowe and Becker, 1992), relatively few records are from Tunisia, Libya or the countries of West Africa, possibly indicating that most western birds take a more direct route south-eastward from Algeria, but also probably reflecting the difficulty of the terrain and the paucity of ornithological observers. Occasional records from Ghana (Dahm, 1969) and Nigeria (Elgood et al., 1966) suggest their presence as sporadic vagrants. In June 2011, 50 breeding males in the Isle of Coll were fitted with geolocators and five birds re-trapped the following year revealed some astonishing information:

> 'The birds moved rapidly south through Britain and France, into Africa, across the Sahara and arrived in West Africa in October. The five birds were spread over a wide area, from Ghana to Nigeria, yet each individual stayed in a fairly small range. Some 4–6 weeks later, the birds made a further movement, to the western part of the Congo, a move perhaps stimulated by habitats in West Africa becoming increasingly dry.'
>
> (Pitches, 2013)

There have been suggestions that the Corncrake population of the Netherlands may in fact be two distinct subgroups: a western group that migrates in a south-westerly direction to western and southern Africa, and an eastern group that migrates south-east to the eastern parts of southern Africa (Voslamber, 1989). An unknown number of birds may also winter around the Mediterranean and in West Africa, but relatively few birds apparently attempt to cross the Mediterranean between these two major flyways.

Both the eastern and western migration routes appear to be utilised in the northward migration that takes place immediately prior to the breeding season, but the details of the particular journeys of individual birds are almost entirely unknown. There was a suspicion voiced that Corncrakes may return in small groups (Mason, 1941), perhaps because of the almost simultaneous appearance of calling males in loosely-dispersed clusters in suitable breeding habitat – but so far, this too has been quite difficult to confirm or disprove. The normal behaviour of the male Corncrakes is that several days may pass between their arrival from their migratory flights and their appearance in potential breeding areas, before they start singing (Green, Rocamora et al., 1997). It often appears that one day they are absent, and the next day they are present somewhere among the tall grasses – a phenomenon that simply adds to their enigmatic reputation.

CONCLUSION

At the end of the breeding season, Corncrakes generally migrate from their northern hemisphere areas of habitat occupation to spend a few months in Africa. There are two major migration routes into Africa: a main flyway into Egypt and thereafter down the eastern and south-eastern countries of the continent, and a secondary flyway from western Europe over Morocco and the Sahara, with some birds stopping off in West Africa and some central African localities. Although the general movements are known, much of the detail is scanty, which is due to a combination of the huge areas of potential habitat, relatively few ornithological observers and the natural reclusiveness of the birds. Movements within African localities are common, and Corncrakes begin their journeys back to their northern breeding areas from late March onwards.

CHAPTER 9

CALLS AND SIGNALLING

Like almost everything else about the Corncrake, the calls with which individual birds communicate are both superficially very simple and, on deeper investigation, incredibly complex, and our understanding is still incomplete. There may have been more articles written on Corncrake vocalisation than on any other single aspect of their behavioural ecology.

The most characteristic of calls made by the Corncrake is the repetitive 'crex crex' sound that gives the species its scientific name. In French, its name, *râle de genêts* is the derivation of our term 'rail' for the genera, meaning the rasping sound of their calls. Typically, the male stretches its neck upwards when calling, with an open bill and the head and neck nearly vertical (Taylor and van Perlo, 1998). That sound is not the only call made by the Corncrake, however, and six different calls have been documented (Mason, 1940):

1. The most familiar, monotonously repetitive 'crex crex' call,
   commonly known as the broadcast call
2. An intermittent version of the above
3. A gurgling-mewing call, often termed the soft call
4. A grunting noise like the squeal of small pigs, sometimes described
   as a whistling note
5. A low, high-pitched cheep
6. A loud 'tsuck' alarm call by wintering birds

We will mention all of these in this chapter, but the broadcast call signal is so emblematic of the bird that it is worth looking first at this call signal in more detail.

THE BROADCAST CALL

From an early stage in the development of ornithology as a field science, it was noticed that a fairly good imitation of the rasping call of a Corncrake could be imitated by rubbing two dry bones together, if one of the pieces has a serrated edge. In England (Mason, 1940) and Scotland (Gray, 1871), well-seasoned horse ribs were apparently preferred, while in Ireland, Otter bones were believed to be the correct density to imitate the original sound (Arthur, 1996). A similar effect can be produced by drawing a hard plastic comb across the edge of a credit card at the rate of roughly two scrapes per second.

The second significant feature to note is that it is only the male birds that make this characteristic call, although as recently as 1996 there appeared to be some lingering doubt about this (Tyler et al., 1996). As Corncrakes invariably select dense vegetation for cover, this is a useful behaviour to assist in population counting, with contemporary ornithologists frequently employing playback recordings of birds to stimulate a response from likely areas of habitat, but as we will see below, there are certain limitations to this technique.

There is a loose distinction between bird calls and bird songs, and there is evidence that different neurological pathways are involved in the production of each, but there is a general belief that calls are less spontaneous than songs and are related to particular functions of communication (May, 1998a). The male birds usually return to the breeding areas from migration about two weeks earlier than the females (Green, Rocamora et al., 1997), and after two or three days settling into a suitable habitat they begin to call. In broad terms, the calling (or singing) of birds has two main functions: to defend or announce the possession of territory to other members of the same gender, and for signalling in courtship to attract a mate (Brenowitz, 1991). The exact function of the Corncrake broadcast call may contain coded signals to indicate a double function of both repelling rivals and attracting females (Cramp and Simmons, 1980), but at present these multiple effects have not been distinguished adequately in field studies. What is more certain is that returning males initially commence their repetitive and monotonous 'crex crex' broadcast call when they first acquire territory, but then largely cease calling during the reproductive cycle when they acquire a mate, and so singing activity is a good indicator of the breeding stage of a male bird (Ręk and Osiejuk, 2010). At this early stage, fights between males are occasionally witnessed, and birds may chase each other. Although females also wander widely, this stops when the nest-building period begins (Stowe and Hudson, 1988). In several studies, no individuals were known to both sing and incubate, or sing and tend young (Tyler and Green, 1996). Single birds that inhabit territories away from concentrations of other birds may sing less frequently (Hudson et al., 1990). Interestingly, the Corncrake is considered to be silent outwith its breeding season while it is in Africa (Newman, 2002), although it may occasionally give the broadcast call while on migration (Taylor and van Perlo, 1998).

The male broadcast call is highly repetitive at night during this initial period, most frequently between 23:00 and 04:00 and often at a rate of 35–55 calls per minute, resulting in around 10,000 calls per night; normally the birds call only sporadically during the daytime (Peake et al., 1998). One observer in Ireland noted:

> *'Once, indeed, after I had counted 847 "crake-crakes", it took breath for the time that would have allowed one crake, but no longer. With this exception I never knew it to pause at all.'*
>
> (Moffat, 1938)

From an early period of investigation into Corncrake behaviour, a distinction was recognised between territorial aggression and courtship displays (Mason, 1950). Earlier studies (Mason, 1941) of rudimentary experiments with a stuffed dummy Corncrake accompanied by the use of notched bones to simulate a broadcast call, produced several effects including birds approaching the dummy, attempted copulation, frequent physical assault on the dummy and also a change in the sort of call emitted by the approaching bird. This latter point will be discussed later.

Soon after the Corncrakes return from Africa to their potential breeding areas they seek out suitable habitat. This is usually established grasslands and meadows, where the vegetation is tall (at least 20–30 cm) and dense (Green, Rocamora et al., 1997) as it provides ideal cover to obscure the movement of the birds and helps contribute to its reputation as a 'secretive' species. It might be expected that this thick vegetation, which certainly impairs easy visual recognition of birds both to human observers and to other birds, results in the distortion or absorption of their calls. Complex vegetative habitat and landscape can result in degradation of the signal characteristics, but 'most of the energy in Corncrake calls can be found above 2kHz' (Ręk and Kwiatkowska, 2016), resulting in the signal quality and transmittance of most Corncrake calls being preserved over distances of at least 1 km or more (Schäffer and Koffijberg, 2004). Unsurprisingly, the wide frequency spectrum characteristics of the Corncrake call appear to be ideal for communicating in their feeding and breeding habitat.

Broadcast calls 'are loud repeated pulse signals (approximately 96dB SPL at 1 m)' (Ręk, 2013b) consisting of two similar syllables (which we hear as the 'crex crex' sound). Actually, this is where it gets really interesting, for the repetitive two-syllable 'crex crex' broadcast call that may sound monotonous and is made when Corncrakes initially return to their breeding grounds, is highly structured. Some researchers have compared it to a simple Morse code system or a form of syntax for communication (Ręk and Osiejuk, 2010). The individual syllables are short (0.18–0.22 seconds), with the first syllable usually being shorter than the second one (Kenyeres et al., 2000). The two syllables together are repeated again and again in a regular pattern, often for hours at a time. The time interval between the first and second syllables, and between each pair of syllables, is very precise and can be slightly different for each bird, although occasional calls may be atypical, as with other animals. The term

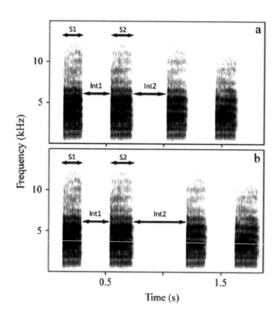

Figure 9.1: *The time structure of Corncrake calls: (a) monotonous and (b) intermittent. In the latter, the second interval is always longer than the first.* Source: Ręk and Osiejuk (2010).

'rhythm' has been defined in this context as the ratio of the length of the second interval to the sum of the first syllable plus the first interval and the second syllable together (Ręk et al., 2011). The information encoded in the call signals (for example, the possible level of aggressiveness of the caller) appears to be contained in the syntactic pattern, rather than in the fixed direction of pulses and syllables (Ręk and Osiejuk, 2013).

There are two main variants of this call: a non-aggressive (monotonous) signal and an aggressive (intermittent) form (see Figure 9.1). Detailed work has observed that:

> *'the rhythm of the Corncrake calls is very specific; both aggressive and non-aggressive signals use the same vocalizations and hence the same vocal structures.'*
>
> (Ręk and Osiejuk, 2010)

The audible difference between the two forms of call is mainly in the timing of the syllables and the intervals (or pauses of silence). One possible reason for the monotonous broadcast call is that:

> *'a male is advertising for females or territory ownership without wanting to interact aggressively (leaving no silent gaps and ignoring any replies), whereas the intermittent pattern means that the male is leaving a silent gap to listen for replies from other males and trying to keep them at bay.'*
>
> (Ręk and Osiejuk, 2010)

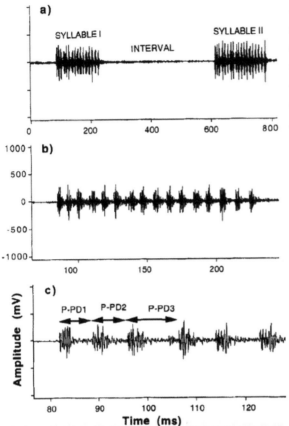

Figure 9.2*: Waveform representations of (a) one complete call; (b) first syllable of the same call; (c) the first six pulses of this syllable. The symbol P–PD refers to pulse-to-pulse duration.* Source: Peake et al. (1998).

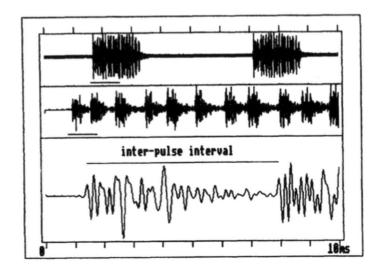

Figure 9.3*: An amplitude display of two call elements with the time scale successively expanded by 10 and 100 times.* Source: May (1998a).

Although calling birds might use these repetitive monotonous calls (with high amplitude and long range) to assess the distance between themselves and another calling bird, there is no firm evidence to confirm that the call is used specifically to locate rival birds (Ręk, 2014). These calls across a distance may be considered as a form of 'exploded lek' (Alonso et al., 2012), in which birds call and/or display across a wide geographical area to attract females. Radio-tracked Corncrakes, whose movements were documented by other researchers, have indicated that a majority of male birds undertook daily visits from their own calling site to the territory of their neighbour, and that males tended to be silent when in their neighbouring territories, 'apparently to prevent confrontation'. Interestingly,

> 'the males who spent a larger part of their time near the neighbour's calling site... tended to sing more frequently near... their own night calling site... and often to sing more often during the day.'
>
> (Skliba and Fuchs, 2004)

In some cases, the males were able to cross an unsuitable habitat to make their visits, and though the purpose of these visits may be foraging for food, researchers have suggested that it was most likely to seek females.

Measurements of call parameters may vary according to a number of factors, including body condition, territorial status, mating status, time of day and season, as well as the overall level of aggressiveness of the caller. Although the 'crex crex' call of an individual Corncrake may sound superficially identical to any other call, according to human hearing, a good way to compare them is to listen to the recordings of several birds in a sound archive such as the Animal Sound Archive (www.animalsoundarchive.org) at the Museum für Naturkunde in Berlin. Websites such as xeno-canto (https://www.xeno-canto.org/species/ Crex-crex) have documented recordings of individual birds throughout the world and are a valuable reference resource. With close comparisons, the subtle distinctions between individual bird calls become apparent. Although significant changes in vocal responses are hard to differentiate, individual Corncrake males have been recorded responding more aggressively to recordings of strangers' calls than to those of neighbouring males, attacking the loudspeaker more frequently when recordings of strangers' calls were played (Budka and Osiejuk, 2013b). This makes sense in evolutionary terms because the recognition of a familiar bird can reduce unnecessary conflicts over territory, in contrast with the need to challenge unfamiliar individuals (Catchpole and Slater, 1995). Taking all the measurable parameters together, it seems logical that the loud broadcast call,

> 'has evolved under a strong pressure towards precise localisation of a sender, which is understandable as Corncrakes inhabit dense vegetation and call almost exclusively at night.'
>
> (Osiejuk and Olech, 2004)

As in all birds, the calls/songs are generated by vibrations in the syrinx which are subsequently preferentially filtered by the vocal tract of the animal. The length and shape of the vocal tract is, to a large extent, related to the size of the bird and therefore can be a good indicator (to other birds of the same species) of the caller's characteristics, such as their sex, age, body size, quality of body condition and even individual identity (Budka and Osiejuk, 2013c). While some animals can apparently falsify this information in the frequency of their signals, for example to imply that they are bigger than they are in reality, it is difficult to maintain this deception (Budka and Osiejuk, 2013c). The Corncrake does not appear to have a single variable in its call that is used to describe the overall body size; however, 'even [a] weak dependence between body size and [the] acoustic properties of signal may be important in natural selection' and is therefore worth further study (Budka and Osiejuk, 2013c). The occasional minor variations in the call of male birds are thought to be largely a matter of body movement, such as a turning of the head or stretching of the neck (Osiejuk and Olech, 2004).

The frequency of single males calling during the night is high (around 92%) compared with only 12% of paired males (Tyler and Green, 1996). Paired males also reduce (or cease) their calling during the egg-laying period, although calling increases again if/when a male establishes a new territory in a second breeding attempt (Osiejuk et al., 2004). Males normally sing on the first night of separating from the first pair bond (Tyler and Green, 1996).

THE INTERMITTENT CALL

A change to a more intermittent rhythm of call is believed to indicate a more aggressive motivation of the caller. This rhythm is created by a longer interval between each pair of the syllable–interval–syllable calls, although there is a continuum of variation between continuous and intermittent calling, rather than a clear dichotomy (Ręk, 2013a). Several reasons have been put forward for this intermittent call (Budka and Osiejuk, 2013b), including the supposition that males cannot call and move (towards the intruder) simultaneously, and/or that the caller needs to pause intermittently to (re)locate the intruder. Males signal aggression towards strangers and neighbours who intrude their territory, but they risk attack (provoking fights) significantly more often towards a stranger. Studies have shown that 'during territorial conflicts, fights are uncommon, but the intensity of the signalling increases' and that 'soft calls seem to imply a threat of force,... [by the caller]...while broadcast calls appear to be more similar to an announcement, which is only indirectly associated with a male's aggressive behaviour' (Ręk et al., 2011).

In effect, any territorial intrusion is more frequently settled in 'combat by song' using the call-and-response interaction between males within vocal range (Mason, 1947). A statistical analysis of calling patterns suggest that calls encode information for both male and female Corncrakes in relation to factors such as the level of aggressiveness of the calling bird, an indication of body size (although this might be a bluff), as well as advertising to listening females and giving a general location of the defended territory (Osiejuk et al., 2004). The intermittent rhythm is more frequent towards the very beginning of the breeding season and, to some extent, before the second breeding attempt (Osiejuk et al., 2004). Other Corncrakes in the vicinity are presumably able to interpret these different calls, and their own reaction to the calling bird will be based upon those encoded signals. Males respond more aggressively to the playback of an intermittent rhythm than to that of a regular rhythm (Budka and Osiejuk, 2013b). The aggressive motivation of a calling bird is signalled by the rhythm of the calls, not just by the presence or number of the calls (Ręk and Osiejuk, 2010). The body size of the calling bird also weakly influences the rhythm of calling (Osiejuk and Olech, 2004), but it appears that larger males tend to favour the intermittent call, 'regardless of the testosterone level and other factors' (Osiejuk et al., 2004). This, in turn, often produces an aggressive reaction from a nearby male, indicated by an intermittent calling response. Males calling with a higher rhythm (more intermittent calls) and soft calls 'behaved more aggressively after producing the signal than males calling with a lower (more monotonous) rhythm' (Ręk et al., 2011) To add to the complexity, it,

> 'appears that acoustic recognition by Corncrake males does not simply rely on temporally coded information, such as the information expressed by the distribution of shorter and longer pulses and their intervening intervals... in contrast, males may employ spectral characteristics to identify conspecifics... otherwise known as formant frequencies... [which] may be highly individual-specific in Corncrakes.'
>
> (Budka and Osiejuk, 2014)

Later, the same study acknowledges that between Corncrakes, pulse-to-pulse duration patterns are important sources for communicating information:

> 'and probably P–PD in combination with other parameters, like call spectral characteristics, can be important in individual identification. Nevertheless, P–PD is not crucial in individual identification [between birds].'
>
> (Budka and Osiejuk, 2014)

THE SOFT CALL AND OTHER CALLS

Soft calls are strong predictors of aggressive behaviours (Ręk and Osiejuk, 2011b). At first, this call-type appears counterintuitive because we might expect that self-confident birds in good condition might produce loud calls, rather than quiet ones (Ręk, 2013b).

Observers have recorded that:

> *'Corncrake males display very strong territorial behaviour. The aggressive response to simulated territorial intrusion [by playing recordings] begins with an approach (on foot or in flight) towards the loudspeaker. The males also perform intermittent cracking calls, switch to soft gurgling-mewing calls and finally attack the loudspeaker.'*

(Budka and Osiejuk, 2013b)

When the bird approached the decoy, it did so with its wings open but stretched slightly back, with its neck feathers erect to form a sort of ruff and uttering what has been described as a 'grunt and whistle' note (Mason, 1941). This whistling note appeared always to be accompanied by a courtship display, while the gurgling-mewing call (sometimes described as growling) has been associated with combative males (Mason, 1940). The gurgling-mewing calls have been observed during the playback of recordings, but never

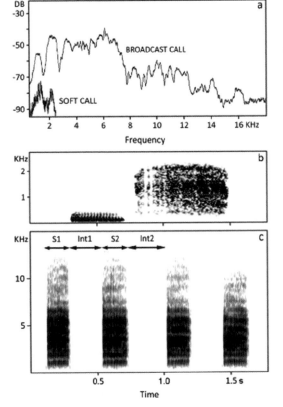

Figure 9.4: Frequency spectra and sonograms of Corncrake calls: (a) frequency spectra of soft and broadcast calls; (b) soft call sonogram; (c) broadcast call sonogram. Source: Ręk and Osiejuk (2011b).

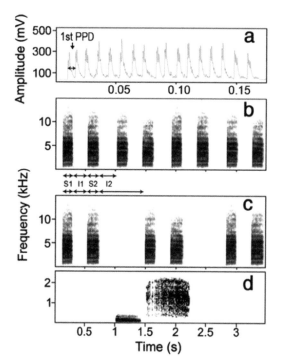

Figure 9.5: Sonogram of Corncrake call: (a) a broadcast call (showing the pulse-to-pulse duration, P–PD); (b) indicating the monotonous rhythm of a broadcast call; (c) a broadcast call with an intermittent rhythm; (d) a soft call. Source: Ręk et al. (2011).

before playback, and they appear to be the equivalent of soft songs in passerine birds and also a signal of increased aggression of the males (Budka and Osiejuk, 2013b). In contrast to the resonate volume of the broadcast call, 'soft calls are quiet (approximately 70 dB SPL at 1 m' and are typically produced closer to the intended receiver (Ręk, 2013b) – another calling Corncrake or a playback recording (Ręk et al., 2011).

It has been suggested that:

> 'the acoustic structure of soft [call] vocalisations can be used to limit the range of the signal, which might be helpful in eavesdropping avoidance, whereas broadcast calls are designed for long-range transmission.'
>
> (Ręk, 2013b)

This soft singing may decrease the chances of the caller being heard by a predator or by another (eavesdropping) male, and it may also give the caller anonymity. As their soft calls are low frequency sounds emitted among dense vegetation, the calls should degrade over a short distance, and are therefore mainly used for close-up aggression and courtship functions. In light of these studies, it, '*seems reasonable to conclude that the maximum limit for communication distance with soft calls in the Corncrake is less than 40 m and even less with gurgling notes only,*' although, '*gurgling notes, despite consistently lower… [signal-to-noise-ratio]…retained their acoustical structures better at larger distances than mewing notes.*'

(Rȩk, 2013b)

Corncrake males are also apparently able to eavesdrop on the vocal interactions between rival birds outside their territories, frequently responding to a distant rival. The strongest response is given by males with a similar rhythm, which indicates a similar level of aggression (Wojas et al., 2018). The reason for this eavesdropping behaviour is probably because it acts as an early warning system to territorial threats, yet also enables a safety-valve to limit the occurrence of potentially dangerous fights.

It seems that, overall, the call of the Corncrake is an adaptation that enables effective transmission through dense vegetation and in positions close to the ground, and that these signals enable a reduction of energy expenditure by facilitating individual recognition between rivals and neighbours, allowing appropriate threat levels to be adopted (Rȩk and Osiejuk, 2011a). As soft calls are given not only in an aggressive context, but also during courtship and the feeding of young, it is now thought that low-amplitude acoustic signals seem to be more widespread than previously thought (Osiejuk, 2011). It is possible that Corncrakes use soft calls when they are close to an opponent because it decreases the possibility of detection and therefore puts the caller at less risk of unintended attack. Experiments with playback recordings suggest that:

'*the responses of Corncrake males to the playback of broadcast calls with and without soft calls at the end of the call series suggest that they recognise soft calls as a signal threat.*'

(Osiejuk, 2011)

The results of several studies have suggested that:

'*soft calls were both effective in provoking a rival to attack as well as in causing the rival to retreat*' and recognise that, '*although singing quietly benefits the sender because it is helpful in driving trespassers off, it can be costly because it prevents the sender from loud singing for [attracting] females and [alerting other] males.*'

(Rȩk and Osiejuk, 2011b)

After captive male birds have attracted the attention of a female, they are known to emit a short sound of medium pitch, which appears to be used initially to attract the female to a nest and is then heard continually when the female is laying (Graham, 2009). A monosyllabic 'tsuck' call by a bird in its African quarters was noted (Taylor, 1984), and it was suggested that this was an alarm call, but this behaviour has not been noted by other observers. The occasional whistling call appears to be associated with courtship and is normally accompanied by a courtship display (Mason, 1940).

THE FEMALE CALL

Although a record has been reported of a female Corncrake singing in captivity (Fisher, 1963), female birds are almost consistently silent in the field (Hudson et al., 1990). Female birds in captivity have been found to give a call almost identical to the male, first when the male in a pair was separated from the female before she had initiated incubation, and second when several females were close together with small chicks (Schäffer et al., 1997). In Sweden, a bird was noted to consistently give an apparently abnormal call, and upon investigation this bird was discovered to be a female (Ottvall, 1999a). This call was described as having a similar rhythm to the male call, but softer (although loud enough to be heard 1–1.5 km away on a windless night) and lacking the harsh rasping effect. A sonogram of the female call indicated a tone-like sound that has harmonics, resulting in a sort of barking effect. In general, however, females have not been reported to call with the same frequency or intensity of the male birds, although it has been suggested that female calls have in the past been disregarded as a variety of the normal male call (Ottvall, 1999a). The female has also been recorded to emit a high-pitched 'cheep' call, and an extended 'oo-oo-oo' sound or a clicking noise to call their chicks (Taylor and van Perlo, 1998). It was also noted that:

> 'when driven away from the chicks the adult [female] bird emitted a call which was like the alarm note of a moorhen repeated several times in succession.'
>
> (Mason, 1941)

This call has also been described as a series of short croaks (Taylor and van Perlo, 1998). It has been further observed that when the chicks were lying still in the long grass the adult bird 'uttered a series of short, hard quacking notes. The chicks all started to run' (Mason, 1941). This may sound like a 'ki' or 'kah' note, and when the nest is threatened, a loud piercing scream may be uttered, starting in a crescendo and fading away (Witherby et al., 1941). On another occasion, a bird made a series of notes similar to a Stonechat, or two stones being struck together. It is worth noting that 'the calls of females do not contain pulses' (Budka and Osiejuk, 2014).

VOCAL IDENTIFICATION

On a scale of interaction,

> *'males compare their rhythm with [their] competitor's rhythm rather than respond to the absolute rhythm... which means that over a short scale, rhythms can transmit clear, discrete messages.'*

> (Ręk, 2013a)

Research from various sources confirmed in the mid-1990s that the pulse patterns of broadcast calls can be subjected to a statistical analysis that enables individual birds to be identified (May, 1998a). The bulk of the energy emitted in a Corncrake broadcast call occurs between 2 and 7 kHz, with the spectrogram showing only indistinct bands throughout the frequency range (Peake et al., 1998). The rhythm of these patterns, however, can be quite distinctive of an individual bird and, within limitations, is consistent for an individual bird throughout the season and from year to year. Close analysis of the pulse pattern shows that:

> *'each syllable is made up of a number of pulses of sound (usually 14–22). Pulses are on average 3–5 milliseconds in length and separated by intervals of 4–8 ms.'*

> (Peake et al., 1998)

The time from the start of one pulse to the start of the next is the pulse-to-pulse duration (P–PD) (Peake et al., 1998). Significantly,

> *'While small differences occurred between the distributions of the same bird on different nights... the P–PD characters of different birds showed greater differences... [and] ... temporal features of the loud advertising vocalizations of male Corncrakes varied little within 24h, within years and, to a lesser extent, between years.'*

> (Peake et al., 1998)

It appears that the pulse-to-pulse duration is specific to individual birds, varying less within than between individual birds, and that this remains constant throughout the life of the bird (Budka et al., 2015). The use of discriminant function analysis of the pulse-to-pulse call patterns, enables 98–100% certainty in identification of known birds within a known population (Peake et al., 1998; Budka et al., 2015) and this may provide a useful way to distinguish between individual birds for the duration of a breeding season, and possibly over a short (two-season?) cycle (Peake et al., 1998). Attempts have also been made to use these distinctive vocal signals of individual birds to determine their site fidelity, and this may be an area for future investigations (Kenyeres et al., 2000). Unfortunately, at present, 'unambiguous identification is impossible when the number of individuals [in the local population] is unknown' (Budka et al., 2015). In particular, it may assist in the individual identification of calling males who change territories in between the first and second clutches within a single breeding season. Opportunities to use call recognition for the individual monitoring of known males may be a useful tool to aid species conservation and local habitat management (Ręk and Osiejuk, 2011a). These methods of identifying individual male Corncrakes might also (eventually) be useful to determine whether migrating birds make use of any specific sites as staging posts (May, 1998b), but the huge potential variability within a narrow acoustic range might render this hope unachievable in practice. Studies have shown that more than 98% of individual birds can successfully be identified even at a sample size of more than 100 individuals in the population (Budka et al., 2015). Researchers are aware, however, that the range of variation of the repetitive pulse-to-pulse duration of the syllables during calls is very small (May, 1994), and consequently the more males that are recorded, the more likelihood there is of finding two or more birds with indistinguishable calling characteristics (Osiejuk et al., 2004).

As a non-passerine, the Corncrake is regarded as a 'non-learning species' of bird, with a very limited repertoire of calls, but the Corncrake has been shown to be able to modify calls by its ability to adapt its signal strategy to respond to new circumstances (Ręk, 2013a). These modifications may include characteristics such as call rate or the intensity of calling (Budka and Osiejuk, 2017). Within a few minutes of being exposed to a new playback recording, males were able to 'understand' the new signalling strategy and to respond by signalling their aggressive motivation with a new pattern of call.

GEOGRAPHICAL AND TEMPORAL VARIATION

The variations in bird songs and calls have been studied extensively, both from a macrogeographical perspective (across large distances) and also in a more local microgeographical context (Podos and Warren, 2007). In relation to the calls of the Corncrake, both aspects have been considered (Peake and Mcgregor, 1999). Differences at the macrogeographic scale might be expected in bird populations that are relatively isolated from each other or in areas that do not overlap, and therefore may be caused by the effects of reproduction within a relatively closed breeding pool.

In a study of several local European Corncrake populations, there appears to be clear similarities between the British and Irish subpopulations of birds and a distinction between those birds and Corncrake subpopulations on mainland Europe (Peake and Mcgregor,

1999). In addition, 87.5% of analysed Corncrake calls from the Inner Hebrides of Scotland and 71.1% of birds from the Outer Hebrides were able to be correctly attributed to their respective island groups. Taken as a whole, the results suggest that there is an element of a slight geographical variation in call over large areas, but there is not sufficient individual variation that the distinctions are clear-cut. Two possible reasons for this are either a variation in migration patterns (if birds learn their call before they return to breed) or a variation in site fidelity of adult birds (if the call is learned during their first breeding season).

The movements of a significant number of individual birds between subpopulations might help to explain these results, but ringing recaptures suggest that this is unlikely, with the majority of birds returning to their natal populations each season. Subsequent studies (Budka et al., 2014) analysed the pulse-to-pulse pattern, as well as the spectral frequencies of calls from localised subpopulations from across mainland Europe, and found significant geographical variations (Peake, 1997). The pulse pattern differed in most cases and the spectral characteristics varied between all local populations, with distant populations showing larger differences in call than neighbouring populations. In so-called non-learning species (such as the Corncrake), vocalisations should mainly reflect genetic and ecological differences, such as those due to sexual selection, social interactions, or conditions of the local environment and, at least in theory, different calling patterns may arise in different subpopulations. At present it is uncertain whether variations in calling patterns are due to birds moving between subpopulations in different years, or due to acoustic adaptations to a particular environment.

Microgeographical call variation is perhaps more difficult to explain, but this has been widely reported in several species, with some slight evidence that neighbouring Corncrakes 'share significantly more call structures than more distant birds from the same population' (Peake and Mcgregor, 1999). This may reflect the genetic relatedness of birds and of a relatively high site fidelity. At a local level, larger males may occupy better quality habitat, and this may produce lower frequency signals, which may also be influenced by the slight differences in anatomy of the sound-producing apparatus (Budka and Osiejuk, 2017). As male Corncrakes apparently have the ability to interpret the calls of neighbouring males (for example, in assessing the level of caller aggressiveness) and are able to respond by modifying their own signalling strategy, it is possible that such social interactions may also be responsible for call variations locally. As the pattern of pulse-to-pulse duration is stable over the life of a bird and appears to be highly individual, it is likely that this is a genetic feature, which also governs the vocal anatomy of the individual bird.

CONCLUSION

The call of the Corncrake is perhaps the most well-known characteristic of the species, and its unmistakable '*crex crex*' call, although only given by the male birds, has been used to identify the presence of a Corncrake in a field and also to count the local population. Usually they sing during the night, mostly between 23:00 and 04:00, to advertise their presence and attract a mate. Males sing less, or not at all, after they have paired, but may resume again prior to attempting a second brood. Although calls are superficially similar to a human ear, audio analysis of recordings of Corncrake calls has shown that it is possible to identify the call signature of individual birds. Within certain limits, this feature may be used to identify individuals that have relocated to a different geographical locality.

CHAPTER 10

FOOD AND FEEDING BEHAVIOUR

It is perhaps ironic that the 'feast' of published documentation on the Corncrake is in the records of its widespread but reclusive distribution, while the 'famine' of documentation is in the number of accounts of its diet. The large majority of reports of what a Corncrake feeds upon and its feeding behaviour are generally asides in articles focusing on other relevant topics, rather than on dedicated studies of feeding (Koffijberg and Schäffer, 2006). There are two basic aspects of feeding, namely what type of food is eaten and what behaviour (and therefore habitat) is required to obtain it.

DIET

An early account suggests that the food of the Corncrake:

> *'consists of small fresh-water shells, larvae of beetles, and thick-bodied moths, which seek refuge in the day time among the grass.'*
>
> (Gray, 1871)

As with most rails, the Corncrake is omnivorous, but its main prey is a range of invertebrates, primarily earthworms, molluscs, slugs, snails and larger insects such as Coleoptera (beetles) Diptera (flies) and Orthoptera (grasshoppers and their relatives) (Tyler, 1996). Weevils are also taken, and in southern Africa, dung beetles, termites and cockroaches may be added to the list of prey (Taylor and van Perlo, 1998). Food is normally sought on the ground or among low-lying vegetation, with a bird foraging, mostly by day and within available cover (Green, Rocamora et al., 1997), by probing the litter with its bill

(Taylor and van Perlo, 1998). Arthropods feature regularly in the diet, with an apparent preference for beetles, flies and spiders, but the food of individual Corncrakes seems to be largely determined by the local availability of invertebrates, and they appear to be fairly opportunistic foragers, and so this is not a limiting factor in the distribution of the species (Koffijberg and Schäffer, 2006). As a result of this opportunism, there are records of craneflies, earwigs, hoverflies, crickets, dragonflies and ants being eaten by Corncrakes (Cramp and Simmons, 1980). It has been noted that:

> 'in Scotland and Ireland, earthworms and molluscs are an important part of the diet… whereas in Poland insects are the most common prey.'
>
> (Green, Rocamora et al., 1997)

An analysis of stomach contents found 82.5% of animal food and 17.5% vegetable matter in the samples (Witherby et al., 1941). The shoots of young plants (Cramp and Simmons, 1980), as well as grains and the seeds of grasses, may also form a part of the diet (Prostov, 1964), especially during autumn and the non-breeding period (Schäffer, 1999), although it is uncertain if these are ingested directly or simply consumed along with other foodstuff taken as prey (Green, Rocamora et al., 1997). Material that is not digested is regurgitated as waste pellets, usually around 1 cm in length (Snow and Perrins, 1998). Young frogs may sometimes be taken, and in captivity, small mammals and birds have been recorded (Glutz von Blotzheim et al., 1973), as well as occasional fish and amphibians (Green Rocamora et al., 1997). Corncrakes may become infected by flukes inhabiting the nymphs or insects that they feed upon (Rothschild and Clay, 1953; see also Chapter 11 on predators and threats).

FEEDING BEHAVIOUR

This versatility in the variety of food consumed by Corncrakes raises two significant issues. First, 'the wide range of the Corncrake diet indicates that they can switch to alternative prey if another group becomes scarce' (Tyler, 1996).

Second, the range and abundance of invertebrates available will be conditioned to a greater or lesser extent by the host vegetational assemblages, as well as by local climate and weather conditions. In general, the abundance of insects increases with the biodiversity of the vegetation (Arbeiter, Franke et al., 2017). The implication of this is that, in habitats with a range of various vegetative structures and species combinations, the availability of prey is generally not a limiting factor to the occurrence or even breeding success of the Corncrake. The habitat management conditions, for example the timing and style of mowing, may prove to be a more limiting and more complex consideration (see Chapter 12), but although the more heavily fertilised fields tend to have a lower biomass of invertebrates, the availability of food in agriculturally improved grasslands does not by itself appear to be a constraint on breeding success (Tyler, 1996).

Both of these factors – their omnivorous diet and the local availability of food – will also influence the selection of territories, geographical distribution and daily movements of Corncrakes throughout the year. The availability of food is related to the structure and species composition of the vegetation, but despite accumulating information on the diet of Corncrakes by direct observations, little is known about the importance of food availability on Corncrakes' habitat selection criteria (Borgo and Zoologia Botanica, 2010). The preference for grassland with tall vegetation, for instance, may be primarily due to the shelter it provides and screening from predators (see Chapter 11), or due to better food availability, or a combination of both (Berg and Hiron, 2012). Any changes in the vegetational structure and composition of the habitat, both within and between seasons, are likely to influence food availability (Brambilla and Pedrini, 2011) and, correspondingly, influence the shifting occurrence of Corncrakes throughout the breeding season as they seek optimal habitat conditions (Michalska-Hejduk et al., 2017). Conversely, it has been observed that as the variety in vegetation has declined, so too has the range of food sources (Lorge, 1999). Although some modern agricultural practices may alter habitat conditions, leading to a loss of suitable breeding areas and a reduction in food availability, the precise situations are highly variable locally (Arbeiter and Franke, 2018; see also Chapters 4 and 12). For example, variations in the use of pesticides may locally affect the height and density of the herbaceous layer (Pedrini et al., 2012), and therefore will have a knock-on effect on the invertebrate communities, with a lower invertebrate abundance contributing to a decline in Corncrake numbers (Joest and Koffijberg, 2016). A corresponding absence or decrease of pesticide treatments along field margins may help to increase floristic diversity and also improve the abundance of arthropods and earthworms (Broyer, 2003). Arthropod richness is significantly higher in areas of less intensive land use (Batáry et al., 2011) and, similarly, unmown strips of grassland may serve as refuges for arthropods, which can then potentially recolonise the mown meadows and provide prey for Corncrakes (Arbeiter, Franke et al., 2017). In the few studies that have investigated the influence of different mowing regimes on the invertebrate populations of grasslands, the meadows with cutting delayed until at least mid-July had densities of Orthopterans that were around five times greater than fields which were mown from mid-June, and meadows with uncut refuge areas were at least twice as dense (Buri et al., 2013). This observation is particularly important because it indicates that slight changes in grassland management can make a significant difference for biodiversity, and because Orthoptera are regarded as key components of grassland food chains and sensitive indicators of ecosystem health, this is especially interesting. In wetter areas of the ground, aquatic invertebrates may be more accessible due to a reduced vegetational cover (Berg and Gustafson, 2006).

The diet of young birds appears to be similar to that of the adults (Gilmour, 1972), and two-day old chicks have been observed being fed by the mother on 'flies and other winged insects that she caught around the nest' (Brown, 1938). Females tend to feed near the nest when incubating (Stowe and Hudson, 1988) and to forage in hay meadows, nettle patches and perhaps among oats or potatoes (Duffy, 2018), as well as in other areas of tall vegetational cover, especially early in the breeding season (Stowe and Hudson, 1988). Field margins are frequently favoured for foraging because they can provide tall cover and also a contrasting structural variety to the adjacent meadows (Arbeiter, Franke et al., 2017), although in Africa they occasionally feed on open tracks in grassland and at the edges of dirt roads (Taylor and van Perlo, 1998). In areas such as the Hebrides, the preference of Corncrakes for agriculturally improved meadows, rather than 'natural' grassland, may be a combination of the amount of cover provided, the variety of invertebrates available for the young, and the density of the grass structure to enable mobility (Cadbury, 1980a).

The regular availability of food resources is also of key importance for mating success (Joest and Koffijberg, 2016), and it is common that the male display areas may contain food that initially attracts the interest of a female. In the so-called 'exploded lek', in which Corncrake males gather in a loose cluster, the extent of the male display area and the proportion of the food resources contained in it are strongly correlated, which in turn is related to the abundance of females attracted to the area (Alonso et al., 2012). There is at least one observation of a male Corncrake presenting a green caterpillar to a decoy as part of a mating display, but there is no understanding of how common this behaviour is (Mason, 1945). Food availability is also likely to be a significant factor in determining the extent and shape of home range sizes (Koffijberg et al., 2007).

In general, meadow biomass is encouraged by higher rainfall and higher temperatures during the growing period, and greater vegetational growth may also increase the availability of food (Frühauf, 2016). The farmland management of potential Corncrake habitats needs careful attention because of the effects that any actions will have on the variety and abundance of prey species. Mowing is a good example to illustrate this relationship (see Chapter 12). Areas of Corncrake habitat that are late-cut, or uncut from year to year, may host a greater abundance and diversity of invertebrate food for some birds, but this benefit needs to be set against a deterioration in the vegetational structure (more dense ground layer and the incursion of shrubs and trees) that eventually make that habitat less attractive for successful breeding (Arbeiter, Helmecke et al., 2017). Grassland abandonment not only leads to changing vegetational assemblages as small shrubs and trees take hold, but the resultant spread of alien invasive species can lead to a reduction in invertebrates, and consequently in the loss of ornithological diversity (Tryjanowski et al., 2011). Undersowing a spring crop can produce a weedy understory that will be rich in invertebrates in the grassland of the following year, as well as providing cover for young chicks (Aebischer et al., 2000). An expanse of continually grazed grassland reduces both cover and potential food sources (Newton, 1991).

In areas of the Netherlands, where Corncrakes are frequently (although atypically) found in crops (see Chapter 4), it is speculated that the specific combination of crop types, together with rich calcareous soils, may be the reason for the abundance of appropriate food (Joest and Koffijberg, 2016). In addition, both the main crops (Alfalfa and Caraway) are normally grown for more than one year and, consequently, they probably have a higher biomass of invertebrates than crops that are ploughed-in annually (Koffijberg and Nienhuis, 2003). Some scientists consider that a simplistic approach to agri-environmental management emphasises the importance of tall vegetational cover, without due recognition that the presence of invertebrate food for Corncrakes within that cover is also critical. Ecological complexity varies from farm to farm (Bignal and McCracken, 2000) and the abundance of invertebrates will not be equal across all fields, and so although late mowing will provide good cover for longer and may benefit some species, it will not benefit all. For this reason, an emphasis has emerged that favours staggered mowing dates to provide a landscape mosaic with a mix of refuge areas (see Chapter 12). The enhanced complexity provided by a landscape that has a vegetational mosaic, especially in areas of less intensive, traditional agriculture, also tends to encourage a greater biomass of arthropods and therefore better availability of prey items for Corncrakes (Batáry et al., 2011).

Outwith their wide breeding region, the Corncrake diet is even more patchily understood. At one of the regular stopover sites during migration, in the Gilan Province of northern Iran, the analysis of 16 crop contents indicated that although some rice seeds and insects were taken, the preferred food was herbs, and Cockspur grass in particular (Ashoori and Zolfinejad, 2008; see also Figure 10.1). In central and southern Russia,

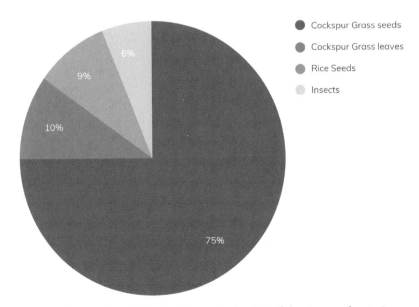

Figure 10.1: Proportion of the food items in the diet of the Corncrakes in Iran.
Source: Redrawn after Ashoori and Zolfinejad (2008).

insects and Oat seeds were also found in Corncrake stomachs, while in Ukraine, 10 stomachs contained mainly animal matter, including Hymenoptera (mainly ants), Carabid beetles, grasshoppers and Borage seeds (Ashoori and Zolfinejad, 2008).

CONCLUSION

Corncrakes are omnivorous, but they mainly feed on invertebrates that they pick up on the ground or from the vegetation in their habitat. They are known to eat a wide variety of insects, spiders, beetles and so on, but will also feed upon seeds at times. Their wide choice of food means that they can be opportunistic feeders and take advantage of a range of habitat situations.

CHAPTER 11

PREDATORS, PARASITES AND PROBLEMS

NATURAL PREDATORS

The prize for 'Young Naturalist of the Year' should surely have gone to Magda Browne-Clayton (aged 11) who in 1948 had a short note published in *Irish Naturalists' Journal*, observing that:

> '*A few days ago at about 8 p.m. I saw from my window a baby Corncrake come out of some long grass on to our lawn. He was followed by his mother who spread her wings over him, when a Magpie appeared. The Magpie landed about 2 ft. off, whereupon mother Corncrake flew at him and chased him away. She then returned to her baby, picked it up in her claws and flew away with him. I would be interested to know if Corncrakes often do this.*'

(Browne-Clayton, 1948)

We would all be interested to find out more about this behaviour, but such are the serendipitous observations of natural history.

Other than the loss of life through accidents or land management changes to their habitat (see Chapter 12), the main cause of Corncrake death is predation by mammals and raptors. Because the nests of ground-nesting birds are usually easily accessible, they are especially vulnerable to predation. A study in Germany (Arbeiter and Franke, 2018) identified potential predators as Fox, Weasel, Stoat, European Polecat and American Mink, in addition to Raven and Hooded Crow, and named these species as the main predators of Corncrake nests in the study locality. Wild Boar are known to prey on Corncrake nests in Hungary, and probably in other European locations (Boldogh, Szentirmai et al., 2016). These same predators have also been noted in other geographical areas. It has also been recorded that the daily predation risk for the birds increased closer to the edge of the meadow and with a decreasing height of the ground vegetation which provides cover. This was related to a higher frequency of mammalian predators being active along field edges and corridors of vegetation, as well as the density of cover at ground level providing screening from avian predators overhead. In view of what we know about the habitat choices of Corncrakes, this indicates the imperative for them to select a balance between the extra cover that is often provided at meadow edges and the increased risk of encountering a mammalian predator in this micro-habitat.

There are records of adults and chicks being taken by Otter, American Mink and household cats, both domestic and feral (Green, Rocamora et al., 1997). In certain areas, the Fox and the feral Ferret may also be regular predators (Taylor and van Perlo, 1998), as well as introduced species such as the Hedgehog and American Mink that have escaped from captivity (Koffijberg and Schäffer, 2006). A study (Reynolds and Reynolds, 2003) in the Outer Hebrides, at a site classified as nationally important for breeding Corncrakes, has suggested anecdotally that Hedgehog do prey on Corncrakes, and though local predation on other ground-nesting birds is known, further investigation on Corncrake mortality is required. Stoat have also been reported as preying on young Corncrakes (Gilmour, 1972). In many areas, it is certain that the tendency for Corncrake males to advertise their presence continually has a fascination for many cats, with half of the dead adult Corncrakes reported to one conservation officer in South Uist being recovered from domestic cats (Pickup, 1985). In Egypt, the Fox, the Fennec Fox and the Desert Monitor are known predators (Eason et al., 2010). Observations of migrating birds in North Sinai have noted that Corncrakes (probably tired from long-distance flying) tend to seek shelter among any tall vegetation where they rely on their cryptic colouration and stay motionless to remain undetected. They are slow to flee, and typically permit humans to approach within 3 m before taking flight (enabling trappers with nets to get sufficiently close) and they normally fly to a refuge more than 100 m away from their original location (Eason et al., 2010). It is on documentary record that the African Crake, the closest living relative of the Corncrake, has been preyed upon by Leopard (Hill, 2001) and Serval cat, as well as by a range of birds including the African Hawk-eagle, Wahlberg's Eagle, Black-headed Heron and the Dark Chanting Goshawk (Taylor and van Perlo, 1998). As the Corncrake and the African Crake are sympatric (a related species inhabiting the same geographical area) in southern Africa, it is not unrealistic to suspect that these predators are also a threat to the Corncrake. That the Boomslang, a large and very poisonous snake, is recorded taking the chicks of the African Crake (Haagner and Reynolds, 1988) is also significant, given the habit of the Corncrake to hide in similar habitats. Predation by the Racoon Dog has been reported from Lithuania (Koffijberg and Schäffer, 2006).

Predation by raptors is also common, with Buzzard (Swann, 1986), Peregrine (Forrester et al., 2007; Ratcliffe, 1980) and Red Kite (Deceuninck, 1999) known to kill adult Corncrake. A Marsh Harrier was observed catching a Corncrake as it was migrating through Egypt

(Baha el Din, 1993), and field observations in an experimental study in north-east Poland noted both Marsh Harrier and Montagu's Harrier as the chief suspects for egg predation in the nests of Corncrake and Spotted Crake (Hirler, 1999). Another Corncrake was recorded taken by a Black-shouldered Kite in the Kruger National Park, South Africa (Walther et al., 2013b), and in Gabon at least one bird was caught by a Black Sparrowhawk that had been trained for falconry, but there is no indication on how common this practice may be (Brosset and Erard, 1986). Among the owls, both the Barn Owl (Glue, 1972) and the Eagle Owl (Frühauf, 1999) are sufficiently adept to take Corncrakes. A pioneering study noted while attempting to lure a Corncrake to a decoy to photograph it that:

> 'When it was approaching [the decoy] a barn owl flew overhead and the corncrake crouched and was silent until the owl passed.'
>
> (Mason, 1940)

Chicks have been eaten by White Stork in Lithuania (Koffijberg and Schäffer, 2006) and also in Latvia, where a colleague has informed me that they regularly prey on chicks and appear quite capable of killing an adult bird. Flocks of White Storks are often observed in central and eastern Europe when hay mowing is in progress (Tyler et al., 1998). Hooded Crows, Ravens and other crows have been recorded preying on young, and various species of gulls will steal eggs and harry and kill chicks, especially when the young are forced out into open ground, for example when mowing the harvest (Venables and Venables, 1950). Several instances have been recorded of Common Gulls mobbing Corncrakes when they are forced out onto open ground (Bahr, 1907; Kinnear, 1907). Significantly, in areas of relatively strong Corncrake populations in the tall grasslands of eastern Hungary, the rich biodiversity associated with the Corncrake territories also results in a higher level of raptors than in the local control sites, with up to 10 raptor species in total (Wettstein and Szép, 2003). This observation supports studies of habitat preferences for Corncrakes that have indicated that the optimal habitat requirements include a relatively open lower layer of grassland (allowing easy movement for feeding and escape), and a greater density provided by taller grass in the higher layer (providing overhead cover from predators) (Borgo and Zoologia Botanica, 2010). In the grasslands of southern Hungary, the Corncrake habitat tends to be relatively open close to the ground, but 90–100% closed at a height of 1 m (Kiss, 2004). This gives an insight into why predation at the nest site generally seems to be quite low, with a major study reporting that 93% of clutches survived the period between laying and hatching (Tyler, 1996).

PARASITES

The threats to the health and life of Corncrakes, in common with all living organisms, are not simply from the larger predators.

Bacteria such as the *Campylobacter* genera are commonly found in wild birds and, unsurprisingly, have been identified in Corncrakes, specifically *Campylobacter jejuni* and *Campylobacter coli* (Mudenda et al., 2008). Corncrakes can be asymptomatic carriers of these bacteria, which they may pick up from infected invertebrates, other birds or from contaminated soil or vegetation. The birds themselves may suffer from ill-health, and if a human frequently handles captive birds and becomes infected, the bacteria can cause gastroenteritis, although this is unlikely to be a significant source for human infection. Similarly, the Corncrake is among the many species of birds that may become periodically infested with Ticks, although from the little we know, they appear to be less susceptible than many other avian species. In what must have been a painstaking study (Hoogstraal et al., 1964) conducted on the Mediterranean coast of Egypt, 10,612 birds of 24 species and subspecies were examined during their southward migration in 1962, at the end of the northern hemisphere summer. Of these, 66 birds were Corncrakes, but only five of them had Ticks attached and, on average, only one Tick per bird. These parasites were identified as *Haemaphysalis punctata*, *Haemaphysalis sulcata* and three of the *Ixodes* species, probably *Ixodes ricinus*. This study was continued when birds migrated northwards again but, somewhat significantly, no Corncrakes were among the species caught and examined by the study team as the birds made their return journey to their breeding areas (Hoogstraal et al., 1964).

Flukeworm is a common parasite in many bird species, including Corncrakes, who often become infected by the invertebrates that they eat, such as dragonflies or their nymphs (Rothschild and Clay, 1953). Intestinal parasitic worms (Helminths) have been recorded from many avian species, and specifically from Corncrakes on a number of occasions, including in Slovakia (Macko, 1971), Poland (Okulewicz, 1993) and Ukraine (Syrota et al., 2020). Helminths are not the most engaging of organisms, and even their existence may bypass most birdwatchers, but for completeness here, the species of Helminth that are known (Yildirimhan et al., 2011) to infect Corncrakes are:

- Brachylaima fuscata
- Cardiofilaria pavlovskyi
- Dilepsis undulata
- Echinostoma revolotum
- Leucochloridium holostomum
- Prosthogonimus cuneatus
- Prosthogonimus ovatus
- Rallitaenia pyriformis
- Rallitaenia rallida

Other intestinal parasites include highly specific protozoan species of the *Eimeria* genera that may result in coccidiosis development in their host, and these include *Eimeria crecis* and *Eimeria nenei*, which have been found in both captive chicks and in wild birds in Scotland (Jeanes et al., 2013). The former species was the more common, and was discovered in Corncrakes of all ages, while the latter species was more prevalent in older birds. In both cases, infection may be fatal for the host bird (Serna et al., 2018), so it is certainly a concern for the reintroduction of any captive chicks into the wild (Sainsbury, 2015). The blood-feeding parasitic fly *Ornithomyia avicularia* has been recorded in the Corncrake in Moscow and, as it is commonly found in many species of birds, it may be a more regular parasite in Corncrakes than is currently understood (Matyukhin and Krivosheina, 2008).

Infectious agents that spread disease also include parasites in the blood, often transmitted to birds by mosquitoes, midges and biting flies, both in their breeding areas and on their migratory travels. There are few studies in this area relating specifically to the Corncrake, but such as there are, provoke interest (Fourcade et al., 2014). There are indications that the infection rate of key pathogens, including malarial parasites, varies strongly across the European range of the Corncrake, with increasing prevalence in the local Corncrake populations further to the east. The gradation is not directly associated with genetic differences, and a strong relationship to the intensity of agricultural practices indicates that ecological factors are the most likely explanation. Although there is generally greater wetland drainage, pesticide use and regular human disturbance in the west of Europe, the different migration flight paths (eastern and western routes across the Mediterranean) may also be a contributory factor to this geographical variation in levels of infection. The tendency of Corncrakes to cluster together in their breeding areas, along with the losses of habitat which encourage higher densities of birds in the remaining suitable areas, is also likely to facilitate transmission of infection between birds. This is an area of study that requires more work, not only to gain a better understanding of the conservation measures necessary to reduce avian disease, but also to help predict the spread by birds of some diseases that may impact upon human populations, such as avian influenza.

PROBLEMS

Despite the many other potential accidents and misadventures that might befall Corncrakes, few seem to be recorded in the literature, and those that do are fairly general and can occur over a widespread geographical area.

As might be expected of a species that frequents farmland meadows and grazing pasture, disturbance by humans and domesticated animals is a regular low-level threat. The impact of domestic (and feral) cats has already been mentioned, and dogs, too, can be opportunistic hunters (Stendall, 1935), by killing Corncrakes (Duffy, 2018) or simply pursuing birds while out walking with their owners (Patterson, 1901). It has been reported that an injured bird may crawl into a hole in the ground and feign death (Cramp and Simmons, 1980). One study in Africa reported using a dog to effectively flush Corncrake out of the long grass to count them more easily (Taylor, 1984). Hunting with dogs has also been reported in Bulgaria (Koffijberg and Schäffer, 2006). Although an adult Corncrake with young may fly at a dog to deter its continuing interest (Swiney, 1892), the usual response to disturbance by a human intruder is to run under the vegetational cover, but a bird might also swim in an emergency or may pretend to be dead to discourage further attention (Taylor and van Perlo, 1998). In grassland, while the main threat to life is during mowing (see Chapter 12), there may be a danger of accidental damage to Corncrake eggs or chicks by cattle standing or lying on them (Swiney, 1892), but with what frequency this happens it is nearly impossible to tell.

The deliberate shooting of Corncrake, whether by accident, commonly in mistake for Woodcock (Turtle, 1935) or Common Quail (Radovic and Dumbovic, 1999) or intentionally (Campbell, 1903) is fortunately now relatively rare in western Europe, but in eastern Europe, in Russia (Mischenko, 2008), Ukraine and Georgia (Koffijberg and Schäffer, 2006), and in parts of Asia and Africa, the Corncrake is still regarded as a game species, although hunting pressure is reputed to be low (BirdLife International, 2020). There is a note that numbers shot in European Russia average around 31,000 birds per season, ranging from 9,000–48,000 over different years (Mischenko, 2016). Although the Corncrake is officially protected in most of its breeding range (BirdLife International, 2020), frequently with legal enforcement (Herkenrath, 1997), illegal hunting is known in several countries, including France (Deceuninck, 1999), Greece (Walther et al., 2013a), Croatia (Koffijberg and Schäffer, 2006), Slovenia (Grobelnik and Trontelj, 1999) and the wider Balkans (Tadic, 1999). The relatively slow flight of the Corncrake can make it an easy target in the confusion while shooting other game species.

During migration, Corncrakes often fly in mixed flocks along with the Common Quail when crossing the Mediterranean (Taylor and van Perlo, 1998). They are also frequently shot or caught in the nets of trappers, who collectively erect nets along the entire Mediterranean coastline of Egypt, and to a lesser extent in other African countries in the region (Grieve and Salama, 2003), while primarily hunting for Common Quail and other migratory birds (Eason et al., 2016). Most trappers operate on a part-time basis during the migration period, with captured Corncrakes retained for personal food and most of the Quail sent to local markets (Baha el Din et al., 1996). Accurately establishing the numbers caught annually is difficult, but most estimates are that it is millions of Common Quail and tens of thousands, possibly hundreds of thousands, of Corncrakes (Eason et al., 2016).

Nor is the threat of hunting and trapping the only danger for migrating Corncrakes, as their tendency to fly at a relatively low altitude means that there have been numerous reports of collisions with fences, overhead wires (Green, Rocamora et al., 1997) and power lines. Death from collision or by electrocution may be locally substantial in certain flight corridors, but numbers are hard to confirm as carcasses may be removed by foxes and cats (Shobrak, 2012).

For a migratory species, such as the Corncrake, the adherence (or lack of it) to different environmental and health standards in the different countries in Europe, Africa and Asia make it difficult to judge the effect of transnational problems such as pollution from pesticides and insecticides (Bibby, 1992). There is, however, little doubt that it must have at least a minor effect in certain localities, and further research is needed to clarify the full extent of the issue.

Conclusion

The main cause of Corncrake deaths, other than chick mortality at grass mowing time, appears to be predation by a small range of mammals and raptors. Losses due to predation on the eggs and young by other animals, particularly crows and gulls, seem mainly to be opportunistic and it is not thought to be a major systematic threat to the survival of the total population. There is an incidental risk of hunting in some areas, mainly in eastern Europe, and a substantial seasonal loss of birds due to trapping as flocks migrate through Egypt, but again this is a relatively low proportion of overall fatalities.

CHAPTER 12

HABITAT MANAGEMENT
AND CONSERVATION

This was possibly the hardest chapter to write about the Corncrake. The reason for that is not just because the fine-grained details of Corncrake ecology are still being discovered, but because of the large number of studies and speculations that have already been published on this particular topic. At least 10% of the total academic literature on the Corncrake deals in one way or another with the management of its habitat and reports on various experiments to improve the conservation of the species. A great many other articles and reports manage a passing mention, at some point in their text, to the effects of agricultural mowing and of grassland management. The three top points that would be highlighted in any comprehensive literature review would probably be the 'secretiveness' of the Corncrake, the fact that it migrates to Africa and that its habitat is under threat due to grass mowing. All of these points are true, of course, but there is much more subtlety and nuance to the full story than just those simplified highlights. Some of the key points of habitat management for Corncrakes have already been mentioned earlier in this book, but to gain a true appreciation of the complexity, a good starting place would be to begin with a short historical review of landscape management practices.

There are three main land management aspects that are crucial to understand in order to appreciate the ecology and conservation of the Corncrake. These aspects are:

- Vegetational cover across the landscape
- Habitat change
- Structure of the vegetation in that habitat

Each of these aspects are interlinked in ecology and agricultural land management, and each aspect consists of several subpoints that demand consideration; therefore, to begin to make sense of it all, we need to take these points one at a time, and then reassemble all the resulting information to try to give some coherence and consistency to the topic.

RANGING BEHAVIOUR AND HABITAT SELECTION

Early shelter for Corncrakes returning from Africa to northern Europe is a crucial factor in their habitat selection. Numerous studies have noted that the early arrivals frequently seek initial shelter among tall vegetation, such as Common Nettles, Yellow Iris, Reed Canary-grass or Common Reed (Green, 1996). A typical example of this behaviour is shown on their return to the crofting landscape of the Hebrides of Scotland. While the birds may return individually, and although calling Corncrakes already on the ground may attract other incoming birds to form loose clusters of the same species, the type of shelter they seek is determined by the early-season shortage of any other convenient vegetational cover (Cadbury, 1980a). In May and early June, Corncrakes tend to call from tall clumps of Yellow Iris and from the field margins, but by July these areas are hardly used at all as the birds have moved into the adjacent fields of hay or silage (Stowe and Hudson, 1988). In the Hebridean Islands, these are usually semi-natural grasslands that have been agriculturally improved with additional seed and/or fertiliser. This 'improved' grassland provides good cover for the majority of Corncrakes, but these fields tend to have less diversity of plants and invertebrate food than the more untended meadows (Cadbury, 1980a). These facts, together with the possibility of the resultant grass crop being mown before the chicks have time to become mobile enough to escape, means that this preference by the Corncrakes for fields managed for hay, silage or haylage is not without its attendant risks. Nevertheless, the small-scale patchwork of croft fields, mown or left unmown at different times, allows birds to seek shelter throughout the landscape, and is a prime reason why Corncrake numbers have historically remained relatively high in the Scottish islands. In this respect, the abandonment of crofts and the subsequent cessation of grass management (or its conversion to solely sheep grazing) is also a serious threat to the maintenance of suitable Corncrake habitat. The causes of abandonment are many, but a profile of human demography skewed towards the aged, together with the lack of agricultural facilities, livestock and fewer active crofters may all contribute to the under-utilisation of croft land (Beaumont and England, 2016). In a similar situation to the crofting areas, the Eastern Alps of Italy also have many very small patches of land belonging to different owners, and these too are facing land abandonment (Borgo and Zoologia Botanica, 2010). This potential threat, however, could also offer new opportunities for Corncrake reproduction if a different whole-landscape style of land management were to be adopted (this is expanded upon later).

In these crofting areas of Scotland (and it may also apply in other less intensive agricultural regimes elsewhere in Europe) there has long been a tendency to leave an unmown patch where a Corncrake nest with eggs is spotted, or to move the nest to adjacent cover for protection from the mower and from the gulls and crows waiting to prey (Venables and Venables, 1950). I have personally talked with crofters in the Outer Hebrides, in South Uist and in north Lewis, who made this their normal practice. In the north of Ireland, echoing the anecdotes from other areas, there are tales of children chasing the adult Corncrakes and chicks through the hayfields at harvest time (Arthur, 1996). The downy, black chicks were sometimes called 'black chickens' by rural people in England (Brown, 1938). Another game delighted in actually seeing a Corncrake among the tall grass, after having been lured closer by rasping together dry bones. Sometimes,

> 'We used to lure them to mirrors when we were boys and watch them fight with their own reflections. They're almost gone now.'
>
> (Arthur, 1996)

It is self-evident that the loss of suitable habitat for Corncrakes, in either their breeding or non-breeding habitats (including the temporary occupation of sites on migrations), is likely to lead to a reduction in the total population. In the breeding regions, the lack of suitable habitat may also lead to some birds being forced into suboptimal areas or indeed to the complete exclusion from breeding for some individuals (Dolman and Sutherland, 1995).

VEGETATIONAL COVER AND MANAGEMENT STYLE

It is worth remembering that although the general decline of the Corncrake population in western Europe has been observed and recorded for more than a century, and the link with the intensification of grassland management suspected as a major cause, it was not until relatively recently that habitat management for Corncrake conservation was studied in any detail (Stowe et al., 1993). Earlier studies had identified the possible link between the increased mechanisation of mowing (producing earlier and faster cutting of meadows) and the destruction of nests with eggs and young (Norris, 1963), but the conclusive evidence of this was slow to be confirmed. Eventually, the lack of rapid declines prior to the introduction of mechanised mowing, and the connection between these regional declines and the timing of mowing, was established (Green, Rocamora et al., 1997). So, too, was the realisation that although Corncrakes may prefer the new species of grass being cultivated for hay and silage to the older permanent meadows of 'natural' grass, the trend towards the earlier mowing of hay fields made this a more dangerous habitat, with consequently higher chick mortality. In many cases still, Corncrakes are more likely to breed and successfully rear young to fledging in the cover areas than they are in the fields being intensively managed for hay or silage (Corbett and Hudson, 2010). This is partly because the specific structure of the grassland habitat is crucially important, and partly because the cover benefits of attempting to breed in managed meadow vegetation may be offset by the disturbances occurring in those fields due to the mowing dates overlapping with Corncrake hatching and the consequent risk of mortality caused by the lack of chick mobility during mowing operations. The practical and economic permutations of different mowing regimes have been considered in substantial detail in both Scotland and Ireland (Aberdeen Centre for Land Use, 1991), but the tension between securing winter fodder and maintaining cover vegetation for breeding Corncrakes is not an easy compromise. Managing the timing of mowing is important, but so too is ensuring the optimum grassland structure. Overall, Corncrakes favour extensively managed (low-intensity) grassland that is dominated by species such as False oat-grass, as this provides a good combination of a low density of vegetation at ground level that permits easy movement (and possibly a drier environment for chicks) together with higher level cover giving protection from predators (Arbeiter, Franke et al., 2017).

It is now recognised that Corncrakes generally prefer tall vegetation for shelter and for feeding, and that the diverse combination of unmanaged meadows, mown and moist meadows, rough field edges, headlands, forest boundaries and occasional arable areas can provide a mosaic of rich biodiversity that is used at different times throughout the year (Berg and Hiron, 2012). Corncrake males frequently make use of trees and bushes as landscape markers for calling sites during the breeding season (Besnard et al., 2016), and they seem to be less averse to hedgerow proximity than many other species of grassland birds. This raises interesting possibilities for the management of landscapes in northern Europe, where abandoned farmland is commonly a component of the local vegetational mosaic. Some abandoned or uncultivated areas may only require minimal management to ensure that they provide suitable breeding habitat for Corncrakes in the future (Orlowski, 2010). The precise composition of these landscape mosaics can vary widely, with correspondingly variable opportunities for feeding, breeding and the general movement of Corncrakes. This is important to appreciate, because we know that both male and female Corncrakes tend to relocate around the landscape through the year in response to habitat change or anthropogenic disturbances, as well as seeking optimal breeding territories for sequential polygamy (Michalska-Hejduk et al., 2017). The breeding success of grassland birds may vary in a single locality from year to year, not simply due to habitat changes, but also due to a variety of other factors, including weather, disease, disturbance and the social dynamics of the species (Bignal and McCracken, 2000). This may suggest that some calling males have been counted twice in field surveys, but it also emphasises the importance of the provision of extensive areas of suitable habitat availability in the overall mosaic of the managed countryside (Mikkelsen et al., 2013).

In Serbia, for instance, National Protected Areas (NPA) are designated for a variety of reasons – aesthetic, economic, historical – rather than solely for species protection. As a result, the suitable Corncrake habitat within all the NPAs is only around 12%, and the

NPAs themselves cover only about 7% of Serbia (Radišić et al., 2019). Although an accurate assessment of the distribution of Corncrakes in Serbia is uncertain because of the lack of systematic surveys, it is clear that large areas of habitat suitable for Corncrakes in east and south-west Serbia are located outside of NPAs (Radišić et al., 2019), although of course not all potential sites will be occupied. In Hungary, as few as 25% of known Corncrakes have been located in the protected Environmentally Sensitive Areas in certain years, and so the need to extend conservation management practices for Corncrake habitats into the wider countryside is important (Boldogh, Visnyovszky et al., 2016). In Austria, the Corncrake is considered to be critically endangered, yet only 5–10% of Corncrake territories are covered by late-mowing agreements (only around 50% of farmers agreed to participate) and the region of Ennstal is the only Austrian site with a Special Protection Area that has a targeted management plan for Corncrake conservation (Frühauf, 2016). Blanket prescriptions on tight management controls will need to integrate with local farming circumstances, otherwise the overall impacts may be counter-productive (Bignal and McCracken, 2000). Effective Corncrake conservation in the future will certainly depend upon increasing appropriate agricultural land management outwith the network of the currently protected sites.

It is significant for the enigma that is the Corncrake that we often hear of the land favoured for its habitat as being regarded as 'High Nature Value' for wildlife conservation, but more commonly referred to simply as 'marginal' agricultural land. Although traditional family farming is steadily decreasing across the whole of Europe, there is substantial evidence that low-input/low-output land management systems are valuable because they have a high ecological value (Bignal and McCracken, 1996). In fact:

> *'environmental or nature conservation value is highest on farms with low inputs and low outputs and where farming practices are to a greater degree shaped by the constraints of the natural environment.'*
>
> (Bignal and McCracken, 2000)

Furthermore, and of great importance for the Corncrake:

> *'Virtually all the remaining high nature conservation value grasslands across Europe are associated with low-intensity livestock systems.'*
>
> (Bignal and McCracken, 2000)

Studies in Romania, however, show clearly that although High Nature Value landscapes of small farming units tend to create a mosaic of rich biodiversity, and are favoured by grassland species such as Corncrakes, grassland-focused conservation strategies alone might not be sufficient for their protection (Page and Popa, 2016). Poorly-constructed agri-environmental schemes that unintentionally encourage the conversion of hay meadows into grazing pasture, that synchronise rather than stagger mowing times (thereby reducing vegetational cover simultaneously), and that do not consider the small traditional field sizes will actually work against Corncrake protection. Under these conditions, the historical behaviour of local farming communities is being destabilised by so-called 'support' schemes that are not sufficiently targeted towards supporting good Corncrake habitats, and therefore risk reducing the diversity of the mosaic available across the entire landscape. Encouraging staggered mowing dates, alone, would encourage a mixture of more favourable habitat diversity (Todorova, 2016). Several studies have suggested that greater assistance should be made directly available to small-scale farming communities to maintain the ecosystem-based approach to the provision of a diverse landscape mosaic (Page and Popa, 2016).

In many regions of rural Europe, this low-intensity agricultural management, often mixed-farming with extensive grazing of sheep and/or cattle, is at the margin of agricultural productivity and socio-economic viability, and several regions face a growing problem of the abandonment of even these small-scale, non-intensive farmlands. In Sweden, for example, the availability of wet meadows for Corncrake breeding has steadily reduced since the mid-1940s as fields have been more intensively managed for arable crops, intensive grazing or fodder production, or simply left to return to swampy scrubland (Berg and Gustafson, 2006). While abandoned meadows may be an attraction for Corncrakes during the first few seasons, they tend to become too dense and ultimately unfavourable for Corncrakes (Budka and Osiejuk, 2013a). The effects of farmland abandonment are complex and can, in different circumstances, be either positive or negative depending on the prior vegetation and the landscape-scale of abandonment. In addition, it is not just the encroachment of subclimax scrub that can be problematic for Corncrakes, but also that alien invasive species such as Goldenrod or Reed can negatively influence the arthropod population, leading to a reduction of food availability (Tryjanowski et al., 2011). Unfortunately, the opposing agricultural environments of intensive management (no cover and possible disruption) and field abandonment (overly-dense vegetation and scrub encroachment) are both detrimental to Corncrake breeding success (Rassati and Rodaro, 2007). As a result, Corncrakes usually survive best in meadows that are intermittently mown, or in a landscape that is mown in stages to create a patchwork mosaic pattern, leaving uncultivated fragments, rough field margins and fallow areas to enable free movement.

In the floodplain environments favoured by many Corncrakes, such as the Rhine valleys in the Netherlands, two factors in particular combine to make an attractive breeding habitat for the species. First, the wet, low-lying meadows are frequently damp late into the growing season and therefore require to be mown later, if they can be mown at all, giving a longer period to enable chicks to become mobile and avoid the mowing machines. Second, the periodic flooding of the habitat has the effect of removing the dead materials of ground litter, allowing a more open sward and preventing the development of a climax vegetation that would eventually impede the relatively free movement of the birds (Atsma, 2006). A long-term management strategy needs to find a workable balance between the economic interests of farmers and the protection of habitat for Corncrakes. Such a balance might include leaving refuge strips unmown, the late cutting of grass and perhaps finding potential alternative uses for late-cut, poor-nutrient grass other than for use as animal fodder (Arbeiter et al., 2018). The regular late mowing of floodplain meadows can be used to maintain a favourable vegetational structure for Corncrakes, and that relatively open structure may also help to reduce the risk of predation in the following breeding season (Arbeiter and Franke, 2018). There is, therefore, an argument that the regular ground clearance of floodplain meadows, whether by natural causes or by managed flooding, could be employed to maintain favourable breeding habitats for Corncrakes.

In north-eastern Hungary, where the wet meadows and abandoned pastures are the most important breeding areas for Corncrakes, the local bird population fluctuates considerably and is frequently associated with the flood level – the higher the flood, the less land available for nesting. This flooding may be another motivation for some birds relocating during the breeding season, and another important reason to maintain potentially suitable habitat outwith the main protected sites in the flood-affected areas (Boldogh, Visnyovszky et al., 2016). In the Alps, the frequent movements of Corncrakes during a single season shift from an early presence at the low altitudes to a later presence at higher elevations, which have later vegetation growth and later harvesting, and this needs to be factored into any habitat management activities (Brambilla and Pedrini, 2011). It is significant, for instance, that the substantial increase in the population of the Corncrake in the core areas in Scotland coincided with the introduction of a range of agri-environmental schemes which were intended to support farmers and crofters to modify mowing techniques, and also to increase the provision of early and late-stage cover to provide refuge areas (O'Brien et al., 2006). Without an effort to increase the vegetational cover (with an appropriate structure) in the current areas of potentially suitable breeding habitat, the Corncrake may have reached the limit of the carrying capacity of the land in some areas, for example in the north-west mainland of Scotland (Wotton et al., 2015).

Delayed mowing

It is worth remembering that the cause-and-effect link between the steady decline of the European Corncrake population and the steady creep of land management intensification (and mechanised mowing in particular) was conclusively established only relatively recently. Early studies (Norris, 1947) posit a connection caused by the replacement of manual mowing with scythes by horse-drawn harvesting machines. Over time, the introduction of tractors and increasingly more efficient mowing machines led to quicker and earlier harvesting, and in some areas a switch from hay to silage or haylage (which does not require to be thoroughly dried by consistent lengthy spells of good weather). A preference by crofters for silage rather than hay is usually not about the intensification of production, but rather on simple economic and logistical decisions of convenience, and therefore proposals for a 'hay premium scheme' to preferentially harvest hay (Williams et al., 1991) have not been widely adopted. Later studies (Tyler et al., 1998) established stronger links between the high mortality of Corncrake chicks and mechanised mowing, and the style(s) of grassland management. In particular, the timing of the grassland harvest strongly influences the breeding success (Green, Tyler et al., 1997), as earlier mowing tends to overlap with the incubation and early maternal care of the first brood of Corncrakes. Early mowing of hay and silage is known to have a strong correlation with low breeding success for Corncrakes (Ottvall and Pettersson, 1998b), and replacement broods (or second broods) are less likely in those situations. Corncrake population dynamics have a high mortality rate and those successful second broods are necessary to at least maintain the population levels.

Although delayed mowing is a more secure way of ensuring that Corncrake chicks are protected from the fatal effects of the mechanical mower, this is often not a feasible option for farmers, particularly in north-western oceanic regions with highly changeable weather. Floodplain habitats are also problematic because later harvests usually produce poorer quality fodder, encouraging many farmers to abandon meadow management altogether, which is not beneficial to Corncrakes as the vegetational structure tends to become more dense and produces a less attractive habitat (Arbeiter, Helmecke et al., 2017). Even relatively small changes to grassland management can have a big knock-on impact. There is evidence that in extensively managed meadows delaying the first mowing for one month, until around mid-summer, can boost the density of invertebrates such as Orthoptera, for example grasshoppers and crickets, by a factor of five (Buri et al., 2013).

In a Swedish study (Berg and Gustafson, 2007), the majority of Corncrakes were found in areas of tall vegetation, frequently produced without any farming subsidy, rather than in the intensively managed meadows. As a general recommendation, it may be that an investment in the future of successfully breeding Corncrakes would benefit by a greater emphasis on payments to crofters and farmers to create a landscape mosaic that can provide cover for Corncrakes, rather than the current emphasis on simply delayed mowing (Corbett and Hudson, 2010). In the localities where winning a crop of good winter fodder for grazing animals is a constant challenge with fickle weather, it is always going to be problematic to miss an early opportunity to harvest the season's hay or silage. In addition, in some regions, the standard practice of delayed mowing can even prove to be counter-productive because the synchronisation of this management activity results in the area-wide homogenisation of the height of the vegetation, which reduces the availability of cover over a wider landscape, and in turn negatively affects Corncrakes (Dorresteijn et al., 2015). In the Shannon Callows in Ireland, a very high proportion of the available meadow is managed by delayed mowing, but the danger of removing all cover for any late-breeding Corncrakes has been partially offset by the introduction of an increased payment for farmers to provide cover by staggering the mowing dates to encourage different stages of growth (Copland, 2001). Despite these management activities, by 2015 no Corncrakes were being recorded on the Shannon Callows (Duffy, 2018), partly due to severe flooding of the meadows in the early 2000s.

In the Italian Alps, the introduction of agricultural subsidies for grassland conservation without giving sufficient consideration to the ecology of target species has actually impacted negatively on Corncrakes (Brambilla and Pedrini, 2013). By encouraging mowing without considering the timing, and the cumulative impact of small changes across the whole landscape, past agri-environmental measures have failed to promote effective Corncrake conservation. It is worth remarking that the historical system of a mosaic of small-scale, individual land managers, where the culture of mowing was spread over days or weeks, is in sharp contrast to the present system of synchronised mowing and the removal of landscape features to maximise yields.

CORNCRAKE-FRIENDLY MOWING

A Russian study in the early 1970s first proposed the idea of mowing from the centre of the field towards the outer limits of the field (now termed Inside–Outward mowing or I–O mowing) because the converse O–I mowing tends to drive both chicks and adult birds into the unmown area in the centre of the field, only to be killed in the final swathes of cutting (Manush, 1974). This proposal, however, took more than two decades to be widely appreciated and put into practice in western Europe, and was only appropriate then in certain land management contexts.

Certainly, the inside–outward style of mowing encourages the adult birds and chicks to move towards the edges of the fields where taller vegetation generally remains to provide some cover. As they move towards the field margins, the uncut hay/silage also provides shelter from the watchful eyes of predators. Chicks, in particular, are usually reluctant to cross areas of newly-mown grass where they are visible and vulnerable. As female Corncrakes usually remain in close proximity to their chicks until they become fully independent, this method of mowing can enable most birds to escape from the harvester into the protection of the surrounding vegetation if a mosaic of uncut grassland, refuge areas or other less intensively managed land is sufficiently available (Tyler et al., 1998).

REFUGE STRIPS

There has been a considerable amount of literature that has documented the decline of the breeding population of European Corncrakes, but although our understanding is becoming clearer, there is often a lack of evidence for assessing which specific elements of different management practices are the most effective in different circumstances to increase the breeding numbers (Corbett and Hudson, 2010). The full extent of the cumulative effects of changes in land management has been difficult to determine precisely, due to the lack of knowledge both of specific aspects of the breeding ecology of the Corncrake and of the extent of international (European) changes in farming practices (Tyler, 2001). For large fields of grass, it has been proposed that leaving strategically placed strips of uncut grass can provide a temporary refuge that may help to reduce the mortality of birds, especially of unfledged chicks and juvenile birds (Broyer, 2003). A recommendation was made that these strips should be a minimum of 10 m wide (when cutting inwards towards the centre of the field) or to leave two 5-m wide strips along field margins (when mowing from the centre outwards; Arbeiter, Helmecke et al., 2017). This so-called 'Corncrake-friendly mowing' from the centre of the field, spiralling out towards the field margins, can allow birds to survive the mowing and move safely to the refuge areas, or adjacent unmown fields, but it is only appropriate in certain limited circumstances. It is favoured for large fields (Arbeiter, Helmecke et al., 2017), but in the heartland of the UK Corncrake population, in the Hebrides, croft fields are frequently long and narrow (perhaps only 20 m wide by 200–300 m long), so inside–outwards mowing is often impossible, and indeed farcical to contemplate. An individual crofting township may cover hundreds of small fields and dozens of individual crofters in a single 1 km² of a census (Beaumont and England, 2016). A similar situation exists in other European regions, including Romania, where small land units are often long and narrow, meaning that a condition of agri-environmental management to leave 3-m wide field margins is often impractical and inadvertently discourages farmers from hay production, to the detriment of making suitable habitat available for Corncrakes (Page and Popa, 2016). Although some larger farms in Europe might manage two crops of grass in a growing season, in the Highlands and Islands of Scotland, the vagaries of unpredictable weather mean that most crofters are grateful to grab at the chance of fine weather to secure even one good crop for the winter, and any delay in mowing can be expensive.

One study (Green et al., 2019) recommended the modification of mowing techniques within 500 m of the calling sites of male Corncrakes, and while this may be applicable in large hayfields in some parts of Europe, it is largely impracticable in crofting areas. To put this into perspective, in areas such as north Lewis, many crofts have elongated, linear fields, perhaps only 10 m wide but 1 km long, and a 500 m 'management zone' around a single calling bird might have a landscape footprint of an entire village covering several dozen entire crofts. Nor is this an unusual situation for traditional farming in Europe: for example, a healthy Corncrake population remains in southern Transylvania, where arable land is used mainly for subsistence farming and most fields are generally smaller than two hectares (Dorresteijn et al., 2015). In 2011, Poland had more than 2.5 million farms, nearly half of which were 'smaller than 2 hectares, and this field mosaic is enriched by a dense network of semi-natural field margins' (Tryjanowski et al., 2011).

Studies show that:

> 'land cover homogenization in a traditional farming landscape could drastically reduce suitable habitat for farmland species such as the Corncrake. This underlines the need for conservation strategies that consider land cover diversity across entire landscape mosaics, and that are specifically geared towards traditional farmland.'
>
> (Dorresteijn et al., 2015)

Elsewhere, studies have shown that a 10-m refuge strip can be effective in protecting about half of all observed chicks during mowing activities. Although adult females frequently remain in the vicinity of their (even already independent) chicks, the adults can normally move ahead of the mower fast enough to escape (Tyler, 1996). These refuge areas are especially important when using modern mowing machines, as they tend to have a longer cutting blade and travel faster, and so it may be necessary to consider a slower mowing speed to allow a better chance for birds to escape (Copland, 2001). Flightless chicks appear reluctant to cover more than 20 m of open ground, and predators such as the Red Fox, White Stork and various raptors are frequently noted to be present in the vicinity during and immediately after mowing to take advantage of any feeding opportunity (Arbeiter, Helmecke et al., 2017).

This whole-landscape style of management is complex because it will require the involvement of many individuals, some of whom are active land managers, others less so (or have even abandoned working their holding). It therefore needs the engagement and collaboration of entire rural communities (Rennie, 1983). In many situations, the land managers in those communities will be part-time (Grant, 1984) or even hobby-farmers, whose ability to maintain pluriactivity in several simultaneous occupations enables them to remain living in these rural locations and to continue their low-input/low-out agricultural practices at a small scale (Rennie, 1991). There is an unmissable connection, which is often glossed over in conservation management prescriptions, that healthy, viable Corncrake populations are co-dependent upon healthy, viable rural communities and extensive (often labour-intensive) farming styles that have often been followed for several human generations.

MIXED METHODS

A key point to note here is that there is no single solution for mowing practices. Management solutions vary with the function and practice of local land management requirements, and in areas where there are multiple owners and land managers, the whole-landscape mosaic of diverse habitat types needs to be available to Corncrakes. This will not be provided simply by applying a blanket of 'protected area' management constraints to the entirety of a rural region, and it indicates that policies and practices need to encourage mixed-farming styles to maintain the biodiversity of the vegetational cover of the region. Throughout Europe, traditional farming practices are long established, and are the results of centuries of intimate interaction between rural people and the natural environment (Bignal and McCracken, 2000). Successive studies over a number of years have shown that the mixed-farming practices of traditional agriculture can simultaneously provide the important habitat requirements for Corncrakes, including areas for shelter, feeding, nesting and cover for their mobility (Dorresteijn et al., 2015). In addition, a major review of agri-environmental practices emphasised that:

> *'Biodiversity conservation cannot rely on protected areas alone, as sustainable conservation requires strategies for managing whole landscapes including areas allocated mainly to production.'*
>
> (Batáry et al., 2011)

They concluded, however, that:

> *'the one-size-fits-all approach of many agri-environmental programmes is not a very efficient way of spending the limited funds available for biodiversity conservation on farmland'* and argued that *'programmes should be targeted to the nature of the landscapes of the regions in which they are implemented and the type of species groups at which they are targeted.'*
>
> (Batáry et al., 2011)

In practice, a mixture of delayed mowing, 'Corncrake-friendly mowing' techniques and the enhancement of a habitat mosaic across the landscape that can provide refuges of cover for young birds would appear to be the best combination for Corncrake protection and their successful reproduction. In the crofting areas of the Highlands and Islands of Scotland, several studies have shown the value of a landscape mosaic of meadows, ungrazed areas and arable patches of land. This landscape allows birds to move under cover throughout the breeding season. Frequently, in the Outer Hebrides and Inner Hebrides, small field sizes (the average size of an entire croft might only be about 5 acres) result in small batches of hay being cut and baled before more is cut (Newton, 1991), enabling birds to move to nearby refuges. Habitat surveys have been conducted in the islands of the Outer Hebrides (Booth and Milne, 1999), as well as in the Inner Hebridean islands of Tiree (Leitch, 1999) and neighbouring Coll (Grant, 2002) to assess the extent of currently available Corncrake habitat, to establish baseline data and to monitor future habitat change, with the future potential of creating Special Protection Areas for Corncrakes.

These areas are similar to other regions where marginal farmland is supporting a human demography skewed towards older age groups, and optimum Corncrake habitat management becomes problematic at the two extremes: where meadows are either grazed heavily or abandoned completely. A study in Tiree, which in the late 1990s supported almost a quarter of the entire UK Corncrake population, illustrates that this problem is often more complex than it at first appears (Jones et al., 1998). A combination of the intensification of grazing/mowing in some areas of very active crofting, together with the abandonment or near-disuse of other crofts and a reduction in the rotational cropping of arable land, has resulted in the redistribution of Corncrakes. They now frequently seek to utilise the cover provided by cereal crops, field margins and the edges of wetland areas. Unlike European farmland that is intensively managed for milk production (where Corncrake numbers are less abundant; Green and Rayment, 1996), many rural areas have identified a need to increase cattle production, as this maintains the demand for growing fodder locally (Newton, 1991), which in turn results in a greater extent of Corncrake-friendly habitat. In at least two regions of mainland Europe, in the Oldambt area of the Netherlands and the Hellwegbörde region of western Germany, both of which record large local Corncrake populations, the main breeding habitats are, unusually, in cereal crops such as winter Wheat and Alfalfa (Joest and Koffijberg, 2016). There is sufficient evidence that most birds breed there successfully, even though the chicks are at least as much at risk from early summer harvests as those birds nesting in grasslands. The fact that crops like Alfalfa provide high vegetative cover that has a rather open structure at ground level, may be part of the attraction for Corncrakes, as will be the adjacent areas of set-aside land that are relatively undisturbed during an entire season and therefore can provide stable refuge sites. Significantly for Corncrake conservation, the encouragement of set-aside grassland in the crofting areas that can be left as refuge patches in the annual landscape mosaic (even by less active crofters) was seen as one of the key factors with the greatest potential in an early habitat management study (Aberdeen Centre for Land Use, 1991), but it seems that little progress has been made on this option. This is not so much a result of the potential 'compensation' costs of such a scheme, but rather because the relevant agencies have baulked at the collective effort required to engage effectively and in sufficient detail with multiple land users covering the whole of a rural community. Despite that, a combination of conservation measures in Scotland has gained a modicum of success after almost a century of steady decline (Stowe and Green, 1997a).

AGRI-ENVIRONMENTAL INITIATIVES

Several countries in Western Europe have formulated Corncrake Action Plans, with various levels of detail and diligence in their implementation, and this attempted implementation is frequently reflected in some sort of agri-environmental scheme and/or government policy intended to encourage conservation-friendly farming (Beaumont and England, 2016). In addition, key lessons from these national action plans have been collated and summarised in an International Single Species Action Plan for the Conservation of the Corncrake (Crockford et al., 1996; Crockford et al., 1997) and this is a good historical source for quick reference to the development of these regional plans (Koffijberg and Schäffer, 2006). Most schemes have been geared towards species protection or to the maintenance of the local population of a target species. Although there have been examples of attempts to reintroduce Corncrakes to the wild, for example a project in England, the reintroduction of any species is not without its risks (Carter and Newberry, 2004). In most cases, compensation to farmers and crofters to manage land in specific ways that might encourage Corncrakes to establish safe territories and therefore breed successfully is based on payments for land management in the vicinity of the location of calling males, on the basis that the female bird and her nest are normally within 200 m of that location. This, however, frequently overlooks the importance of the mosaic effect of adjacent habitats to provide cover and feeding locations, and a whole-landscape approach needs to be strongly considered in the conservation strategy for any future agri-environment schemes, rather than the minimalist approach of current location-based management (Green, Tyler et al., 1997). A good example of this is the Environmentally Sensitive Area scheme in the Hebrides of Scotland that has attempted to incorporate Corncrake management requirements into agricultural practices (Aebischer et al., 2000), although this has also focused mainly on the machair grassland and the worked croftland, without acknowledging that the traditional croft management strategies also include the integral use of other areas, such as adjacent moorland (which is ineligible for support) that makes the whole agricultural system viable.

In Ireland, in addition to providing payments to support changes in land management practices, for example different mowing techniques, to conserve the Corncrake, considerable attention has been given to the philosophy and practice of how farmers themselves might contribute financially to support such schemes (Hynes et al., 2007). Perhaps unsurprisingly, one of the outcomes of the research was that farmers who still had Corncrakes on their land (usually small farms with more traditional management) were willing to pay more than the farmers with larger, more intensive farms, who would be required to make substantial changes to their farm operations. There are difficulties in trying to generalise from a small number of sample sites to propose lessons for the wider countryside, but the broad indications are that the income value of Corncrake conservation to the countryside of Ireland is approximately six times the cost of current agri-environmental programmes established to encourage Corncrake conservation (Hynes and Hanley, 2009).

It could further be argued that the total benefits to Irish society as a whole are substantially greater than even these estimates of worth. If the application of Corncrake management schemes were to be extended to land beyond the current requirement for a calling male to be present, to include potential suitable areas of the wider countryside, a much greater benefit could be expected, especially because of the large geographical variations in the annual population numbers (Duffy, 2018). Only focused measures such as these are likely to ensure the restoration of the Corncrake as a common species of the Irish countryside. This is not an atypical story: in Switzerland, the Corncrake population is considerably diminished compared to historical records, and their current annual presence is unpredictable. The tendency is to 'rarely settle in the same meadow in consecutive years' (Inderwildi, 2016), which means that a whole-landscape approach, rather than just concentrating on small 'protected areas', is required for effective Corncrake restoration, although without an attractive agri-environmental compensation to farmers it is highly doubtful that any Corncrakes will successfully breed in Switzerland (Inderwildi and Müller, 2015). Although farmers are encouraged to maintain 'ecological compensation' areas, these efforts are small, do not have enforceable minimum standards and are generally of low ecological quality, with poor species richness. In the Swiss lowlands, agriculture has intensified to such a level that more than half the farmland bird species are on the Red Data list, and in a key study (Birrer et al., 2007) the Corncrake, which was listed as Critically Endangered in the country, was not recorded in any of the study areas.

The big picture is clear: the survival and flourishing of Corncrake populations requires the active engagement of rural human communities, who are encouraged to employ a whole-landscape approach to ensuring a balance between viable economic farming and a Corncrake-friendly environment. An overemphasis on 'special sites' and reserves ignores the fact that more than 50% of the most highly valued biotopes in Europe occur on low-intensity farmland (over 2 million hectares in the UK, with over 65% of it outwith designated Environmentally Sensitive Areas (Bignal and McCracken, 1996). The active collaboration of land managers of all sorts, together with conservation activities targeted as specifically as possible within the broad landscape of potentially suitable habitat for the species, is likely to be the minimum required combination for breeding success (Broyer et al., 2014). Unfortunately, many of the recent and current Corncrake management schemes narrowly target only the management of the breeding habitat, for example hay meadows, rather than rewarding crofters/farmers to take a large-scale perspective on land management. In all countries, land-use policies, both national and transnational, will continue to heavily influence the distribution of agriculture and conservation priorities in the future, and although the historical fragmentation of semi-natural habitats has in many areas led to the focus of nature conservation only on protected areas, it is clear that this in itself is not enough (Pienkowski et al., 1996). A mosaic of connected habitat areas is required by many species to ensure the continuity of range and the opportunities for nesting, shelter and feeding in the wider countryside, not only in discrete areas of 'protected' land, or locations where the species has been recorded. The large-scale availability of complex mosaics of different habitats is an important characteristic enabling the presence of the large Corncrake population across Russia (Mischenko, 2016). In the UK, generally less than 10% of the known Corncrake population is recorded from dedicated bird reserves (Aebischer et al., 2000), and so a method of safeguarding and enhancing the habitat of the other 90% of the Corncrake population will require the engagement of a wider community base. As has been noted on more than one occasion:

> *'Fine-tuning farming methods to provide conditions for Corncrakes is desirable but will not be possible if the farming systems themselves cease to exist.'*
>
> (O'Brien et al., 2006)

Likewise, in the Saône Valley of France, the land areas under past agri-environmental schemes were considered to be too small and too fragmented to efficiently support the maintenance of the Corncrake population, and the regional population declined sharply (Broyer et al., 2014). As grazing requirements, the physical environment and human intervention will all vary widely in different regions, there is a need to tailor conservation management policies and incentives to more closely support appropriate regional diversity. Although agricultural practices often lead to intensified land management, this need not mean a requirement to return to former farming methods, nor is it guaranteed that simply limiting surplus production in intensive farming will automatically produce sympathetic ecological conditions that provide optimum habitat for targeted species.

> *'If we understood the complex processes better and knew why they work, then modern methods could be adapted to take this into account.'*
>
> (Pienkowski et al., 1996)

LAND ABANDONMENT OR REJUVENATION

Although the local/regional details may differ in the specifics, this broad trend is mirrored in other areas all across Europe. This issue was particularly highlighted in a review that considered the variations in local/regional habitat conditions between western Europe and the east of Russia and Asia in relation to the accuracy of Corncrake population counts and the need to adjust the local implementation of agri-environmental schemes (Fourcade et al., 2013). In Latvia, for instance, during 1984–2004, the area of abandoned agricultural land increased significantly at the expense of cultivated pastures (Keišs, 2005). Although the highest breeding density of Corncrakes was seen in the abandoned grasslands, the projected trends show a significant long-term decrease due to the future loss of suitable habitat. As meadows rich in grass species and arable fields cease to be farmed, the steady encroachment of trees and bushes and the reduction of open grasses will make the habitat unfavourable for Corncrakes. One study noted that:

'Corncrakes were mainly recorded in old fields dominated by herbs but still with minimal invasion of trees, i.e. fields that were abandoned between 5 and 15 years ago.'

(Grishchenko and Prins, 2016)

Eventually, however, without intervention, fewer Corncrakes will favour this environment as the forest scrub replaces grassland. These ongoing transitions make the long-term future of the Corncrake population trend unclear. Changes in political systems are often reflected in changes in the intensity of agriculture and land use, which may cumulatively have rapid ecological consequences (Beaumont and England, 2016). In Russia, as well as in the Baltic states and other Eastern European countries, these changes have been substantial in the past three decades. Since the 1990s, Russia has experienced the cessation of farming over more than 48 million hectares of land, much of this in European Russia (Mischenko et al., 2019). As in other regions, the termination of cattle grazing has resulted in no need for local hay production, and consequently the large-scale abandonment of meadows and floodplain grasslands from systems of farm management.

The example of plant succession resulting from farm abandonment is well-illustrated by the long-term studies in Russia. In one area, cattle grazing and arable production stopped completely between 1986 and 2000, with only 4–17% of the region still used for hay production. Although the regional peak of Corncrake numbers was recorded in abandoned farmland in the early stages, this soon fell away. Plant succession typically followed the general trend of:

1. Managed meadows
2. Tall weeds and individual low bushes becoming established
3. Sites with tall weeds extending and young bushes and several trees starting to appear
4. Areas of bushes spreading rapidly and trees developing in the drier sites
5. Trees and bushes occupying the main area, increasing their density, and leaving tall weeds and open spaces only in smaller, discrete patches (Mischenko et al., 2019)

The effects of the different forms of land restoration projects to encourage Corncrake breeding, and the habitat differences caused by the various permutations of grazing intensity, mowing every few years and mixed management methods are still poorly understood (Berg and Gustafson, 2006). Furthermore, a farmland management scheme that produces optimal grassland habitat for the Corncrake may be suboptimal for other bird species, so careful targeting and monitoring will be required. An example of this is the preference of the Chough (another species of concern) for access to early mown fields in June in search of leatherjackets (the larvae of the Cranefly) rather than of the Corncrake for mowing in late August, by which time the larvae will have hatched and flown. One result of the lack of proper targeting of agri-environmental schemes for habitat management is that while the benefits to the target species are generally measured, the costs to other species are not, and there is little or no 'risk-assessment' in terms of the outcomes of overall ecological accountancy. The variation of farmland biodiversity across the spread of the European continent and the associated styles of agricultural management are such that it is clear that Corncrake conservation, and bird conservation in general, will require careful regional customisation of farm economics, environmental sensitivity and species targeting to be effective (Tryjanowski et al., 2011). Several studies have criticised recent agri-environmental schemes as being insufficiently supportive of the conservation of species such as the Corncrake, due to the variability of regional conditions and local land management practices, but also to the poorly customised local implementation of the schemes (Bellebaum and Koffijberg, 2018). One size does not fit all.

On the whole, however, carefully designed agri-environmental schemes can also provide wider ecological benefits in terms of species diversity and abundance, as well as benefiting the target species such as Corncrakes (Wilkinson et al., 2012). Agricultural intensification is not a single process, and the multiple components, such as grazing and stock levels, drainage, crop rotation and harvesting, make it difficult to assess the individual impact of changes on different species (Newton, 2004). In a review of the decline of Corncrake numbers breeding in Ireland, and the ways in which this trend may be contained or reversed (Copland, 2001), the importance of site-specific management objectives was noted. This will require the application of management objectives that are tailored to targeted sites, together with local community collaboration, but these small-scale operations make it difficult to fully understand the complex ecological requirements needed for wider countryside management. As I write this chapter, there was a social media post drawn to my attention advertising a new PhD position to explore such opportunities for improving the conservation status of the Corncrake throughout Ireland. Small nature reserves and other 'protected areas' can play a role, but, at the grand scale:

'land acquisition and reserve management is [sic] *likely to be inappropriate to conserve a dispersed species such as Corncrake.'*

(Green and Williams, 1992)

The ideal solution is for national and international support for the implementation of environmentally-friendly land management implemented by rural communities themselves, within a framework of available specialist advice and educational support. In terms of the requirements for the period of their lives spent on the continent of Africa, much more needs to be understood about the movements, distribution and habitat choices of Corncrakes. It is not wise to generalise too often, but it seems that they are not unduly threatened from any specific sources in Africa, other than hunting/trapping during migration and the generic possibilities of local habitat loss (Walther et al., 2013a). The majority of studies in these regions have concluded that at the moment, there continues to be abundant suitable available habitat in Africa (Walther et al., 2013a), and that the capture of migratory birds in Egypt, while not condoned and in need of greater protection enforcement, is not currently a primary cause of Corncrake population decline (Eason et al., 2016).

In its breeding areas, the implementation of agri-environmental schemes that focus on grassland management alone will not be sufficient to ensure successful Corncrake conservation. In 2018, barely 6% of the total EU Corncrake populations were in areas covered by agri-environmental schemes (Bellebaum and Koffijberg, 2018). The precise habitat requirements for one species may be inappropriate for another species, and also varies within the context of the physical environment of the landscape. This means that schemes designed for intensive farming in one region cannot be simply transferred to traditional farming landscapes in a different region (Dorresteijn et al., 2015). A study on the costs, benefits and opportunities of agri-environmental management resulting from the inclusion of new member states into the EU, presented 34 specific recommendations for policy implementation (Keenleyside, 2006). These detailed recommendations reflect the complexity and necessary inter-relatedness of economic, social and environmental priorities for effective rural development. In view of the regularly changing nature of all of those factors, the report can be regarded as a general manifesto for agri-environmental management throughout the whole of Europe, not only the countries of the EU.

If it is possible to derive a single message from this detailed report, it is that the benefits of traditional mixed-farming systems are under threat from both intensification and abandonment, and that this combined threat will not be effectively addressed without specifically embedding a robust and integrated response into investment in land management by, for and in rural communities. The 'high nature conservation benefits' of farmland that is managed under low-intensity systems continue to be marginalised by many policy-makers, despite the fact that these biotopes have been created and maintained by rural communities. The clear conclusion is that support for the retention of such systems is a better social *and* environmental investment than either the single benefit of special 'reserves' or minor gains at the periphery of intensive farming activities (Bignal and McCracken, 1996). This is where the future of the European Corncrake population really lies.

CONCLUSION

Like so many other aspects of the ecology of Corncrakes, the management of their habitat is both apparently simple and as complex as a labyrinth. The general conditions that are required for an optimal breeding territory are well known. The ideal habitat provides tall grasses and similar vegetation that have an open structure at ground level to permit easy mobility of movement but are closed at a higher levels to shield the birds from predators. Traditionally, fields grown for hay have provided this environment, but often the best times to mow the hay/silage overlap with the hatching and early days of the young Corncrakes. This can lead to high mortality of chicks as they fail to escape from mowing machines. Various tactics have been tried to minimise this mortality, including delayed mowing and patterns of mowing that allow the birds to escape to refuges, but most of these efforts are an uneasy compromise between bird conservation and mainstream farming activities. Corncrake protection has a financial cost for the farmer, and current agri-environmental schemes designed to compensate for this are often too specific or too limiting to make any significant long-term improvements. A clear shift is needed, away from the constraints of the protection that is provided for Corncrakes on special sites/reserves, to a large-scale area-wide form of countryside management. By the creation of a landscape mosaic of favourable vegetational assemblages, providing access to shelter and food throughout the breeding season, it is hoped that mixed-farming styles can effectively complement species conservation requirements and reverse the decline of the Corncrake population, to the benefit of both Corncrakes and humans in rural areas.

CHAPTER 13

FURTHER RESEARCH

Some people may find it daunting, but I am exhilarated that at the end of this book there are so many unanswered questions remaining. Despite the vast amount of knowledge that we have accumulated on Corncrakes, there is still much more to be observed. Many of our insights so far have simply been observations. We have observed the selection of habitat, for example, but we have only vague clues as to why they chose *that* specific environment and *that* particular time, and why they may subsequently move on to visit another location.

Working systematically through the academic literature of the past hundred years or so, it has been striking to read the unfolding narrative of Corncrake ecology. Some initial ideas have later been shown to be inaccurate, or at least only temporarily true, and eventually updated with more accurate information as better knowledge became available. Invariably this has raised new questions and has tended to deepen interest in the Corncrake, rather than resolving the enigmas. Surprisingly, several of the key characteristics of Corncrakes that we currently recognise (and think that we understand) were only discovered comparatively recently, often within the past couple of decades. The broad picture might now be discernible, but there are large gaps in our understanding. There are still good opportunities to conduct meaningful research on a whole range of aspects of Corncrake ecology.

A better networking of our collective intelligence, combined with wider and more accurate geographical surveys, has revealed new patterns of the global distribution and total numbers of Corncrakes. Historically the survey focus has been on the more populous countries of western Europe, and so the recent inclusion of the vast, hard-to-reach regions of eastern Russia, abundant in potential Corncrake habitat but frequently lacking humans, has dramatically increased the known global population numbers and distribution. Much of this data, however, remains simply as better-educated guesswork, and further ground-truthing is required to consolidate this as evidence. Refinements in census techniques, such as a new mobile phone app for recording in the field, non-invasive location-finding using thermal imaging or passive acoustic monitoring or possibly the audio-identification of specific individuals moving between local populations and new records of nocturnal migration calls are tentatively offering innovative ways to improve the ease and accuracy of surveys. Similarly, reasons for the frequent long-distance movements of Corncrakes within a single breeding season are only partially understood.

What are the factors that trigger these movements? Are there subtle habitat differences or knock-on impacts of global climate change that are detectable by Corncrakes but (at least so far) invisible to us? In some cases, regional weather patterns, such as the flooding of breeding territories, may provide obvious clues, but definitive reasons for other regional movements are less clear. Are late arrivals in breeding locations simply birds relocating from other European areas or are they late arrivals from migration? Are they failures of an earlier mating or simply a second breeding attempt in a potentially more favourable habitat? Can such movements explain the well-documented local fluctuations in annual population numbers, and what are the key factors that Corncrakes prioritise to differentiate apparently similar (to us, at least) habitat conditions? The scale of the geographical relocation of Corncrakes can vary across large distances, so a large-scale, transnational approach to conservation management is required. Local detail is needed, but the long-term solutions to the problems require transnational collaboration. The answers to these questions should certainly help to better inform future habitat management activities.

Corncrake geographical movements, at the local and international level, are generally often difficult to follow. Ringing recoveries tend to be poor, partly due to the variance in the number of birds that are ringed in different regions of Europe (for example, fewer birds are ringed in eastern Russia or western Asia) and partly also due to the low probability that ringed birds will be found, recognised and reported in the huge, little-inhabited regions of Africa. Do different local populations in the separate breeding areas migrate to different areas of Africa during the non-breeding part of their year, and if so, what are the factors influencing these differences? Are the movements consistent, or do they also vary from year to year? Is there any systematic variation in the movements between the localities within the African continent, and are these movements in response to regional climatic or environmental stimuli, or caused by something else entirely? Much more detail is needed about the presence and behaviours of Corncrakes during this non-breeding period, and any new information could perhaps contribute towards species protection and the management of potential habitats.

Two broad migration pathways are noted that are followed from the northern hemisphere breeding areas into Africa, but there seems quite a large variation in the flightpaths of individual birds, and perhaps in the routes and stopover sites used by different regional populations, so detailed satellite tracking may prove a more reliable option than ringing. This in turn will require cheaper, lighter and more robust tracking technology, and may need to be combined with other procedures, such as comparing the subtly distinct genetic markers of different local populations to pinpoint the complexity of these movements. Can specific molecular markers be used to measure the mixing of geographical populations, and therefore enable better understanding of whether reports of increased numbers are a result of successful breeding locally, or because of the in-migration from a different geographical population?

The females are very reclusive, and their behaviour is poorly understood. Their silent manner means that they are noticed less frequently than noisy neighbouring males, that they are captured and ringed less often, and even their use of the habitat and their movements throughout the landscape are almost mysterious. Information on female dispersal is scarce, in relation to any relocation of breeding territories between the first and second brood, and to their subsequent destinations during migrations. Can new techniques provide better detail on these behaviours?

On return to the habitats of their breeding areas, what is it that stimulates the apparent clustering effect during territory establishment by males? Presumably this behaviour has some evolutionary advantage, but does the spatial distribution of an 'exploded lek' have any other profound consequences apart from the possible allocation of optimal and suboptimal territories according to a hierarchy of male dominance? What influence does this process have (if any at all) in how males and females select their breeding partners? Interesting new possibilities for research are appearing as a result of novel applications in the identification of genetic markers that are specific to Corncrakes, and linking these markers to consequent behavioural traits, morphological characteristics, and even to different regional breeding populations, could open the doors to a deeper level of ecological understanding. Not only could these genetic markers help to clarify issues such as gene flow across the global Corncrake population, enable rapid gender identification in the field, spot minute adaptations to the local environment, and quantify the extent and frequency of transnational population fluctuations, but the techniques may also assist in understanding and predicting the occurrence of human diseases spread by avian carriers.

In terms of habitat use by Corncrakes, there is deeper research needed to better understand the locality changes that are made by both males and females within the breeding season, and what might be their preferences for 'first choice' nesting habitat versus their selection of forage areas. For proactive habitat management, there are ongoing experiments with the restoration of suitable natural environments by growing patches of Common Nettle and Oats, or by the creation of a mosaic of refuge zones and areas where early or late-season vegetation cover can be improved to retain breeding birds and their young. An important and often underrated factor needs research to focus not just on the types of vegetative cover favoured by Corncrakes, but also on the community of invertebrates that these habitats can support.

The use of grassland and hay fields is well documented, but less is known about the value and utilisation by the Corncrake of other vegetational assemblages in the landscape mosaic. This, of course, will need to incorporate the needs of other species – ecology is often a delicate balance. There is an urgent requirement to better understand the functional integration between farming systems and environmental conservation, especially traditional and mixed-farming systems. This should stimulate a serious political consideration of the potentially negative effects of landscape homogenisation on biodiversity, and the different impacts of multiple combinations of various management techniques. For example, the changing numbers and ratios of cattle and sheep grazing regimes, combined with variations in the patterns and timing of grass mowing activities, will present a wide variety in the continuum of farmland biodiversity, with consequently profound effects on both local and landscape-scale management. Some current agri-environmental measures, including precisely defined grass mowing procedures, are effectively distancing the natural system of farming and crofting from the effective provision of good Corncrake habitats. Redressing this mismatch will require research in human ecology – that is, the intimate interaction between human social and environmental sciences. How this landscape mosaic is likely to alter as a result of global climate change and regional and national changes in agricultural management throughout the entire breeding and non-breeding range occupied by the Corncrake is, as yet, only speculation. Such changes can occur rapidly and dramatically, as well as slowly and stealthily, and future agri-environmental schemes will need sensitive but robust evaluations of their effectiveness if they are to be successful in the long term.

In some geographical regions, habitat types such as floodplains, uncultivated fields or abandoned farmland, may only require minimal management in the future to ensure they are able to provide suitable breeding habitat for Corncrakes. In all areas, while the continued protection of the targeted species is essential, the short-term benefits of conservation organisations owning 'nature reserves' need to be weighed carefully against the longitudinal necessity of intimately involving rural communities in wildlife management as a mainstream land-use activity. Management of the wider natural environment outwith 'special protected areas' is crucially important. Ecological management needs to work in close partnership with local communities. In this respect, the solution presented for Corncrakes surviving, even thriving, as a species, moves way beyond conventional biological science to encompass broader environmental and societal goals. The development of a form of 'Corncrake tourism' that contributes to the rural economy and rural culture without posing any threats to the source of those benefits – the Corncrakes themselves – is an exciting possibility. If this is sensitively managed, it might usher in the arrival of a public engagement with Corncrake population dynamics that can stabilise, or even reverse, the sustained trajectory of declining numbers and range in western Europe that has been the story of the Corncrake for the past hundred years. Even if this is successfully achieved, I doubt if it would remove the wonderful intrigue of Corncrake ecology and, for me at least, it would certainly not make the species any less enigmatic.

CHAPTER 14

REFERENCES

I have attempted to compile the most comprehensive reading list available on the Corncrake so that it may be useful for future naturalists and researchers. In this, I have tried to avoid notes that simply mention the presence of a Corncrake, such as in regional bird guides, unless that information builds on, or is directly relevant to, the understanding of other issues in the main text. The specific regional references that are given in the bibliographies of the cited papers will provide leads to those other records and locations. Some article titles are also given in their original language, and these may be found by copying and pasting this title into a web search engine. For a similar reason, I have tried to give a link to the online version of relevant articles where that is known, for easier access for future readers (although some URLs may be lengthy or may be subject to broken links at a future date).

Aberdeen Centre for Land Use (1991). *Corncrakes and Grassland Management in Britain and Ireland*. Sandy: RSPB.

Adamian, M. S. and Klem, D. (1999). The Corncrake (*Crex crex*) in Armenia. In: Schäffer, N. and Mammen, U. (eds.), Proceedings of the International Corncrake Workshop 1998, Hilpoltstein, Germany, pp. 7–8. https://web.archive.org/web/20081120124206/http://www.corncrake.net/Download/armenia.pdf

Adomatitis, E., Barauskas, R., Kirstukas, M. and Preiksa, Z. (1998). How many Corncrakes are there in Lithuania? *Ciconia* 6, 5–7. (In Lithuanian).

Aebischer, N. J., Green, R. E. and Evans, A. D. (2000). From science to recovery: Four cases of how science has been translated into conservation action in the UK. In: Aebischer, N. J., Evans, A. D., Grice, P. V. and Vickery, J. A. (eds.), *Ecology and Conservation of Lowland Farmland Birds*, pp. 43–54. Tring: British Ornithologists' Union. https://www.gwct.org.uk/research/scientific-publications/2000–09/2000/aebischer2000/

Alcover, J. A., Mcminn, M. and Segui, B. (2005). *Fossil rails (Gruiformes: Rallidae) from the Balearic Islands*. In: Alcover, J. A. and Bover, P. (eds.), Proceedings of the International Symposium 'Insular Vertebrate Evolution: The Palaeontological Approach'. *Monografies de la Societat d'Història Natural de les Balears*, 12, 9–16.

Alexander, H. G. (1914). A report on the Land-Rail inquiry. *British Birds* 8, 82–92.

Alnås, I. (1974). Die Ortstreue der gotländischen Wachtelkönige *Crex crex* (L.). [Territory fidelity of the Corncrake *Crex crex* (L.) in Gotland]. *Ornis Scandinavica* 5 (2), 123–129. https://www.jstor.org/stable/3676056 (In Swedish with English abstract).

References

Alonso, J. C., Magaña, M. and Álvarez-Martínez, J. M. (2012). Male display areas in exploded leks: The importance of food resources for male mating success. *Behavioral Ecology* 23 (6), 1296–1307. doi: https://doi.org/10.1093/beheco/ars121

Anderson, G. Q. A. and Green, R. E. (2009). The value of ringing for bird conservation. *Ringing & Migration* 24 (3), 205–212. doi: https://doi.org/10.1080/03078698.2009.9674393

Angus, S. (2001). *The Outer Hebrides: Moor and Machair.* Cambridge: White Horse Press.

Anonymous (2014). Scottish Corncrake populations reach highest levels since counts began. *Am Pàipear*, 2 October 2014. http://www.ampaipear.org.uk/corncrake-populations-reach-highest-levels-since-counts-began/

Arbeiter, S. and Franke, E. (2018). Predation risk of artificial ground nests in managed floodplain meadows. *Acta Oecologica* 86, 17–22. doi: https://doi.org/10.1016/j.actao.2017.11.012

Arbeiter, S., Franke, E., Helmecke, A. and Tanneberger, F. (2017). Habitat preference of female Corncrakes *Crex crex*: implications for the conservation of breeding sites in a secretive species. *Bird Study* 64 (2), 255–263. doi: https://doi.org/10.1080/00063657.2017.1318107

Arbeiter, S., Helmecke, A. and Bellebaum, J. (2017). Do Corncrakes *Crex crex* benefit from unmown refuge strips? *Bird Conservation International* 27, 560–567. doi: https://doi.org/10.1017/S0959270916000447

Arbeiter, S., Roth, T., Helmecke, A., Haferland, H. J. and Bellebaum, J. (2017). How to count a vagabond? - Population estimation in the Corncrake *Crex crex*. *Vogelwelt* 137, 75–79.

Arbeiter, S., Roth, T., Helmecke, A., Haferland, H. J., Tanneberger, F. and Bellebaum, J. (2018). Conflict between habitat conservation and Corncrake *Crex crex* brood protection in managed floodplain meadows. *Agriculture, Ecosystems & Environment* 265, 15–21. doi: https://doi.org/10.1016/j.agee.2018.05.030

Arthur, C. (1996). The last corncrake. *Contemporary Review* 268 (1565), 315–317.

Ashoori, A. and Zolfinejad, K. (2008). The ecology of the Corncrake *Crex crex* in stubble paddyfields in the South Caspian Lowlands. *Podoces* 3 (1), 92–96.http://www.wesca.net/Podoces/Podoces3/PODOCES%203_1-2_%20Corncrake%20in%20Iran.pdf

Asikainen, M. (1999). The Corncrake (*Crex crex*) in Finland. In: Schäffer, N. and Mammen, U. (eds.), Proceedings of the International Corncrake Workshop 1998, Hilpoltstein, Germany, pp. 31–32.

Atemasov, A. A., Gorban, I. M., Dudkin, O. V., Mykytiuk, O. Y. and Domashevskiy, S. V. (2016). Number and distribution of Corncrakes *Crex crex* in the Ukraine in the 2000s. *Vogelwelt* 136 (2–3), 145–152.

Atsma, G. (2006). *Habitat selection by the Corncrake Crex crex: Importance of ecotope distribution and landscape composition in river floodplains. Corncrake distribution along the Dutch Rhine branches in the period 2001–2005.* Report Environmental Science nr. 294 SOVON Report 2006/06. Radboud Universiteit Nijmegen.

Baha el Din, S. (1993). *The Catching of Corncrakes Crex crex and Other Birds in Northern Egypt*. Cambridge: BirdLife International, Study Report No. 55.

Baha el Din, S. M., Salama, W., Grieve, A. and Green, R. E. (1996). Trapping and shooting of Corncrakes *Crex crex* on the Mediterranean coast of Egypt. *Bird Conservation International* 6, 213–228. https://www.cambridge.org/core/services/aop-cambridge-core/content/view/4C41F66DDAE1FAA3798782EA58D3DED7/s0959270900003117a.pdf/trapping_and_shooting_of_corncrakes_crex_crex_on_the_mediterranean_coast_of_egypt.pdf

Bahr, P. H. (1907). Some bird notes from the Outer Hebrides during a month spent there, May-June 1907. *Annals of Scottish Natural History* 1907, 208–215. https://www.biodiversitylibrary.org/item/16994

Bannerman, D. A. (1963). *The Birds of the British Isles, Vol. 12*, pp. 173–184. Edinburgh: Oliver and Boyd.

Barke, J. (ed.) (1955). *Poems and Songs of Robert Burns*. Glasgow: Collins.

Batáry, P. Andras, B., Kleijn, D. and Tscharntke, T. (2011). Landscape-moderated biodiversity effects of agri-environmental management: A meta-analysis. *Proceeding B of the Royal Society: Biological Sciences* 278 (1713), 1894–1902. doi: https://doi.org/10.1098/rspb.2010.1923

Baxter, E. V. and Rintoul, L. J. (1953). *The Birds of Scotland. Vol. 2*, pp. 699–703. Edinburgh.

Beaumont, D. J. and England, B. J. (2016). The Corncrake *Crex crex* population in Scotland from 1993 to 2015 with an overview of conservation measures taken during this period. *Vogelwelt* 136, 153–161.

Bechstein, J. M. (1803). *Ornithologisches Taschenbuch von und für Deutschland oder kurze Beschreibung aller Vogel Deutschlands*. [Paperback by and for Germany or a brief description of all birds in Germany] (In German). Vol. 2. Leipzig: Richter. p. 336 doi: http://doi.org/10.5962/bhl.title.62820. https://www.biodiversitylibrary.org/page/727060#page/172/mode/1up

Beeton, I. (1861). *The Book of Household Management*. Recipe 1033: Roast Landrail of Corn-Crake, pp. 522–523. https://archive.org/details/b21527799/page/522/mode/2up

Bellebaum, J. and Koffijberg, K. (2018). Present agri-environment measures in Europe are not sufficient for the conservation of a highly sensitive bird species, the Corncrake *Crex crex*. *Agriculture, Ecosystems and Environment*, 257, 30–37. doi: https://doi.org/10.1016/j.agee.2018.01.018

Bellebaum, J., Arbeiter, S., Helmecke, A. and Koffijberg, K. (2016). Survival and departure of Corncrakes *Crex crex* on managed breeding grounds. *Annales Zoologici Fennici* 53, 288–295. doi: https://doi.org/10.5735/086.053.0606

Bellebaum, J., Grüneberg, C. and Karthäuser, J. (2016). Status and population trend of Corncrakes *Crex crex* in Germany. *Vogelwelt* 136, 113–120.

Berg, Å. and Gustafson, T. (2006). Meadow birds in Sweden – population trends, effects of restoration and management. *Osnabrücker Naturwissenschaftliche Mitteilungen* 32, 99–106.

Berg, Å. and Gustafson, T. (2007). Meadow management and occurrence of corncrake *Crex crex*. *Agriculture, Ecosystems & Environment* 120, 139–144. doi: https://doi.org/10.1016/j.agee.2006.08.009

Berg, Å. and Hiron, M. (2012). Occurrence of Corncrakes *Crex crex* in mosaic farmland landscapes in south-central Sweden – effects of habitat and landscape structure. *Bird Conservation International* 22, 234–245. doi: https://doi.org/10.1017/S0959270911000116

Besnard, A. G., Fourcade, Y. and Secondi, J. (2016). Measuring difference in edge avoidance in grassland birds: the Corncrake is less sensitive to hedgerow proximity than passerines. *Journal of Ornithology* 157 (2), 515–523. doi: https://doi.org/10.1007/s10336-015-1281-7

Best, J. B. J. (2013). *Living in Liminality: An Osteoarchaeological investigation into the use of avian resources in North Atlantic island environments*. PhD thesis, Cardiff University. http://orca.cf.ac.uk/58668/1/2014bestjbphd.pdf

Bibby, C. J. (1992). Conservation of migrants on their breeding grounds. *Ibis* 134 (Suppl. 1), 29–34. doi: https://doi.org/10.1111/j.1474-919X.1992.tb04730.x

Bignal, E. M. and McCracken, D. I. (1996). Low-intensity farming systems in the conservation of the countryside. *Journal of Applied Ecology* 33 (3), 413–424.

Bignal, E. M. and McCracken, D. I. (2000). The nature conservation value of European traditional farming systems. *Environmental Reviews* 8 (3), 149–171 doi: https://www.jstor.org/stable/10.2307/envirevi.8.3.149

BirdLife International (2015). The IUCN Red list of Threatened Species. *Crex crex* (Corncrake). European Red List of Birds: Supplementary Material. http://datazone.birdlife.org/userfiles/file/Species/erlob/supplementarypdfs/22692543_crex_crex.pdf

BirdLife International (2016). *Crex crex*. The IUCN Red List of Threatened Species 2016: https://dx.doi.org/10.2305/IUCN.UK.2016-3.RLTS.T22692543A86147127.en

BirdLife International (2020). Species factsheet: *Crex crex*. http://www.birdlife.org

Birrer, S., Spiess, M., Herzog, F., Jenny, M., Kohli, L. and Lugrin, B. (2007). The Swiss agri-environment scheme promotes farmland birds, but only moderately. *Journal of Ornithology* 148 (Suppl. 2), S295–S303. doi: https://doi.org/10.1007/s10336-007-0237-y

Boev, Z. (2000). Late Pleistocene Avifauna of the Razhishkata Cave, Western Bulgaria. *Historia Naturalis Bulgarica* 12, 71–87. https://www.researchgate.net/publication/301215512_Late_Pleistocene_Avifauna_of_the_Razhishkata_Cave_Western_Bulgaria

Boev, Z. (2015). *Porzana botunensis* sp. N., a New Early Pleistocene Crake (Aves: Rallidae) from Bulgaria. *Acta Zoologica Bulgarica* 67 (2), 283–290. https://www.researchgate.net/publication/279201332_Porzana_botunensis_sp_n_a_New_Early_Pleistocene_Crake_Aves_Rallidae_from_Bulgaria

Boldogh, S. (1999). The Corncrake (*Crex crex* L. 1758) in Hungary. In: Schäffer, N. and Mammen, U. (eds.), Proceedings of the International Corncrake Workshop 1998, Hilpoltstein, Germany, pp. 13–23. https://web.archive.org/web/20030911130429/http://www.corncrake.net/Download/hungary.pdf

Boldogh, S. A., Visnyovszky, T., Szegedi, Z., Habarics, B., Horváth, R., Krajnyák, C. and Lengyel, S. (2016). Where can flood refugees go? Re-distribution of Corncrakes (*Crex crex*) due to floods and its consequences on grassland conservation in North-eastern Hungary. *Ornis Hungarica* 24 (2), 18–31. doi: https://doi.org/10.1515/orhu-2016-0012

Boldogh, S., Szegedi, Z., Szentgyörgyi, P. and Petrovics, Z. (2009). Distribution, population size and conservation of Corncrake *Crex crex* in North-east Hungary, 1997–2006. *Vogelwelt* 130, 153–158.

Boldogh, S., Szentirmai, I., Nagy, K. and Habarics, B. (2016). Distribution, population trends and conservation status of the Corncrake (*Crex crex*) in Hungary, 2007–2015. *Vogelwelt* 136, 121–126.

Booth, A. B. and Milne, F. (1999). *Western Isles Corncrake Habitat Survey*. Central Environmental Surveys, Scottish Natural Heritage Commissioned Report F99LC03.

Borgo, A. and Zoologia Botanica (2010). Check-list habitat requirement, threat and conservation of the *Crex crex*

(Rallidae) in the Italian Alps. *Gortania* 32, 193–201. https://www.researchgate.net/publication/309610310_
Check-list_habitat_requirement_threat_and_conservation_of_the_Crex_crex_Rallidae_in_the_Italian_Alps

Božič, L. (2005a). The population of corncrake *Crex crex* at Ljubljansko barje (Central Slovenia) is declining due to early mowing and destruction of the extensively farmed meadows. *Acrocephalus* 26, 3–21. (In Slovenian with English summary). https://www.dlib.si/stream/URN:NBN:SI:doc-5ZSYT5EY/735973d6-dd5a-4e7f-877f-0c2a-fa437a32/PDF

Božič, L. (2005b). Gnezditvena razširjenost in velikost populacije kosca *Crex crex* v Sloveniji leta 2004. [Breeding distribution and population size of Corncrake *Crex crex* in Slovenia in 2004]. *Acrocephalus* 26 (127), 171–179. (In Slovenian with English summary).

Braaksma, S. (1962). Voorkomen en levensgewoonten van de Kwartelkoning. [Distribution and habits of the Corncrake *Crex crex*]. *Limosa* 35 (3), 230–259. http://limosa.nou.nu/limosa_search2.php (In Dutch with English summary).

Brambilla, M. and Pedrini, P. (2011). Intra-seasonal changes in local pattern of Corncrake *Crex crex* occurrence require adaptive conservation strategies in Alpine meadows. *Bird Conservation International* 21, 388–393. doi: http://10.1017/S0959270910000572

Brambilla, M. and Pedrini, P. (2013). The introduction of subsidies for grassland conservation in the Italian Alps coincided with population decline in a threatened grassland species, the Corncrake *Crex crex*. *Bird Study* 60 (3), 404–408. doi: http://dx.doi.org/10.1080/00063657.2013.811464

Braunlich, A. and Rank, M. (1999). Notes on the occurrence of the Corncrake (*Crex crex*) in Asia and in the Pacific region. In: Schäffer, N. and Mammen, U. (eds.), Proceedings of the International Corncrake Workshop 1998, Hilpoltstein, Germany, pp. 9–14. https://web.archive.org/web/20120112205326/http://www.corncrake.net/Download/asia.pdf

Brenowitz, E. A. (1991). Evolution of the vocal control system in the avian brain. *Seminars in the Neurosciences* 3, 399–407. doi: https://doi.org/10.1016/1044-5765(91)90030-R

Brock, H. H. (1896). *Crex crex* in Maine. *The Auk* 13 (2), 173–174. https://www.jstor.org/stable/4068712

Brosset, A. and Erard, C. (1986). Les oiseaux des régions forestières du nord-est du Gabon. Vol. 1. Paris: Société Nationale de Protection de la Nature.

Brown, R. H. (1938). Notes on the Land-rail. *British Birds* 32, 13–16.

Browne-Clayton, M. (1948). Corncrake carrying young. *Irish Naturalists' Journal* 9 (8), 217. https://www.jstor.org/stable/25533685

Broyer, J. (2003). Unmown refuge areas and their influence on the survival of grassland birds in the Saone valley (France). *Biodiversity and Conservation* 12, 1219–1237. doi: https://doi.org/10.1023/A:1023099901308

Broyer, J. and Renaud, C. (1998). Conservation du Râle des genêts et calendrier agricole: contribution à l'étude du rôle des refuges disponibles en période de fenaison [The protection of the Corncrake and the effect of agricultural activities: A contribution to the role of refuges during the hay-making season]. *Nos oiseaux* 45, 13–18. (In French with English summary)

Broyer, J., Curtet, L. and Chazal, R. (2014). How to improve agri-environmental schemes to achieve meadow bird conservation in Europe? A case study in the Saone valley, France. *Journal of Ornithology* 155, 145–155. doi: https://doi.org/10.1007/s10336-013-0996-6

Budka, M. and Osiejuk, T. S. (2013b). Neighbour-stranger call discrimination in a nocturnal rail species, the Corncrake *Crex crex*. *Journal of Ornithology* 154, 685–694. doi: https://doi.org/10.1007/s10336-013-0933-8

Budka, M. and Osiejuk, T. S. (2013c). Formant frequencies are acoustic cues to caller discrimination and are a weak indicator of the body size of corncrake males. *Ethology* 119, 960–969. doi: https://doi.org/10.1111/eth.12141

Budka, M. and Kokocinski, P. (2015). The efficiency of territory mapping, point-based censusing, and point-counting methods in censusing and monitoring a bird species with long-range acoustic communication – the Corncrake *Crex crex*. *Bird Study* 62, 153–160. doi: http://dx.doi.org/10.1080/00063657.2015.1011078

Budka, M. and Osiejuk, T. S. (2013a). Habitat preferences of Corncrake (*Crex crex*) males in agricultural meadows. *Agriculture, Ecosystems & Environment* 171, 33–38. doi: https://doi.org/10.1016/j.agee.2013.03.007

Budka, M. and Osiejuk, T. S. (2014). Individually specific call feature is not used to neighbour-stranger discrimination: The Corncrake case. *PLoS ONE* 9 (8) e104031. doi: https://doi.org/10.1371/journal.pone.0104031

Budka, M. and Osiejuk, T. S. (2017). Microgeographic call variation in a non-learning species, the Corncrake (*Crex crex*). *Journal of Ornithology* 158, 651–658. doi: http://dx.doi.org/10.1007/s10336-017-1438-7

Budka, M., Mikkelsen, G., Turčokavá, L., Fourcade, Y., Dale, S. and Osiejuk, T. S. (2014). Macrographic variation in the call of the corncrake *Crex crex*. *Journal of Avian Biology* 45, 65–74. doi: http://dx.doi.org/10.1111/j.1600-048X.2013.00208.x

Budka, M., Ręk, P., Osiejuk, T. S. and Jurczak, K. (2012). Zagęszczenie samców derkacza *Crex crex* na wybranych powierzchniach w Polsce. [Density of the Corncrake *Crex crex* in selected areas in Poland]. *Ornis Polonica* 53, 165–174. http://www.ornis-polonica.pl/_pdf/OP_2012_3_165–174.pdf (In Polish with English abstract).

Budka, M., Wojas, L. and Osiejuk, T. S. (2015). Is it possible to acoustically identify individuals within a population? *Journal of Ornithology* 156, 481–488. doi: https://doi.org/10.1007/s10336-014-1149-2

Bürger, P., Pykal, J. and Hora, J. (1997). Der Wachtelkönig *Crex crex* L. In der Tschechischen Republik. [The Corncrake *Crex crex* L. In the Czech Republic]. *Vogelwelt* 118, 209–213.

Bürger, P., Pykal, J. and Hora, J. (1998). Rozšíření, početnost a výsledky kroužkování chřástala polního (*Crex crex*) v České republice v letech 1993–1997. [Distribution, numbers and ringing results of Corncrake (*Crex crex*) in the Czech Republic in the period 1993–1997]. *Sylvia* 34 (1), 73–84.

Burgos, K. and Olmos, F. (2013). First record of Corncrake *Crex crex* Rallidae for South America. *Revista Brasileira de Ornitologia* 21 (3), 205–208. https://pdfs.semanticscholar.org/b45e/3ad8548fddb8494e702b603a-0f87e73a8a5c.pdf

Buri, P., Arlettaz, R. and Humbert, J.-Y. (2013). Delaying mowing and leaving uncut refuges boosts orthopterans in extensively managed meadows: Evidence drawn from field -scale experimentation. *Agriculture, Ecosystems & Environment* 181, 22–30.

Burkitt, J. P. (1921). Migration season of the Corncrake. *The Irish Naturalist* 30 (1), 16. https://www.jstor.org/stable/25525006

Cadbury, C. J. (1980a). The status and habitats of the Corncrake in Britain 1978–79. *Bird Study* 27, 203–218.

Cadbury, C. J. (1980b). The 1978/9 survey of Corncrakes in Britain. *Scottish Birds* 11 (2), 53–55.

Cadbury, C. J. (1989). Corncrake and Corn Bunting status and habitats on Tiree and Coll, Inner Hebrides. In: Stroud, D. A. (Ed.), *Birds of Coll and Tiree: Status, habitats and Conservation,* pp. 51–66. Edinburgh: Nature Conservancy Council and the Scottish Ornithologists Club.

Campbell, D. C. (1903). A winter Corncrake near Lough Swilly. *The Irish Naturalist* 12 (4), 112. https://www.jstor.org/stable/25522335

Carmichael, A. (1992). 'The speech of birds: The Corncrake said'. In: *Carmina Gadelica: Hymns and Incantations.* Edinburgh: Floris Books. p. 326.

Carter, I. and Newberry, P. (2004). Reintroduction as a tool for population recovery of farmland birds. *Ibis* 146 (Special Issue No. 2), 221–229.

Casey, C. (1999). Distribution and conservation of the Corncrake in Ireland, 1993–1998. *Irish Birds* 6, 159–176.

Catchpole, C. K. and Slater, P. J. B. (1995). *Bird Song: Biological Themes and Variations.* Cambridge: Cambridge University Press.

Chylarecki, P., Gromadzka, J. and Zielinski, P. (1998). *Corncrake survey in Poland. Part 1. Final report of the survey in 1997.* Gdansk: OTOP/Gdansk Ornithological Station.

Clare, J. (2004). 'The Landrail'. John Clare – Poems. The World's Poetry Archive. https://www.poemhunter.com/poem/the-landrail/

Cocker, M. and Mabey, R. (2005). *Birds Britannica*, pp. 178–180. London: Chatto and Windus.

Collar, N. J. and Andrew, P. (1988). *Birds to Watch: The ICBP World Checklist of Threatened Birds.* London: International Council for Bird Preservation. doi: https://doi.org/10.1017/S0030605300022468

Congreve, L. H. (1904). A winter Corncrake in Co. Galway. *The Irish Naturalist* 13 (2), 45. https://www.jstor.org/stable/25522510

Copland, A. (2001). Delivering Corncrake *Crex crex* conservation in Ireland: Past, present and future. *Irish Birds* 7, 33–42. https://www.researchgate.net/publication/272134792_Delivering_Corncrake_Crex_crex_conservation_in_Ireland_past_present_and_future

Corbett, P. E. and Hudson, M. D. (2010). Management of cover areas may increase numbers of breeding Corncrakes *Crex crex*. *Bird Study* 57, 553–559. doi: http://dx.doi.org/10.1080/00063657.2010.489601

Cramp, S. and Simmons, K. E. L. (eds.) (1980). *The Birds of the Western Palearctic.* Vol. 2, pp. 570–578. Oxford: Oxford University Press.

Crockford, N. J., Green, R. E., Rocamora, G., Schäffer, N., Stowe, T. J. and Williams, G. M. (1997). A summary of the European Action plan for the corncrake *Crex crex*. *Vogelwelt* 118, 169–173.

Crockford, N. J., Green, R., Rocamora, G., Schäffer, N., Stowe, T. and Williams, G. (1996). Action plan for the corncrake *Crex crex* in Europe. In: Heredia, B., Rose, L. and Painter, M. (eds.), *Globally Threatened birds in Europe: Action Plans,* pp. 205–243. Strasbourg, France: Council of Europe Publishing and BirdLife International. https://ec.europa.eu/environment/nature/conservation/wildbirds/action_plans/docs/crex_crex.pdf

Cuthill, I. (1991). Field experiments in animal behaviour: Methods and ethics. *Animal Behaviour* 42 (6), 1007–1014. doi: https://doi.org/10.1016/S0003–3472(05)80153–8

Dahm, A. G. (1969). A corn-crake, *Crex crex L.*, trapped in Kumasi, Ghana. *Bulletin British Ornithologists Club* 89, 76–78.

Darwin, C. (1994). *The Origin of Species by Means of Natural Selection, or, The Preservation of Favoured Races in the Struggle for Life*. New York: Modern Library.

Decandido, R. and Allen, D. (2018). The Corn Crake (*Crex crex*) in New York State, with comments on its occurrence in the western hemisphere, 1833–2017. *The Kingbird* 68 (1), 4–10. https://nybirds.org/KB_issuesarchive/y2018v68n1.pdf

Deceuninck, B. (1999). The Corncrake (*Crex crex*) in France. In: Schäffer, N. and Mammen, U. (eds.), Proceedings of the International Corncrake Workshop 1998, Hilpoltstein, Germany, pp. 13–23. https://web.archive.org/web/20081120123809/http://www.corncrake.net/Download/france.pdf

Delov, V. and Iankov, P. (1997). National survey of the Corncrake *Crex crex* in Bulgaria in 1995. *Vogelwelt* 118, 239–241.

Dementʹev, G. P., Gladkov, N. A. and Spangenberg, E. P. (1969). *Birds of the Soviet Union*. (English translation). Volume 3. Jerusalem: Israel Program for Scientific Translations.

Demeter, L. and Szabo, Z. D. (2005). Data on the spatial distribution of the Corncrake *Crex crex* in the Eastern Carpathians, Romania. *Biota* 6, 13–20. https://www.researchgate.net/publication/233379498_Data_on_the_spatial_distribution_of_the_Corncrake_Crex_crex_in_the_Eastern_Carpathians_Romania

Demko, M. (1999). The Corncrake (*Crex crex*) in Slovakia. In: Schäffer, N. and Mammen, U. (eds.), Proceedings of the International Corncrake Workshop 1998, Hilpoltstein, Germany, pp. 89–91. https://web.archive.org/web/20081120170007/http://www.corncrake.net/Download/slovakia.pdf

Dervović, I. and Kotrošan, D. (2016). Kosac (*Crex crex*) na visokim planinama i brdovitim područjima Bosne i Hercegovine (2014–2016). Corncrake (*Crex crex*) on high mountains and uplands of Bosnia and Herzegovina (2014–2016). *Bilten Mreže posmatrača ptica u Bosni i Hercegovini* 10–12, 143–144. http://www.wild-herzegovina.com/bibliography/Dervovic-2016b.pdf (Bosnian with English abstract and summary).

Dodds, E. R. (ed.) (1966). *The Collected Poems of Louis MacNeice*. London: Faber & Faber. p. 493.

Dolman, P. M. and Sutherland, W. J. (1995). The response of bird populations to habitat loss. *Ibis* 137, S38–S46. doi: https://doi.org/10.1111/j.1474–919X.1995.tb08456.x

Donaghy, A. M. (2007a). *Management of habitats on the Shannon Callows with special reference to their suitability for Corncrake Crex crex*. PhD Thesis. National University of Ireland, Cork.

Donaghy, A. M., Green, R. E. and O'Halloran, J. (2011). Timing of autumn migration of young Corncrakes *Crex crex*. *Ibis* 153 (2), 425–428. doi: https://doi.org/10.1111/j.1474–919X.2011.01104.x

Dorresteijn, I., Teixeira, L., von Wehrden, H., Loos, J., Hanspach, J., Stein, J. A. R. and Fischer, J. (2015). Impact of land cover homogenization on the Corncrake *Crex crex* in traditional farmland. *Landscape Ecology* 30, 1483–1495. doi: https://doi.org/10.1007/s10980–015–0203–7

Dudkin, O. (2001). *Corncrake Inventory in Ukraine in 2000 and 2001*. Ukranian Union for Bird Conservation.

Duffy, M. (2018). *The Corncrake Conservation Project: Annual Report 2018*. Department of Culture, Heritage and the Gaeltacht, Ireland.

Dwelly, E. (1973). *The Illustrated Gaelic to English Dictionary*. 8th edn. Glasgow: Gairm.

Dyrcz, A., Okulewicz, J., Witkowski, J., Jesionowski, J., Nawrocki, P. and Winiecki, A. (1984). Ptaki torfowisk niskich w Kotlinie Biebrzańskiej. Opracowanie faunistyczne. [Birds of fens in Biebrza Marshes. Faunistic approach]. *Acta Ornithologica*. 20, 1–8.

Eagle Clarke, W. (1915). Corn-crake at St Kilda. *Scottish Naturalist,* p. 333.

Eason, P., Rabea, B. and Attum, O. (2010). Conservation implications of flight initiation distance and refuge use in Corn Crakes *Crex crex* at a migration stopover site. *Zoology in the Middle East* 51 (1), 9–14. doi: https://doi.org/10.1080/09397140.2010.10638435

Eason, P., Rabia, B. and Attum, O. (2016). Hunting of migratory birds in North Sinai, Egypt. *Bird Conservation International* 26, 39–51. doi: http://10.1017/S09592270915000180

Eken, G., Kurt, B. and Aydemir, G. (1999). The Corncrake (*Crex crex*) in Turkey. In: Schäffer, N. and Mammen, U. (eds.), Proceedings of the International Corncrake Workshop 1998, Hilpoltstein, Germany, p. 109. https://web.archive.org/web/20081120124206/http://www.corncrake.net/Download/turkey.pdf

Elgood, J. H., Sharland, R. E. and Ward, P. (1966). Palaearctic migrants in Nigeria. *Ibis* 108, 84–116.

Elts, J. (1997). Der Wachtelkönig in Estland 1995. [Studies of the Corncrake in Estonia in 1995]. *Vogelwelt* 118, 236–238.

Elts, J. and Marja, R. (2007). Counts of calling Corncrakes (*Crex crex*) in Karula National Park in 2003 and 2004 and the effects of song playbacks on counting efficiency. *Hirundo* 20, 54–65.

Emile, W., Noor, N. and Dereliev, S. (2014). *Plan of Action to Address Bird Trapping along the Mediterranean Coasts of Egypt and Libya*. Bonn: UNEP/AEWA.

Enemar, A. (1969). Om förekomsten av kornknarr *Crex crex* i Sverige ar 1968. [The Corn-Crake *Crex crex* in Sweden in 1968]. *Vår Fågelvärld* 28, 194–198.

Faragó, A. and Szentirmai, I. (2014). Az őrségi harisok (*Crex crex*) élőhely-használatának kutatása rádió-telemetriás nyomkövetés segítségével [Research on the habitat selection of the Corncrake (*Crex crex*) in Örseg, using radio-telemetry]. *Cinege* 19, 17–23. From http://chernelmte.extra.hu/cinege2014_19_teljes.pdf

Ferlan, T., Vranetič, M., Sovinc, A. and Hudoklin, A. (1998). Popis kosca *Crex crex* v Jovsih. [Survey of the Corn Crake *Crex crex* at Jovsi]. *Acrocephalus* 19, 147–151. (In Slovenian with English summary).

Feustel, K. (2018). A Corn Crake (*Crex crex*) at Cedar Beach, Suffolk County, Long Island. The Kingbird 68 (1), 2–3. https://nybirds.org/KB_issuesarchive/y2018v68n1.pdf

Fiedler, W. (2009). New technologies for monitoring bird migration and behaviour. *Ringing & Migration* 24 (3), 175–179. doi: https://doi.org/10.1080/03078698.2009.9674389

Fisher, G. (1963). The Park's Corncrakes. *Report of the Royal Zoological Society Scotland* 51, 13–14.

Fitter, R. S. R. and Richardson, R. A. (1968). *Collins Pocket Guide to Nests and Eggs: The Complete Identification Book*. London: Collins. p. 55.

Flade, M. (1991a). Die Habitate des Wachtelkönigs während der Brutsaison in drei europäischen Stromtälern (Aller, Save, Biebrza) [The habitats of the Corncrake during the breeding season in three European stream valleys - Aller, Save, Biebrza] *Vogelwelt* 112, 16–40. (In German with English summary).

Flade, M. (1997). Wo lebte der Wachtelkönig in der Urlandschaft? [Habitat of the Corncrake *Crex crex* in primaeval landscapes]. *Vogelwelt* 118, 141–146.

Florit, F. and Rassati, G. (2013). Il monitoraggio di una specie prioritaria per l'Unione Europea promosso dalla Regione Autonoma Friuli-Venezia Giulia: Il re di quaglie *Crex crex*. [Monitoring of a priority species for European Union promoted by autonomous Region of Friuli-Venezia Giulia: The Corncrake, *Crex crex*]. *Riv. Ital. Orn. Milano 82 (1–2), 177–179.* (Italian with English abstract).

Florit, F. and Rassati, G. (2016). Distribution and trends of Corncrakes *Crex crex* in Friuli-Venezia Giulia (north-eastern Italy). *Vogelwelt* 136 (2–3), 131–134.

Folvik, A. and Øien, I. J. (1999). The Corncrake (*Crex crex*) in Norway. In: Schäffer, N. and Mammen, U. (eds.), Proceedings of the International Corncrake Workshop 1998, Hilpoltstein, Germany, pp. 67–68. https://web.archive.org/web/20081120122949/http:/www.corncrake.net/Download/norway.pdf

Forrester, R., Andrews, I., Mcinerny, C., Murray, R., Mcgowan, B., Zonfrillo, B., Betts, M., Jardine, D. and Grundy, D. (eds.) (2007). *The Birds of Scotland* (digital version). Aberlady, UK: The Scottish Ornithologists' Club.

Fourcade, Y., Engler, J. O., Besnard, A. G., Rödder, D. and Secondi, J. (2013). Confronting expert-based and modelled distributions for species with uncertain conservation status: A case study from the corncrake (*Crex crex*). *Biological Conservation* 167, 161–171. doi: http://dx.doi.org/10.1016/j.biocon.2013.08.009

Fourcade, Y., Keišs, O., Richardson, D. S. and Secondi, J. (2014). Continental-scale patterns of pathogen prevalence: A case study of the corncrake. *Evolutionary Applications* 7, 1043–1055. doi: https://doi.org/10.1111/eva.12192

Fourcade, Y., Richardson, D. S. and Secondi, J. (2019). No evidence for a loss of genetic diversity despite a strong decline in size of a European population of the Corncrake *Crex crex*. *Bird Conservation International*, 1–7. doi: https://doi.org/10.1017/S0959270919000327

Fourcade, Y., Richardson, D. S., Keišs, O., Budka, M., Green, R. E., Fokin, S. and Secondi, J. (2016). Corncrake conservation genetics at a European scale: The impact of biogeographical and anthropological processes. *Biological Conservation* 198, 210–219. doi: http://dx.doi.org/10.1016/j.biocon.2016.04.018

Frühauf, J. (1997). Der Wachtelkönig (*Crex crex*) in Österreich: Langfristige Trends, aktuelle Situation und Perspektiven. [The Corncrake *Crex crex* in Austria: Long-term trends, current situation, and perspectives]. *Vogelwelt* 118, 195–207.

Frühauf, J. (1999). The Corncrake (*Crex crex*) in Austria. In: Schäffer, N. and Mammen, U. (eds.), Proceedings of the International Corncrake Workshop 1998, Hilpoltstein, Germany, pp. 13–23. https://web.archive.org/web/20081120125626/http:/www.corncrake.net/Download/austria.pdf

Frühauf, J. (2016). Trends, population, and conservation of Corncrakes *Crex crex* in Austria. *Vogelwelt* 136 (2–3), 93–106.

Gache, C. (1999). The Corncrake (*Crex crex*) in Romania. In: Schäffer, N. and Mammen, U. (eds.), Proceedings of the International Corncrake Workshop 1998, Hilpoltstein, Germany, pp. 75–76. https://web.archive.org/web/20090105170239/http:/www.corncrake.net/Download/romania.pdf

Gache, C. and Trelea, S. (2004). Actual status of the Corncrake (*Crex crex*) in the northeastern part of Romania. *Analele Ştiinţifice ale Universităţii* 34, 337–341. http://www.bio.uaic.ro/publicatii/anale_zoologie/issue/2004/34–2004.pdf

Gautschi, B., Klug Arter, M., Husi, R., Wettstein, W. and Schmid, B. (2002). Isolation and characterization of microsatellite loci in the globally endangered Corncrake, *Crex crex* Linné. *Conservation Genetics* 3, 451–453. https://www.researchgate.net/publication/227291127_Isolation_and_characterization_of_microsatellite_loci_in_the_globally_endangered_Corncrake_Crex_crex_Linne

Gilmour, J. G. (1972). Corncrakes breeding in Stirlingshire. *Scottish Birds* 7, 52.

Glue, D. E. (1972). Bird prey taken by British Owls. *Bird Study* 19 (2), 91–96. https://doi.org/10.1080/00063657209476330

Glutz von Blotzheim, U., Bauer, K. and Bezzel, E. (1973). *Handbuch der Vogel Mitteleuropas.* Vol. 5. Frankfurt: Akademische Verlag.

Götte, R. (2009). Brutnachweis des Wachtelkönigs *Crex crex* im Hochsauerlandkreis. [Breeding record of Corncrake *Crex crex* in Hochsauerland]. *Chradrius* 45 (2), 225–226. http://www.nw-ornithologen.de/images/textfiles/charadrius/charadrius45_4_225_226_goette.pdf (In German with English summary).

Grabovsky, V. I. (1993). Spatial distribution and spacing behaviour of males in a Russian Corncrake (*Crex crex*) population. *Gibier Faune Sauvage* 10, 259–279. http://www.nature.air.ru/models/crex%20crex.htm

Graham, J. (2009). Corn Crake pair-bonding and nesting behaviour. *British Birds* 102, 217.

Grant, E. (2002). *Corncrake habitat survey of Coll Special Protection Area*. Scottish Natural Heritage Commissioned Report FO1LG09.

Grant, J. S. (1984). The part-time holding – an island experience. The Arkleton Lecture 1983. Enstone: The Arkleton Trust. https://arkletontrust.co.uk/wp-content/uploads/2017/12/Arkleton-Lecture-1983.pdf

Gray, R. (1871). *Birds of the West of Scotland including the Outer Hebrides,* pp. 331–333. Glasgow: Thomas Murray and Son.

Green, R. E. (1995a). The decline of the Corncrake *Crex crex* in Britain continues. *Bird Study* 42, 66–75. doi: http://dx.doi.org/10.1080/00063659509477150

Green, R. E. (1996). Factors affecting the population density of the corncrake *Crex crex* in Britain and Ireland. *Journal of Applied Ecology* 33 (20), 237–248. https://www.jstor.org/stable/2404746

Green, R. E. (1999a). Survival and dispersal of male Corncrakes *Crex crex* in a threatened population. *Bird Study* 46 (1) (supplement), S218–S229. doi: https://doi.org/10.1080/00063659909477248

Green, R. E. (1999b). The Corncrake (*Crex crex*) in the UK. In: Schäffer, N. and Mammen, U. (eds.), Proceedings of the International Corncrake Workshop 1998, Hilpoltstein, Germany, pp. 111–113. https://web.archive.org/web/20081120141329/http://www.corncrake.net/Download/uk.pdf

Green, R. E. (2004a). A new method for estimating the adult survival rate of the Corncrake *Crex crex* and comparison with estimates from ring-recovery and ring-recapture data. *Ibis* 146, 501–508. doi: http://dx.doi.org/10.1111/j.1474–919x.2004.00291.x

Green, R. E. (2004b). Age-dependent changes in the shape of the secondary remiges of individual adult corncrakes *Crex crex*. *Ringing & Migration* 22, 83–84. http://ww2.rspb.org.uk/Images/green_04_b_tcm9–206325.pdf

Green, R. E. (2007). The Corn Crake. In: Forrester, R. Andrews, I., Mcinerny, C., Murray, R., Mcgowan, B., Zonfrillo, B., Betts, M., Jardine, D. and Grundy, D. (eds.) (2007). *The Birds of Scotland* (digital version), pp. 525–528. Aberlady, UK: The Scottish Ornithologists' Club.

Green, R. E. (2008). Demographic mechanism of a historical bird population collapse reconstructed using museum specimens. *Proceedings of the Royal Society B: Biological Sciences* 275, 2381–2387. doi: http://dx.doi.org/10.1098/rspb.2008.0473

Green, R. E. (2010). Timing of breeding, primary moult and duration of maternal care of chicks by adult female Corncrakes *Crex crex*. *Ibis* 152, 826–829. doi: http://dx.doi.org/10.1111/j.1474–919x.2010.01042.x

Green, R. E. and Gibbons, D. (2000). The status of the Corncrake (*Crex crex*) in Britain in 1998. *Bird Study* 47, 129–137. doi: https://doi.org/10.1080/00063650009461168

Green, R. E. and Rayment, M. D. (1996). Geographical variation in the abundance of the Corncrake *Crex crex* in Europe in relation to the intensity of agriculture. *Bird Conservation International* 6, 201–211. doi: http://dx.doi.org/10.1017/S0959270900003105

Green, R. E. and Riley, H. (1999). *Corncrakes*. Battleby: SNH Publications.

Green, R. E. and Stowe, T. J. (1993). The decline of the corncrake in Britain and Ireland in relation to habitat change. *Journal of Applied Ecology* 30 (4), 689–695. https://www.jstor.org/stable/2404247

Green, R. E. and Tyler, G. A. (2005). Estimating the age of Corncrake Crex crex chicks from body weight and the development of primary feathers. Ringing & Migration 22 (3), 139–144. doi: https://doi.org/10.1080/03078698.2005.9674322

Green, R. E. and Williams, G. (1992). The ecology of the corncrake Crex crex and action for its conservation in Britain and Ireland. In: Bignal, E., McCracken, D. 1. and Curtis, D. J. (eds.), Nature Conservation and Pastoralism in Europe, pp. 69–74. Peterborough: Joint Nature Conservation Committee.

Green, R. E., Brekke, P., Ward, H., Slaymaker, M., van der Velde, M., Komdeur, J. and Dugdale, H. L. (2019). Use of microsatellite-based paternity assignment to establish where Corncrake Crex crex chicks are at risk from mechanized mowing. Ibis 161 (4), 890–894. doi: http://10.1111/ibi.12724

Green, R. E., Rocamora, G. and Schäffer, N. (1997). Populations, ecology and threats to the corncrake Crex crex in Europe. Vogelwelt 118, 117–134. https://www.researchgate.net/publication/271390946_Populations_ecology_and_threats_to_the_Corncrake_Crex_crex_in_Europe

Green, R. E., Schäffer, N. and Wend, D. (2001). A method for ageing adult corncrakes Crex crex. Journal of Applied Ecology 20, 352–357. doi: https://doi.org/10.1080/03078698.2001.9674262

Green, R. E., Tyler, G. A., Stowe, T. J. and Newton, A. V. (1997). A simulation model of the effect of mowing of agricultural grassland on the breeding success of the corncrake (Crex crex). Journal of Zoology 243, 81–115. doi: https://doi.org/10.1111/j.1469-7998.1997.tb05758x

Greenoak, F. (1997). British Birds: Their Folklore, Names and Literature. London: Christopher Helm.

Grieve, A. and Salama, W. (2003). The globally threatened Corncrake Crex crex (Egypt). In: Lemons, J., Victor, R. and Schäffer, D. (eds.), Conserving Biodiversity in Arid Regions: Best Practices in Developing Countries, Chapter 32, pp. 423–431. New York: Springer.

Grishchenko, M. and Prins, H. H. T. (2016). Abandoned field succession in Russia and its potential effect on Corncrake Crex crex habitats. Vogelwelt 136, 175–184.

Grobelnik, V. and Trontelj, P. (1999). The Corncrake Crex crex in Slovenia. In: Schäffer, N. and Mammen, U. (eds.), Proceedings of the International Corncrake Workshop 1998, Hilpoltstein, Germany, pp. 93–96. https://web.archive.org/web/20081120161724/http://www.corncrake.net/Download/slovenia.pdf

Groessens van Dyck, M.-C. (1989). The Quaternary avifauna of the Walou Cave (Trooz, Prov. Liege). Bulletin de la Société Belge de Géologie 98–2, 197–199. http://biblio.naturalsciences.be/rbins-publications/bulletin-de-la-societe-belge-de-geologie/098%20-%201989/bsbg_nr98_1989_197–199.pdf

Gromadzki, M. (1999). The Corncrake Crex crex in Poland. In: Schäffer, N. and Mammen, U. (eds.), Proceedings of the International Corncrake Workshop 1998, Hilpoltstein, Germany, pp. 69–71. https://web.archive.org/web/20081120134821/http://www.corncrake.net/Download/poland.pdf

Haagner, G. V. and Reynolds, D. S. (1988). Notes on the nesting of the African Crake at Manyeleti Game Reserve, eastern Transvaal. Ostrich 59, 45. doi: https://doi.org/10.1080/00306525.1988.9633925

Haartman, L. Von (1958). The decrease of the Corncrake (Crex crex). Societas Scientiarum Fennica Comment Biology 18 (2), 1–29.

Harvie-Brown, J. A. (1903). On the avifauna of the Outer Hebrides, 1888–1902 (continued). Annals of Scottish Natural History 1903, 7–22. https://www.biodiversitylibrary.org/item/16993

Harvie-Brown, J. A. and Buckley, T. E. (1888). A Vertebrate Fauna of the Outer Hebrides. Edinburgh: D. Douglas. p. 122.

Helmecke, A. (1999). Use of space and habitat by the Corncrake (Crex crex, L.) In the Lower Valley of the Oder. In: Schäffer, N. and Mammen, U. (eds.), Proceedings of the International Corncrake Workshop 1998, Hilpoltstein, Germany, pp. 173–175. https://web.archive.org/web/20081120141739/http://www.corncrake.net/Download/helmecke.pdf

Hennique, S., Deceuninck, B., Mourgaud, G. and Chanson, C. (2013). Deuxième plan national d'actions en faveur du Râle des genêts (Crex crex) 2013–2018. LPO, LPO Anjou, Ministère de l'Ecologie, du Développement Durable et de l'Energie, DREAL des Pays de la Loire, 2013, pp. 140. (In French with English summary). https://www.ecologie.gouv.fr/sites/default/files/PNA_Rale-des-genets_2013–2018.pdf

Herkenrath, P. (1997). Der Wachtelkönig Crex crex im Paragraphendschungel-Gesetzliche Grundlagen des Wachtelkönigschutzes in Deutschland. [The Corncrake Crex crex in the jungle of paragraphs – the legal basis of Corncrake conservation in Germany]. Vogelwelt 118, 157–159.

Hill, R. A. (2001). Leopard cub kills crake. CCA Ecological Journal 3, 63.

Hirler, A. (1999). Losses from birds' nests because of predators in different types of vegetation – an experimental investigation. In: Schäffer, N. and Mammen, U. (eds.), Proceedings of the International Corncrake Workshop 1998, Hilpoltstein, Germany, pp. 187–188. https://web.archive.org/web/20081120152615/http://www.corncrake.net/Download/hirler.pdf

Holloway, S. (1996). *The Historical Atlas of Breeding Birds in Britain and Ireland 1875–1900*. London: Poyser.

Hoogstraal, H., Traylor, M. A., Gaber, S., Malakatis, G., Guindy, E. and Helmy, I. (1964). Ticks (Ixodidae) on migrating birds in Egypt, spring and fall 1962. Bulletin of the World Health Organisation 30 (3), 355–367. https://www.ncbi.nlm.nih.gov/pmc/articles/PMC2554818/

Horton, J. (2013). Corncrakes tracked to Congo in new study. *Scotsman* (28 April 2013). https://www.scotsman.com/news/environment/corncrakes-tracked-congo-new-study-1577436

Howard, R. and Moore, A. (1980). *A Complete Checklist of the Birds of the World*. Oxford University Press: Oxford.

Hudson, A. V., Stowe, T. J. and Aspinall, S. J. (1990). Status and distribution of Corncrakes in Britain in 1988. *British Birds* 83 (5), 173–186. https://britishbirds.co.uk/wp-content/uploads/article_files/V83/V83_N05/V83_N05_P173_187_A064.pdf

Hull, R. (2001). *Scottish Birds: Culture and Tradition,* pp. 156–157. Edinburgh: Mercat Press.

Hume, R. (2010). Waking up to Corncrakes. *Birds* 23 (2), 10–14.

Hynes, S. and Hanley, N. (2009). The *"Crex crex"* lament: Estimating landowners willingness to pay for corncrake conservation on Irish farmland. *Biological Conservation* 142, 180–188. doi: https://doi.org/10.1016/j.biocon.2008.10.014

Hynes, S., Hanley, N. and O'Donoghue, C. (2007). Using spatial microsimulation techniques in the aggregation of environmental benefit values: An application to Corncrake conservation on Irish farmland. ENVECON 2007 Applied Environmental Economics Conference – UN Network of Environmental Economists, 23 March 2007. http://hdl.handle.net/1893/11740

Inderwildi, E. (2016). Population trend, time of arrival and altitudinal distribution of the Corncrake *Crex crex* in Switzerland – the results of 20 years of conservation. *Vogelwelt* 136, 107–112. https://www.birdlife.ch/sites/default/files/documents/2016-Inderwildi.pdf

Inderwildi, E. and Müller, W. (2015). Auswirkungen eines langfristigen Artenförderungsprogramms auf Verbreitung und Bestand des Wachtelkönigs *Crex crex* in der Schweiz. [Effects of a long-term recovery project for Corncrake *Crex crex* in Switzerland]. *Der Ornithologische Beobachter* 112, 23–40. https://www.birdlife.ch/sites/default/files/documents/2015-OB_Wachtelkoenig_DEF_kl.pdf

Ingersoll, E. (1923). *Birds in Legend, Fable and Folklore*. New York, London: Longmans, Green and Co.

International Corncrake Research Group (1997). Repeatability of measurements of Corncrakes *Crex crex*. *Vogelwelt* 118, 245–247.

Jacob, J.-P. (1988). Kwartelkoning *Crex crex*. In: Devillers, P., Roggeman, W., Tricot, J., Del Marmol, P., Kerwijn, C., Jacob, J.-P. and Anselin, A. (eds.), *Atlas van de Belgische broedvogels,* pp. 108–109. Brussels: Koninklijk Belgisch Instituut voor Natuurwetenschappen.

Javakhishvili, Z. (1999). The Corncrake (*Crex crex*) in Georgia. In: Schäffer, N. and Mammen, U. (eds.), Proceedings of the International Corncrake Workshop 1998, Hilpoltstein, Germany, pp. 47–48. https://web.archive.org/web/20081120140514/http://www.corncrake.net/Download/georgia.pdf

Jeanes, C., Vaughan-Higgins, R., Green, R. E., Sainsbury, A. W., Marshall, R. N. and Blake, D. P. (2013). Two new *Eimeria* species parasitic in Corncrakes (*Crex crex*) (Gruiformes: Rallidae) in the United Kingdom. *Journal of Parasitology* 99 (4), 634–638. https://www.jstor.org/stable/41982064

Joest, R. and Koffijberg, K. (2016). Corncrakes *Crex crex* in crops – population dynamics, habitat use and conservation strategy in two intensively managed arable farming areas in the Netherlands and Germany. *Vogelwelt* 136, 163–174.

Jones, D. G. L., Bignal, E. M. and McCracken, D. I. (1998). Ecological effects of changes in mixed farming on the Hebridean island of Tiree (Scotland) between 1960 and 1997. In: van Keulen, H., Lantinga, E. A. and van Laar, H. H. (eds.), *Mixed Farming Systems in Europe: Workshop Proceedings Dronten, The Netherlands*, 25–28 May 1998, pp. 53–60.

Juszczak, K. and Olech, B. (1997). Liczebnosc i rozmieszczenie derkacza *Crex crex* na terenach otwartych Kampinoskiego Parku Narodowego i jego okolic w latach 1996–1997]. [Numbers and distribution of the Corncrake *Crex crex* in the open areas of the Kampinoski National Park and its surroundings in 1996–1997]. *Notatki Ornitologiczne* 38 (3), 197–213. (In Polish with English summary).

Keenleyside, C. (2006). *Farmland birds and agri-environment schemes in the new member States*. A report for the Royal Society for the Protection of Birds. Sandy: RSPB. https://www.birdlife.org/sites/default/files/attachments/Farmland%20birds%20and%20agri-environment%20schemes%20in%20the%20new%20Member%20States.pdf

Keišs, O. (1997). Results of a randomised Corncrake *Crex crex* survey in Latvia 1966: population estimates and habitat selection. *Vogelwelt* 118, 231–235.

Keišs, O. (2003). Recent increases in numbers and the future of Corncrake *Crex crex* in Latvia. *Ornis Hungarica* 12–13, 151–156.

Keišs, O. (2004). Results of a survey of Corncrake *Crex crex* in Latvia, 1989–1995. In: Anselin, A. (Ed.) *Bird Numbers 1995*, Proceedings of the International Conference and 13th Meeting of the European Bird Census Council, Parnu, Estonia. *Bird Census News* 13 (2000), 73–76.

Keišs, O. (2005). Impact of changes in agricultural land use on the Corncrake *Crex crex* population in Latvia. *Acta Universitatis Latviensis (Biology)* 691, 93–109. https://www.researchgate.net/publication/228365387_Impact_of_changes_in_agricultural_land_use_on_the_Corncrake_Crex_crex_population_in_Latvia

Keišs, O. and Kemlers, A. (2000). Increase in numbers of Corncrake (*Crex crex*) in Latvia in late 1990 - results of conservation efforts or accidental circumstances? (In Latvian with English summary). *Putni dabā* 10.3, 22–30.

Keišs, O. and Mednis, A. (2006). Impacts of land-use on the Corncrake population in Latvia: Trends and population structure. *Journal of Ornithology* 147, 192.

Keišs, O., Granāts, J. and Mednis, A. (2004). Use of biometrical data to study Corncrake *Crex crex* population in Latvia. *Acta Universitatis Latviensis (Biology)* 676, 119–126.

Keišs, O., Granāts, J. and Mednis, A. (2007). Estimated population dynamics of the Corncrake *Crex crex* in Latvia and Europe in the 20th century by ringing data analysis. *Acta Universitatis Latviensis (Biology)* 723, 71–97. https://www.researchgate.net/publication/259192704_Estimated_population_dynamics_of_the_Corncrake_Crex_crex_in_Latvia_and_Europe_in_the_20_Crex_crex_in_Latvia_and_Europe_in_the_20_Crex_crex_th_century_by_ringing_data_analysis

Kempe, V. (2008). *Changed genetic variation in the vulnerable Swedish Corncrake (Crex crex) population: Sign of immigration?* Biology Centre and Department of Population Biology, Uppsala University.

Kenyeres, A., Wetstein, W. and Szép, T. (2000). Haris egyedek felismerése hangelemzés alapján [Individual recognition of Corncrakes (*Crex crex*) by sound analysis]. *Ornis Hungarica* 10, 65–70. (In Hungarian with English Summary).

Kinnear, N. B. (1907). Notes on birds seen in the Outer Hebrides during the spring of 1906. *Annals of Scottish Natural History 1907*, 81–85. https://www.biodiversitylibrary.org/item/16994

Kiss, J. (2004). A Haris (*Crex crex*) állományvizsgálata Baranya Megyében. [Population studies on Corncrake (*Crex crex*) in Baranya county (S. Hungary)]. *Aquila* 111, 59–74.

Koffijberg, K. (1999a). The Corncrake (*Crex crex*) in The Netherlands. In: Schäffer, N. and Mammen, U. (eds.), Proceedings of the International Corncrake Workshop 1998, Hilpoltstein, Germany, pp. 89–93. https://web.archive.org/web/20090105175753/http://www.corncrake.net/Download/netherld.pdf

Koffijberg, K. and Nienhuis, J. (2003). Kwartelkoningen in het Oldambt: een onderzoek naar de populatiedynamiek, habitatkeuze en mogelijkheden voor beschermingsmaatregelen in akkers. Groningen: SOVON report https://www.sovon.nl/sites/default/files/doc/Kwartelkoningen%20in%20Oldambt%20en%20onderzoek%20naar%20populatiedynamiek%20habitatkeuze%20en%20beschermingsmaatregelen%20in%20akkers_rap2003_04.pdf

Koffijberg, K. and Schäffer, N. (eds.) (2006). International Single Species Action Plan for the Conservation of the Corncrake *Crex crex*. CMS Technical Series No. 14 and AEWA Technical Series No. 9, Bonn, Germany.

Koffijberg, K. and van Dijk, A. J. (2001). Influx van Kwartelkoningen *Crex crex* in Nederland in 1998. [Influx of Corncrakes *Crex crex* in the Netherlands in 1998]. *Limosa* 74, 147–159. (in Dutch with English summary). http://www.nou.nu

Koffijberg, K., Hallman, C., Keišs, O. and Schäffer, N. (2016). Recent population status and trends of Corncrakes *Crex crex* in Europe. *Vogelwelt* 136, 75–88. https://repository.ubn.ru.nl/handle/2066/163328

Koffijberg, K., van Kleunen, A. and Majoor, F. (2007). Kwartelkoningen in de peiling territoriumactiviteit in terreingebruik met zendertechniek in kaart gebracht. [Territorial behaviour and habitat use of Corncrakes *Crex crex* in the Netherlands revealed by radio-tracking]. *Limosa* 80 (4), 167–171. http://limosa.nou.nu/limosa_search2.php (In Dutch with English summary).

Kolb, K.-H. (1997). Der Wachtelkönig *Crex crex* im Biosphärenreservat Rhön. [The Corncrake *Crex crex* in the Biosphere Reserve Rhön]. *Vogelwelt* 118, 185–189.

Kramer, M. and Armbruster, G. (1997). Bestandsentwicklung, Verbreitung und Status des Wachtelkönigs *Crex crex* in Baden-Württemberg. [Distribution, status and population trend of the Corncrake *Crex crex* in Baden-Württemberg, SW Germany]. *Vogelwelt* 118, 179–183.

Lambrecht, K. (1933). *Handbuch der Palaeornithologie*. 1024p Berlin: Gebruder Borntraeger.

Latham, R. (1964). Another Corn Crake record for Long Island. *The Kingbird* 14 (1), 28–29.

Leitch, A. (1999). *Corncrake Habitat Survey of Tiree Proposed Special Protection Area*. Scottish Natural Heritage Commissioned Report F99LF06A.

References

Leuven, R. S. E. W., Atsma, G., Koffijberg, K. and Schipper, A. M. (2006). Riverine habitat use of the Corncrake (Crex crex) in the Netherlands. In: Augustijn, D. C. M. and van Os, A. G. (eds.), *Proceedings of NCR-days 2006*, pp. 38–39. Enschede: Netherlands Centre for River Studies.

Linnaeus, C. (1758). Systema naturae per regna tria naturae, secundum classes, ordines, genera, species, cum characteribus, differentiis, synonymis, locis. Tomus I. Editio decima, reformata (in Latin). 1. Holmiae (Stockholm): Laurentii Salvii. p. 153. https://www.biodiversitylibrary.org/page/727060#page/172/mode/1up

Lippens, L. and Wille, H. (1972). *Atlas des Oiseaux de Belgique et d'Europe occidentale*. Tielt, Belgium: Lannoo.

Livezey, B. C. (1998). A phylogenetic analysis of the Gruiformes (Aves) based on the morphological characters, with an emphasis on the rails (Rallidae). *Philosophical Transactions of the Royal Society London* 353B, 2077–2151. doi: https://doi.org/10.1098/rstb.1998.0353

Lockwood, W. B. (1984). *Oxford Book of British Bird Names*. Oxford: Oxford University Press. p. 47.

Lorge, P. (1999). The Corncrake (*Crex crex*) in Luxembourg. In: Schäffer, N. and Mammen, U. (eds.), Proceedings of the International Corncrake Workshop 1998, Hilpoltstein, Germany, pp. 71–72. https://web.archive.org/web/20081120132920/http://www.corncrake.net/Download/luxembg.pdf

Lorimer, J. (2008). Counting Corncrakes: The Affective Science of the UK Corncrake census. Social Studies of Science 38 (3), 377–405. doi: https://www.jstor.org/stable/25474585

Love, J. A. (2009). *A Natural History of St Kilda*. Edinburgh: Birlinn.

Ma Ming and Wang Qishan (2002). New records of Corncrake *Crex crex* in Xinjiang, China. *Forktail* 18, 158.

Macconnell, S. (2008). Endangered corncrake once a culinary delicacy. *Irish Times* (29 September 2008). https://www.irishtimes.com/news/endangered-corncrake-once-a-culinary-delicacy-1.941307

Macgillivray, J. (1842). An account of the island of St. Kilda, chiefly with reference to its natural history; from notes made during a visit in July 1840. *Edinburgh New Philosophical Journal* 32, 47–178.

Macko, J. K. (1971). Die Helminthenfauna von *Crex crex* aus die Ostslowakei. [The helminth fauna of *Crex crex* from East Slovakia]. *Helminthologia* 10, 297–305.

Mandl, W. and Sandner, J. (1997). Verbreitung und Habitatwahl des Wachtelkönigs *Crex crex* im südlichen Chiemgau, Oberbayern. [Distribution and habitat selection in southern Chiemgau, Upper Bavaria]. *Vogelwelt* 118, 191–194.

Manush, S. G. (1974). Agricultural machines and game. In: Kolodjazny, J. K. (ed.), *Proceedings of Zavidovsky State Scientific-Experiment Reserve III*. Moscow. (In Russian).

Marja, R., Elts, J., Tuvi, J. and Phillips, J. (2015). Rukkiräägu (*Crex crex*) arvukuse varieeruvus elupaigatüüpide lõikes Lahemaa rahvuspargis 2014. [Corncrake (*Crex crex*) habitat dynamics in Lahemaa National Park during 2014]. *Hirundo* 2, 43–52. https://www.etis.ee/Portal/Publications/Display/f9e702b3–36fe-42de-86fd-0bc3db5cd74a (In Estonian with English summary).

Martin, M. (1698). *A Late Voyage to St Kilda*. London: D. Brown and T. Goodwin.

Martin, M. (1716). *A Description of the Western Isles of Scotland*. London: Andrew Bell.

Marvell, A. (1651). *Upon Appleton House*. http://www.luminarium.org/sevenlit/marvell/appleton.htm

Mason, A. G. (1940). On some experiments with Corncrakes. *Irish Naturalists' Journal* 7 (9), 226–237. doi: https://www.jstor.org/stable/25532979

Mason, A. G. (1941). Further experiments with Corncrakes. *Irish Naturalists' Journal* 7 (12), 321–333. doi: https://www.jstor.org/stable/25533069

Mason, A. G. (1944). Combat display of Corncrake. *Irish Naturalists' Journal* 8 (6), 200–202. https://www.jstor.org/stable/25533259

Mason, A. G. (1945). The display of the Corncrake. *British Birds* 38, 351–352.

Mason, A. G. (1947). Aggressive behaviour of Corn-Crake and Ringed Plover. *British Birds* 40, 191–192.

Mason, A. G. (1950). The behaviour of Corncrakes. *British Birds* 43, 70–78. https://britishbirds.co.uk/wp-content/uploads/article_files/V43/V43_N03/V43_N03_P070_078_A016.pdf

Mason, A. G. (1951). Aggressive display of the Corn-crake. *British Birds* 44, 163–166. https://www.biodiversitylibrary.org/item/188483#page/15/mode/1up

Matyukhin, V. and Krivosheina, M. G. (2008). Contribution to the knowledge of Diptera (Insecta) parasitizing on birds. *Entomological Review* 88 (2), 258–259. doi: https://doi.org/10.1134/S0013873808020115

Maumary, L. (1999). The Corncrake (*Crex crex*) in Switzerland. In: Schäffer, N. and Mammen, U. (eds.), Proceedings of the International Corncrake Workshop 1998, Hilpoltstein, Germany, pp. 107–108. https://web.archive.org/web/20081120132118/http://www.corncrake.net/Download/switzerl.pdf

May, L. (1994). Individually distinctive Corncrake *Crex crex* calls: A pilot study. *Bioacoustics* 6, 25–32. doi: http://dx.doi.org/10.1080/09524622.1994.9753269

May, L. (1998a). Individually distinctive Corncrake *Crex crex* calls: a further study. *Bioacoustics* 9 (2), 135–148. doi: https://doi.org/10.1080/09524622.1998.9753388

May, L. (1998b). Vocalizations in the magpie and the corncrake: methods of analysis, individual differences and geographical variation. PhD thesis (Unpublished). Manchester Metropolitan University.

Mayr, G. (2009). *Paleogene Fossil Birds,* pp. 93–103. Berlin: Springer.

Mccormick, F., Buckland, P. C., Carter, S. P. and Sadler, J. P. (2003). Faunal change. In: Edwards, K. J. and Ralston, B. M. (eds.), *Scotland after the Ice Age: Environment, Archaeology and History 8000 BC–AD 1000,* Chapter 6, pp. 83–108. Edinburgh: Edinburgh University Press. https://www.jstor.org/stable/10.3366/j.ctvxcrd9j.13

McDevitt, A. and Casey, C. (1999). The Corncrake *Crex crex* in Ireland. In: Schäffer, N. and Mammen, U. (eds.), Proceedings of the International Corncrake Workshop 1998, Hilpoltstein, Germany. pp. 59–68 https://web.archive.org/web/20090105181236/http://www.corncrake.net/Download/ireland.pdf

Mckinlay, J. (1899). The Corn Crake in Nova Scotia. *The Auk* 16 (1), 75–76.

Meek, E. R. (1996). Corn Crake *Crex crex* in Vietnam: The first for South-East Asia. *Forktail* 12, 168–169. https://static1.squarespace.com/static/5c1a9e03f407b482a158da87/t/5c1fb969352f53c7fe2afb10/1545582953686/Meek-corncrake.pdf

Meijer, R. (2007). De teloorgang van de Kwartelkoning in de Biesbosch. [Disappearance of the Corncrake *Crex crex* from the Biesbosch]. *Limosa* 80 (3), 89–95. http://limosa.nou.nu/limosa_search2.php (In Dutch with English summary).

Micevski, B. (1999). The Corncrake (*Crex crex*) in Macedonia. In: Schäffer, N. and Mammen, U. (eds.), Proceedings of the International Corncrake Workshop 1998, Hilpoltstein, Germany. pp. 59–61. https://web.archive.org/web/20081120135635/http://www.corncrake.net/Download/macedoni.pdf

Michalska-Hejduk, D., Budka, M. and Olech, B. (2017). Should I stay or should I go? Territory settlement decisions in male Corncrakes *Crex crex*. *Bird Study* 64 (2), 232–241. doi: https://doi.org/10.1080/00063657.2017.1316700

Mikkelsen, G. (2010). Individual Corncrake *Crex crex* song reveals long distance movements within the breeding season. Masters thesis, Department of Ecology and Natural Resource Management, Norwegian University of Life Sciences.

Mikkelsen, G., Dale, S., Holtskog, T., Budka, M. and Osiejuk, T. S. (2013). Can individually characteristic calls be used to identify long-distance movements of Corncrakes *Crex crex*? *Journal of Ornithology* 154, 751–760. doi: https://doi.org/10.1007/s10336-013-0939-2

Mischenko, A. and Sukhanova, O. (1999a). Corncrake *Crex crex* in Russia (European Part). In: Schäffer, N. and Mammen, U. (eds.), Proceedings of the International Corncrake Workshop 1998, Hilpoltstein, Germany, pp. 77–82. https://web.archive.org/web/20081120150715/http://www.corncrake.net/Download/russia.pdf

Mischenko, A. L. (2008). Corncrake *Crex crex* monitoring in European Russia in 2002–2003: A pilot study. *Revista Catalana d'Ornitologia* 24, 65–70.

Mischenko, A. L. (2016). Corncrake *Crex crex* in European Russia: Habitat characteristics, status and trends. *Vogelwelt* 136, 139–144.

Mischenko, A. L., Sukhanova, O. V., Butjev, V. T., Mosalov, A. A. and Mezhnev, A. P. (1997). Ergebnisse der Wachtelkönig-Erfassung im europäischen Teil Russlands 1995. [Results of Corncrake surveys in European Russia in 1995]. *Vogelwelt* 118, 215–222.

Mischenko, A. L., Sukhanova, O. V., Melnikov, V. N. and Amosov, P. N. (2019). Meadow birds under waning traditional pasture animal husbandry. *Biology Bulletin* 46 (10), 1431–1441.

Mitchell, I. (2006). The truth about the RSPB and the Corncrake. *Country Illustrated Magazine* 79, October 2006.

Moffat, C. B. (1938). Notes on the Corncrake. *Irish Naturalists' Journal* 7 (4), 115–117. https://www.jstor.org/stable/25532885

Moga, C. I., Hartlel, T. and Öllerer, K. (2010). Status, microhabitat use and distribution of corncrake *Crex crex* in a Southern Transylvanian rural landscape, Romania. North-West. *Journal of Zoology* 6, 63–70. http://www.biozoojournals.ro/nwjz/content/v6.1/nwjz.061107.Moga.pdf

Mudenda, N., Sainsbury, A. W., Macgregor, S. K., Flach, E. J. and Owen, R. J. (2008). Prevalence of *Campylobacter* species in corncrakes (*Crex crex*) in a reintroduction programme in the UK. *Veterinary Record* 163 (9), 274–275. Short Communications. https://veterinaryrecord.bmj.com/content/163/9/274

Murin, B., Krištín, A., Darolová, A., Danko, Š. and Kropil, R. (1994). Početnosť hniezdnych populácii vtákov na Slovensku. [Breeding bird population sizes in Slovakia]. *Sylvia* 30, 97–105. https://oldcso.birdlife.cz/www.cso.cz/wpimages/other/sylvia30_2_1Murin.pdf

Newman, K. (2002). *Newman's Birds of Southern Africa,* pp. 120–122. Struik: Cape Town.

Newton, A. V. (1991). Corncrakes, crofting, and conservation. In: Curtis, D. J., Bignal, E. M. and Curtis, M. A. (eds.), *Birds and Pastoral Agriculture in Europe.* Proceedings of the Second European Forum on Birds and Pastoralism 1990. Peterborough: Joint Nature Conservation Committee. pp. 35–36.

Newton, I. (2004). The recent declines of farmland bird populations in Britain: An appraisal of causal factors and conservation actions. *Ibis* 146, 579–600. https://www.researchgate.net/publication/229510800_The_recent_declines_of_farmland_bird_populations_in_Britain_An_appraisal_of_causal_factors_and_conservation_actions

Niemann, S. (1995). *Habitat Management for Corncrakes.* RSPB: Sandy.

Nikiforov, M. and Vintchevski, D. (1999). The Corncrake (*Crex crex*) in Belarus. In: Schäffer, N. and Mammen, U. (eds.), Proceedings of the International Corncrake Workshop 1998, Hilpoltstein, Germany, pp. 13–15. https://web.archive.org/web/20081120124206/http://www.corncrake.net/Download/belarus.pdf

Norris, C. A. (1945). Summary of a report on the distribution and status of the Corncrake (*Crex crex*). *British Birds* 38, 142–148; 162–168. https://www.biodiversitylibrary.org/bibliography/105650

Norris, C. A. (1947). Report on the distribution and status of the Corncrake. British Birds 40, 226–244. https://britishbirds.co.uk/wp-content/uploads/article_files/V40/V40_N08/V40_N08_P226_244_A043.pdf

Norris, C. A. (1963). The distribution of the Corncrake in the British Isles, and the causes of its decrease. In: Bannerman, D. A. *The Birds of the British Isles Vol. 12,* pp. 173–184. Edinburgh: Oliver and Boyd.

O'Brien, M., Green, R. E. and Wilson, J. (2006). Partial recovery of the population of Corncrakes *Crex crex* in Britain, 1993–2004. *Bird Study* 53, 213–224. doi: https://doi.org/10.1080/00063650609461436

O'Donoghue, B. (2019). Corncrake supporting document for Article 12 reporting period 2013–2018. National Parks & Wildlife Service, Killarney, Ireland. https://test.npws.ie/sites/default/files/general/crex-article-12-2019-suppdoc.pdf

Obratil, S. (1999). The Corncrake (*Crex crex*) in Bosnia-Herzegovina. In: Schäffer, N. and Mammen, U. (eds.), Proceedings of the International Corncrake Workshop 1998, Hilpoltstein, Germany, pp. 19–21. https://web.archive.org/web/20090105185349/http://www.corncrake.net/Download/bosnia.pdf

Okulewicz, A. (1993). *Capillariinae* (*Nematoda*) palearktycznych ptaków. Wydawn. Uniwersytetu Wroclawskiego, 1–147. [In Polish].

Olson, S. L. (1973). A Classification of the Rallidae. *Wilson Bulletin* 85 (4), 381–416. https://www.jstor.org/stable/4160386

Olson, S. L. (1977). A synopsis of the fossil Rallidae. In: Ripley, S. D. (ed.), *Rails of the World: A Monograph of the Family Rallidae.* Boston MA: David R. Godine Publishers. Reprinted with a separate bibliography from Chapter 5. https://repository.si.edu/bitstream/handle/10088/12826/VZ_77_Synopsis_fossil_Rallidae.pdf?Sequence=1&isallowed=y

Orlowski, G. (2010). Effect of boundary vegetation and landscape features on diversity and abundance of breeding bird communities of abandoned crop fields in southwest Poland. *Bird Study* 57 (2), 175–182. doi: https://doi.org/10.1080/00063650903449946

Osiejuk, T. S. (2011). Soft song and the readiness hypothesis: comments on Arçay et al. (2011). *Animal Behaviour* 82, e1–e3. doi: https://doi.org/10.1016/j.anbehav.2011.09.011

Osiejuk, T. S. and Olech, B. (2004). Amplitude spectra of Corncrake calls: what do they signalise? *Animal Biology* 54 (2), 207–220. doi: https://doi.org/10.1163/1570756041445218

Osiejuk, T. S., Olech, B., Ratyńska, K., Owsiński, A. and Gromadzka-Ostrowska, J. (2004). Effects of season, plasma testosterone and body size on corncrake (*Crex crex*) call rhythm. *Annales Zoologici Fennici* 41, 647–659. https://www.jstor.org/stable/23735958

Ottvall, R. (1999a). Female Corncrake (*Crex crex*) singing in the wild. *Journal of Ornithology* 140, 453–456.

Ottvall, R. (1999b). The Corncrake (*Crex crex*) in Sweden. In: Schäffer, N. and Mammen, U. (eds.), Proceedings of the International Corncrake Workshop 1998, Hilpoltstein, Germany, pp. 99–101. https://web.archive.org/web/20081120133757/http://www.corncrake.net/Download/sweden.pdf

Ottvall, R. and Pettersson, J. (1998a). Kornknarrens *Crex crex* biotopval, revirstorlek och ortstrohet på Öland: En radiosändarstudie. [Habitat choice, home range size and site fidelity of the Corncrake *Crex crex* in Oland, Sweden: A ratio telemetry study]. *Ornis Svecica* 8: 65–76.

Ottvall, R. and Pettersson, J. (1998b). Is there a viable Corncrake *Crex crex* population on Öland, southeastern Sweden? Habitat preferences in relation to hay-mowing activities. *Ornis Svecica* 8, 157–166. https://cdn.birdlife.se/wp-content/uploads/ornis_svecica/cms_20-s1_Vol%208(4),%20157–166%20Ottvall%20Pettersson%20kornknarr.pdf

Page, N. and Popa, R. (2016). Conservation of Corncrake *Crex crex* in the high nature value farmed landscapes of Transylvania: Theory and practice. *Vogelwelt* 136, 191–196.

Parslow, J. (1973). *Breeding Birds of Britain and Ireland: A Historical Survey,* pp. 71–73. Berkhamsted, UK: Poyser.

Patterson, R. (1901). Corn-Crake in January. *The Irish Naturalist* 10 (4), 93. https://www.jstor.org/stable/25521951

Peake, T. M. (1997). Variation in the vocal behaviour of the Corncrake *Crex crex*: Potential for conservation. PhD thesis (Unpublished). University of Nottingham.

Peake, T. M. and Mcgregor, P. K. (1999). Geographical variation in the vocalization of the corncrake *Crex crex*. *Ethology, Ecology and Evolution* 11 (2), 123–137. doi: https://doi.org/10.1080/08927014.1999.9522831

Peake, T. M. and Mcgregor, P. K. (2001). Corncrake *Crex crex* census estimates: A conservation application of vocal individuality. *Animal Biodiversity and Conservation* 24 (1), 81–90. http://www.bcn.cat/museuciencies_fitxers/imatges/fitxercontingut1401.pdf

Peake, T. M., Mcgregor, P. K., Smith, K. W., Tyler, G., Gilbert, G. and Green, R. E. (1998). Individuality in Corncrake *Crex crex* vocalizations. *Ibis* 140, 120–127. doi: http://dx.doi.org/10.1111/j.1474–919x.1998.tb04548.x

Pedrini, P., Florit, F., Martignago, G., Mezzavilla, F., Rassati, G., Silveri, G. and Brambilla, M. (2016). Corncrake *Crex crex* population trend in Italy. *Vogelwelt* 136, 127–130.

Pedrini, P., Rizzolli, F., Rossi, F. and Brambilla, M. (2012). Population trend and breeding density of corncrake *Crex crex* (Aves: Rallidae) in the Alps: Monitoring and conservation implications of a 15-years study in Trentino, Italy. *Italian Journal of Zoology* 79 (3), 377–384. doi: http://dx.doi.org/10.1080/11250003.2011.651492

Pfützke, S. (1999). Investigations in the Corncrake (*Crex crex*) population in the Bremen Basin. In: Schäffer, N. and Mammen, U. (eds.), Proceedings of the International Corncrake Workshop 1998, Hilpoltstein, Germany, pp. 177–178. https://web.archive.org/web/20081120144617/http://www.corncrake.net/Download/pfuetzke.pdf

Pickup, C. (1985). Corncrakes, land improvements… and cats! *Stornoway Gazette* (25 May 1985).

Pienkowski, M. W., Bignal, E. M., Galbraith, C. A., McCracken, D. I., Stillman, R. A., Boobyer, M. G. and Curtis, D. J. (1996). A simplified classification of land-type zones to assist the integration of biodiversity objectives in land-use policies. *Biological Conservation* 75, 11–25. doi: https://doi.org/10.1016/0006–3207(95)00042–9

Pitches, A. (2013). Corn Crakes – a Scottish conservation success story. *British Birds* 106 (5), 241–242. https://www.biodiversitylibrary.org/item/230833

Podos, J. and Warren, P. S. (2007). The evolution of geographic variation in birdsong. *Advances in the Study of Behavior* 27, 403–458. doi: https://doi.org/10.1016/S0065–3454(07)37009–5

Polak, S., Kebe, L. and Koren, B. (2004). Trinajst let popisov kosca *Crex crex* na Cerkniškem jezeru (Slovenija). Thirteen years of the Corn Crake *Crex crex* census at Lake Cerknica (Slovenia). *Acrocephalus* 25 (121), 59–70. https://www.dlib.si/stream/URN:NBN:SI:doc-B4YWZ7R1/1c25e818-c30b-4490-a46c-e5f4a0ae6335/PDF

Preiksa, Z. (1999). 'The Corncrake (*Crex crex*) in Lithuania'. In: Schäffer, N. and Mammen, U. (eds.), Proceedings of the International Corncrake Workshop 1998, Hilpoltstein, Germany, pp. 57–58. https://web.archive.org/web/20081120143816/http://www.corncrake.net/Download/lithuani.pdf

Prostov, A. (1964). Investigation of the ornithofauna in the region of Burgas. Izv. Na Zool. Inst. S Muzei, BAN, 15, 5–68. (In Bulgarian).

Pykal, J. and Flousek, J. (2016). Numbers and population trends of the Corncrake (*Crex crex*) in the Czech Republic: results of a 20-year monitoring study. *Vogelwelt* 136, 89–91.

Pykal, J., Burger, P. and Hora, J. (1999). The Corncrake (*Crex crex*) in the Czech Republic. In: Schäffer, N. and Mammen, U. (eds.), Proceedings of the International Corncrake Workshop 1998, Hilpoltstein, Germany, pp. 25–27. https://web.archive.org/web/20081120160543/http://www.corncrake.net/Download/czech.pdf

Radišić, D., Mišković, M., Jovanović, S., Nikolić, T., Sekulić, G., Vujić, A. and Milić, D. (2019). Protected area networks are insufficient for the conservation of threatened farmland species: a case study on corncrake (*Crex crex*) and lesser grey shrike (Lanius minor) in Serbia. *Archives of Biological Sciences* 71 (1), 111–121. doi: https://doi.org/10.2298/ABS180924053R

Radovic, D. and Dumbovic, V. (1999). The Corncrake (*Crex crex*) in Croatia. In: Schäffer, N. and Mammen, U. (eds.), Proceedings of the International Corncrake Workshop 1998, Hilpoltstein, Germany, pp. 49–53. https://web.archive.org/web/20081120145133/http://www.corncrake.net/Download/croatia.pdf

Ralph, R. (ed.) (2017). *William macgillivray: A Hebridean Naturalist's Journal 1817–1818.* Stornoway: Acair.

Ramirez, J. C. G. (2014). *The influence of space and time on the genetic architecture of rail species (Aves: Rallidae).* PhD thesis, Massey University, New Zealand.

Rassati, G. and Tout, C. P. (2002). The Corncrake (*Crex crex*) in Friuli-Venezia Giulia (North-eastern Italy). *Avocetta* 26 (1), 3–6.

Rassati, G. and Rodaro, P. (2007). Habitat, vegetation and land management of Corncrake *Crex crex* breeding sites in Carnia (Friuli-Venezia Giulia, NE Italy). *Acrocephalus* 28 (133), 61–68. http://www.dlib.si/stream/URN:NBN:SI:DOC-PFW55E7N/0cb94435-50e1-4c20-ac06-cd1ced597bdb/PDF

Ratcliffe, D. A. (1980). *The Peregrine Falcon.* Calton, UK: Poyser.

Ravkin, Y. S. (1999). The Corncrake (*Crex crex*) in Russia (West Siberian Plain). In: Schäffer, N. and Mammen, U. (eds.), Proceedings of the International Corncrake Workshop 1998, Hilpoltstein, Germany, pp. 83–87. https://web.archive.org/web/20090105182253/http://www.corncrake.net/Download/siberia.pdf

Ręk, P. and Osiejuk, T. S. (2010). Sophistication and simplicity: Conventional communication in a rudimentary system. *Behavioral Ecology* 21, 1203–1210. doi: https://doi.org/10.1093/beheco/arq143

Ręk, P. and Osiejuk, T. S. (2011a). No male identity information loss during call propagation through dense vegetation: The case of the corncrake. *Behavioural Processes* 86, 323–328. doi: https://doi.org/10.1016/j.beproc.2011.01.011

Ręk, P. and Osiejuk, T. S. (2011b). Nonpasserine bird produces soft calls and pays retaliation cost. *Behavioral Ecology* 22 (3), 657–662. doi: https://doi.org/10.1093/beheco/arr027

Ręk, P. and Osiejuk, T. S. (2013). Temporal patterns of broadcast calls in the corncrake encode information arbitrarily. *Behavioral Ecology* 24, 547–552. doi: https://doi.org/10.1093/beheco/ars196

Ręk, P. (2013a). Corncrake males learn new signal meanings during aggressive interactions. *Animal Behaviour* 86, 451–457. doi: https://doi.org/10.1016/j.anbehav.2013.05.042

Ręk, P. (2013b). Soft calls and broadcast calls in the corncrake as adaptations to short and long range communication. *Behavioural Processes* 99, 121–129. doi: https://doi.org/10.1016/j.beproc.2013.07.009

Ręk, P. (2014). Acoustic location of conspecifics in a nocturnal bird: The corncrake *Crex crex. Acta Ethologica* 17, 31–35. doi: https://doi.org/10.1007/s10211-013-0155-3

Ręk, P. and Kwiatkowska, K. (2016). Habitat complexity and the structure of vocalizations: A test of the acoustic adaptation hypothesis in three rail species (Rallidae). *Ibis* 158, 416–427. doi: https://doi.org/10.1111/ibi.12357

Ręk, P., Osiejuk, T. S. and Budka, M. (2011). Functionally similar acoustic signals in the corncrake (*Crex crex*) transmit information about different states of the sender during aggressive interactions. *Hormones and Behavior* 60 (5), 706–712. doi: https://doi.org/10.1016/j.yhbeh.2011.09.011

Rennie, F. (1983). The Corncrake: looking forward to the IDP? *West Highland Free Press* (January 1983).

Rennie, F. (1991). The way of crofting. In: Magnusson, M and White, L. (eds.), *The Nature of Scotland: Landscape, Wildlife and People,* Chapter 9, pp. 123–132. Edinburgh: Canongate.

Reynolds, P. and Reynolds, V. (2003). *Ness and Barvas SPA Hedgehog Surveys 2003.* Commissioned Report for Scottish Natural Heritage.

Ripley, S. D. (1976). Rails of the world: Through inherent adaptive plasticity, this versatile family of marsh birds has spread over a wide range of habitats. *American Scientist* 64 (6), 628–635. https://www.jstor.com/stable/27847554

Ritchie, A. (1983). Excavation of a Neolithic farmstead at Knap of Howar, Papa Westray, Orkney. *Proceedings of the Society of Antiquaries of Scotland* 113, 40–121.

Robinson, M. (ed.) (1985). *The Concise Scots Dictionary.* Aberdeen: Aberdeen University Press.

Robinson, R. A. (2005). *Birdfacts: Profiles of Birds Occurring in Britain and Ireland.* Thetford: BTO. http://www.bto.org/birdfacts

Rogacheva, H. (1992). *The Birds of Central Siberia.* Husum, Germany: Husum-Druck und Verlagsgesellschaft.

Rothschild, M. and Clay, T. (1953). *Fleas, Flukes and Cuckoos. A Study of Bird Parasites,* pp. 204–205. London: Collins. https://archive.org/details/fleasflukescucko00roth/page/204/mode/2up

Ryelandt, P. (1995). Le Râle des Genêts (*Crex crex*) en Fagne et Famenne de 1990 à 1994. *Aves* 32 (1), 1–33. (In French with summary and captions in English). https://www.aves.be/fileadmin/Aves/Bulletins/Articles/32_1/32_1_1.pdf

Ryelandt, P. (1999). The Corncrake (*Crex crex*) in Belgium. In: Schäffer, N. and Mammen, U. (eds.), Proceedings of the International Corncrake Workshop 1998, Hilpoltstein, Germany, pp. 11–16.

Sackl, P., Dervović, I., Kotrošan, D., Topić, G., Drocić, S., Šarac, M., Sarajlić, N., Durst, R. and Stumberger, B. (2013). The distribution and population numbers of Corncrakes *Crex crex* in the Karst Poljes of Bosnia-Herzegovina – results of a large-scale survey in 2012 and 2013. Dinaric Karst Poljes – Floods for Life Conference. Proceedings of the 1st Workshop on Karst Poljes as Wetlands of National and International Importance. Livno, Bosnia-Herzegovina. https://www.researchgate.net/publication/280728178_The_distribution_and_population_numbers_of_Corncrakes_Crex_crex_in_the_karst_poljes_of_Bosnia-Herzegovina_-_results_of_a_large-scale_survey_in_2012_and_2013

Sainsbury, A. W. (2015). Mitigating the risk from disease while conserving parasites in future ecosystems: case studies from cirl buntings and corncrakes. Health and Disease in Translocated Wild Animals: Abstracts and Posters. *Proceedings of Zoological Society of London Symposium*, 14 and 15 May. p. 11.

Salzer, U. (1999). Comparison of the breeding habits and development of the young of the Corncrake *Crex crex*, the Spotted Crake Porzana porzana and the Water Rail *Rallus aquaticus*. In: Schäffer, N. and Mammen, U. (eds.), Proceedings of the International Corncrake Workshop 1998, Hilpoltstein, Germany, pp. 191–192. https://web.archive.org/web/20081120114124/http://www.corncrake.net/Download/salzer.pdf

Salzer, U. and Schäffer, N. (1997). Altersbestimmung von Wachtelkönigen *Crex crex*. [Aging of Corncrakes *Crex crex*] *Vogelwelt* 118, 135–139.

Sánchez-Marco, A., Blasco, R., Rosell, J., Gopher, A. and Barkai, R. (2016). Birds as indicators of high biodiversity zones around the Middle Pleistocene Qesem Cave, Israel. *Quaternary International* 421, 23–31. doi: http://dx.doi.org/10.1016/j.quaint.2015.11.001

Schäffer, N. (1999). Habitatwahl und Partnerschftsystem von Tüpfelralle *Porzana porzana* und Wachtelkönig *Crex crex*. PhD thesis. [Habitat use and mating systems of the Corncrake and Spotted Crake]. *Ökologie der Vögel* 21 (1), 1–267. (In German).

Schäffer, N. (2016). Preface: Corncrakes and Corncrake conservation over time. *Vogelwelt* 136, 73–74. (Special issue devoted to Corncrakes).

Schäffer, N. and Green, R. E. (2001). The global status of the Corncrake. *RSPB Conservation Review* 13, 18–24.

Schäffer, N. and Koffijberg, K. (2004). *Crex crex* Corncrake. *Birds of the Western Palearctic, Update* 6 (1–2), 57–78. London: Oxford University Press.

Schäffer, N. and Koffijberg, K. (2006). Corncrake *Crex crex*. In: *The Birds of the Western Palearctic* on interactive DVD-ROM. 2006 Update. Sheffield/Oxford: Oxford University Press.

Schäffer, N. and Mammen, U. (2003). International Corncrake monitoring. *Ornis Hungarica* 12–13, 129–133.

Schäffer, N. and Münch, S. (1993). Untersuchungen zur Habitatwahl und Brutbiologie des Wachtelkönigs *Crex crex* im Murnauer Moos/Oberbayern. *Vogelwelt* 114, 55–72.

Schäffer, N. and Zub, K. (1994). Tam derkacz wrzasnął z łąki. [There the corncrake called from the meadow]. *Lowiec Polski* 7, 14. https://plamkamazurka.pl/2012/04/tam-derkacz-wrzasnal-z-laki/

Schäffer, N., Salzer, U. and Wend, D. (1997). Das Lautrepertoire des Wachtelkónings *Crex crex*. [Vocalizations of the Corncrake *Crex crex*]. *Vogelwelt* 118, 147–156.

Schoppers, J. and Koffijberg, K. (2008). Kwartelkoningen in Nederland in 2007. SOVON-informatierapport 2006/01., 1–25.

Seebohm, H. (1896). *Coloured Figures of the Eggs of British Birds.* (Edited by Sharpe, R. B.) Sheffield: Pawson and Brailsford. p. 83. https://archive.org/stream/colouredfigureso00seeb#page/82/mode/2up

Serna, H., Pocknell, A., Sainsbury, A. W., Peniche, G., Blake, D. P. and Beckmann, K. M. (2018). *Eimeria* spp. in captive-reared corncrakes (*Crex crex*): Results of a Genescan assay consistent with high prevalence of infection and extra-intestinal life stages. *Avian Pathology* 47 (4), 375–383. doi: https://doi.org/10.1080/03079457.2018.1451621

Sharpe, R. B. (1893). Untitled communication. *Bulletin of the British Ornithologists' Club* 1, 26–29.

Sharrock, J. T. R. (1976). *The Atlas of Breeding Birds in Britain and Ireland,* pp. 156–157; 456. Berkhamsted, UK: Poyser.

Shobrak, M. (2012). Electrocution and collision of birds with power lines in Saudi Arabia. *Zoology in the Middle East* 57, 45–52. http://nwrc.gov.sa/NWRC_ARB/akhr_thdyth_files/ZME57%20045–052%20Shobrak.pdf

Shrubb, M. (2003). *Birds, Scythes and Combines: A History of Birds and Agricultural Change.* Cambridge: Cambridge University Press.

Shufeldt, R. W. (1892). Commentary in Cope, E. A. D. A contribution to the vertebrate palaeontology of Texas. *Proceedings of the American Philosophical Society* 30 (No. 137), 123–131. https://www.jstor.org/stable/983215

Sibbald, R. (1684). *Scotia Illustrata, sive Prodromus historiæ naturalis.* Edinburgh: Jacobi Kniblo, Josuae Solingensis & Johannes Colmarii.

Sibley, C. G. and Ahlquist, J. E. (1985). *The Relationships of Some Groups of African Birds, Based on Comparisons of the Genetic Material, DNA,* pp. 115–162. In: Proceedings of the International Symposium of African Vertebrates. Bonn: Zoologisches Forschungsinstitut und Museum Alexander Koenig.

Sibley, C. G., Ahlquist, J. E. and Monroe, B. L. (1988). A classification of the living birds of the world based on DNA–DNA hybridization studies. *The Auk* 105, 409–423. https://pdfs.semanticscholar.org/6c-d7/8c563914d433547d23f851ebcd64c89cc18e.pdf

Skliba, J. and Fuchs, R. (2002). Preferované prostředí a prostorová aktivita chřástalů polních (*Crex crex*) na Sumave. [Habitat preference and spatial activity of the Corncrake (*Crex crex*) in the Sumava Mts. (southern Bohemia)]. *Sylvia* 38, 83–90. (In Czech with English summary). https://www.birdlife.cz/wp-content/uploads/2017/12/Sylvia53_4Vlcek.pdf

Skliba, J. and Fuchs, R. (2004). Male Corncrakes *Crex crex* extend their home ranges by visiting the territories of neighbouring males. *Bird Study* 51 (2), 113–118. doi: https://doi.org/10.1080/00063650409461342

Smith, J. B. and Ó Laoire, L. (2009). 'The Silly Treun': An odd bird identified. *Folk Life* 47 (1), 51–57. doi: https://doi.org/10.1179/175967009X422693

Snow, D. and Perrins, C. M. (eds.) (1998). *The Birds of the Western Palaearctic*. Vol. 1 (Concise edition), pp. 496–499. Oxford: Oxford University Press.

Songs of Separation (n.d.). 'The echo mocks the Corncrake'. https://lyricstranslate.com/en/songs-separation-echo-mocks-corncrake-lyrics.html

Sršen, A. O., Kralj, J. and Šešelj, L. (2017). The late-Holocene avifaunal assemblage from the island of Palagruža (Croatia): The earliest record of the Northern Gannet in the Adriatic Sea. *The Holocene* 27 (10), 1540–1549. doi: https://doi.org/10.1177/0959683617693897

Steadman, D. W. (1995). Prehistoric extinctions of Pacific Island birds: Biodiversity meets zooarchaeology. *Science* 267, 1123–1131. doi: https://doi.org/10.1126/science.267.5201.1123

Stendall, J. A. S. (1935). Corncrake in January. *Irish Naturalists' Journal* 5 (7), 173. https://www.jstor.org/stable/25532394

Stowe, T. J. and Becker, D. (1992). Status and conservation of the corncrake *Crex crex* outside the breeding grounds. *Tauraco* 2, 1–23.

Stowe, T. J. and Green, R. E. (1997a). Response of Corncrake *Crex crex* populations in Britain to conservation action. *Vogelwelt*, 118, 161–168.

Stowe, T. J. and Green, R. E. (1997b). Threats to Corncrakes *Crex crex* on migration and in the winter quarters. *Vogelwelt* 118, 175–178.

Stowe, T. J. and Hudson, A. V. (1988). Corncrake studies in the Western Isles. *Royal Society for the Protection of Birds Conservation Review* 2, 38–42.

Stowe, T. J. and Hudson, A. V. (1991). Radio-telemetry studies of Corncrakes in Great Britain. *Vogelwelt* 112 (1–2), 10–16.

Stowe, T. J., Newton, A. V., Green, R. E. and Mayes, E. (1993). The decline of the corncrake in Britain and Ireland in relation to habitat. *Journal of Applied Ecology* 30 (1), 53–62. https://www.jstor.org/stable/2404270

Sukhanova, O. V. and Mischenko, A. L. (2003). Monitoring Corncrake *Crex crex* numbers in European Russia: The first stage. *Ornis Hungarica* 12–13, 135–141.

Swann, R. L. (1986). The recent decline of the Corncrake *Crex crex* on the Isle of Canna. *Bird Study* 33, 201–205. doi: https://doi.org/10.1080/00063658609476921

Swiney, J. H. H. (1892). The Corn-Crake (*Crex pratensis*). *Irish Naturalists' Journal* 1 (6), 126–127. https://www.jstor.org/stable/25520243

Syrota, Ya. Yu., Korol, E. M. and Kuzmin, Yu. I. (2020). New records of Helminths of the Corncrake, *Crex crex* (Aves, Rallidae) from Ukraine. *Zoodiversity* 54 (1), 11–16. doi: https://doi.org/10.15407/zoo2020.01.011

Szentirmai, I., Boldogh, S. A., Nagy, K., Habarics, B. and Szép, T. (2016). Preserving an obscure bird: Achievements and future challenges of Corncrake (*Crex crex* Linnaeus, 1758) conservation in Hungary. *Ornis Hungarica* 24 (2), 1–17. doi: https://doi.org/10.1515/orhu-2016-0011

Szép, T. (1991). The present and historical situation of the Corncrake in Hungary. *Vogelwelt* 112, 45–48.

Tadic, A. (1999). The Corncrake (*Crex crex*) in Yugoslavia. In: Schäffer, N. and Mammen, U. (eds.), Proceedings of the International Corncrake Workshop 1998, Hilpoltstein, Germany, pp. 111–113. https://web.archive.org/web/20090105171101/http://www.corncrake.net/Download/yugoslav.pdf

Taylor, B. and Kirwan, G. M. (2020). Corn Crake (*Crex crex*), version 1.0 In: del Hoyo, J., Elliott, A., Sargatal, J., Christie, D. A. and de Juan, E. (eds.), *Birds of the World*. Ithaca, NY: Cornell Lab of Ornithology. doi: https://doi.org/10.2173/bow.corcra.01

Taylor, B. and van Perlo, B. (1998). *Rails: A Guide to the Rails, Crakes, Gallinules, and Coots of the World*. Sussex: Pica Press.

Taylor, P. B. (1984). A field study of the Corncrake *Crex crex* at Ndola, Zambia. *Scopus* 8 (3), 53–59. https://www.biodiversitylibrary.org/page/41803767#page/239/mode/1up

Thom, M. D. F. and Dytham, C. (2012). Female choosiness leads to the evolution of individually distinctive males. *Evolution* 66–12, 3736–3742. doi: https://www.jstor.org/stable/23328280

Thorup, O. (1999a). The Corncrake (*Crex crex*) in Denmark. In: Schäffer, N. and Mammen, U. (eds.), Proceedings of the International Corncrake Workshop 1998, Hilpoltstein, Germany, pp. 29–30. https://web.archive.org/web/20090105174420/http://www.corncrake.net/Download/denmark.pdf

Ticehurst, N. F. (1913). The case of the Land Rail: An enquiry proposed. *British Birds* 7 (1), 4–6.

Todorova, L. (2016). Why do we need an agri-environment package for Corncrakes *Crex crex* in the high nature value area from Romania. *Vogelwelt* 136, 185–189.

Toivanen, L. (2009). Habitat choice of territorial male Corncrakes *Crex crex* in the province of Värmland. D-level Biology thesis, Faculty of Social and Life Sciences, Karlstads University. http://www.diva-portal.org/smash/get/diva2:210700/FULLTEXT01.pdf

Tome, D. (2002a). Effect of floods on the distribution of meadow birds on Ljubljansko Barje. *Acrocephalus* 23 (112), 75–79. http://www.dlib.si/details/URN:NBN:SI:doc-DCHQOESE

Tome, D. (2002b). Ali je populacija kosca *Crex crex* na Ljubljanskem baru (še) stabilna? [Is the Corn Crake *Crex crex* population at Ljubljansko barje (still) stable?] *Acrocephalus* 23 (113–114), 141–143. https://www.dlib.si/stream/URN:NBN:SI:doc-NH4HZNCR/28c5fd32-b0b1-4ce3-be15-488bdc499d64/PDF

Tomialojc, L. (1990). Ptaki Polski. Rozmieszczenie i liczebność. [The Birds of Poland. Their Distribution and Abundance]. Warsaw: PWN.

Tomison, J. (1907). Bird-life as observed at Skerryvore Lighthouse. *Annals of Scottish Natural History* 1907, 20–31. https://www.biodiversitylibrary.org/item/16994

Trezza, J. (2017). Birders drop everything to behold rare Corn Crake that turned up in New York. *Audubon* (9 November 2017). https://www.audubon.org/news/birders-drop-everything-behold-rare-corn-crake-turned-new-york

Trontelj, P. (1995). Popis kosca *Crex crex* v Sloveniji v letih 1992–93. [Census of the Corn Crake *Crex crex* in Slovenia in 1992–93]. *Acrocephalus* 16 (73), 174–180. https://www.dlib.si/stream/URN:NBN:SI:doc-QPSVJOU7/d9015a13-5757-4a1e-8fa1-26c49fc3f3e4/PDF

Trontelj, P. (1997b). Der Wachtelkönig *Crex crex* in Slowenien: Bestand, Verbreitung, Habitat und Schutz. [The Corncrake *Crex crex* in Slovenia: Status, distribution, habitat and conservation]. *Vogelwelt* 118, 223–229.

Trontelj, P. (1999). Molecular markers in Corncrake biology. In: Schäffer, N. and Mammen, U. (eds.), Proceedings of the International Corncrake Workshop 1998, Hilpoltstein, Germany, pp. 85–87. https://web.archive.org/web/20081120171151/http://www.corncrake.net/Download/molekul.pdf

Trontelj, P. (2001). Popis kosca *Crex crex* v Sloveniji leta 1999 kᴀze na kratkoročno stabilno populaijo. [The 1999 Slovenian Corncrake *Crex crex* census indicates short-term stable population]. *Acrocephalus* 22, (108), 139–148. http://www.dlib.si/details/URN:NBN:SI:DOC-YCP6HAM4/?Query=%27keywords%3dacrocephalus%27&pagesize=25&sortdir=ASC&sort=date&language=eng&fyear=2001

Tryjanowski, P., Hartel, T., Báldi, A., Szymański, P., Tobolka, M., Herzon, I., Golawski, A., Konvička, M., Hromada, M., Jerzak, L., Kujawa, K., Lenda, M., Orlowski, G., Panek, M., Skórka, P., Sparks, T. H., Tworek, S., Wuczyński, A. and żmihorski, M. (2011). Conservation of farmland birds faces different challenges in Western and Central-Eastern Europe. *Acta Ornithologica* 46 (1), 1–12. doi: https://doi.org/10.3161/000164511X589857

Tucker, G. M. and Heath, M. F. (1994). *Birds in Europe: Their Conservation Status*. BirdLife Conservation Series No. 3. Cambridge: BirdLife International.

Turtle, L. J. (1935). Corncrake in February and other bird notes. *Irish Naturalists' Journal* 5 (8), 199–200. https://www.jstor.org/stable/25532412

Tutiš, V. (2010). Monitoring Programme for Corncrake *Crex crex* in Croatia. http://www.haop.hr/sites/default/files/uploads/dokumenti/03_prirodne/monitoring_prog/Program%20monitoringa%20Crex%20crex.pdf

Tyler, G. A. (1996). *The ecology of the Corncrake with special reference to the effect of mowing on breeding production*. PhD thesis, University College Cork. https://www.researchgate.net/profile/Glen_Tyler/publication/237544937_The_Ecology_of_the_Corncrake_with_special_reference_to_the_effect_of_mowing_on_breeding/links/5669e-5c308ae62b05f02706e.pdf

Tyler, G. A. (2001). The ecology of the Corncrake with special reference to the effect of mowing on breeding. In: Schäffer, N. and Mammen, U. (eds.), Proceedings of the International Corncrake Workshop 1998, Hilpoltstein, Germany, pp. 181–184. https://web.archive.org/web/20090105184356/http://www.corncrake.net/Download/tyler.pdf

Tyler, G. A. and Green, R. E. (1996). The incidence of nocturnal song by male Corncrakes *Crex crex* is reduced during pairing. *Bird Study* 43, 214–219. doi: https://doi.org/10.1080/00063659609461013

Tyler, G. A. and Green, R. E. (2004). Effects of weather on the survival and growth of Corncrake *Crex crex* chicks. *Ibis* 146 (1), 69–76. doi: https://doi.org/10.1111/j.1474–919X.2004.00225.x

Tyler, G. A., Green, R. E. and Casey, C. (1998). Survival and behaviour of Corncrake *Crex crex* chicks during the mowing of agricultural grassland. *Bird Study* 45 (1), 35–50. doi: https://doi.org/10.1080/00063659809461076

Tyler, G. A., Green, R. E., Stowe, T. J. and Newton, A. V. (1996). Sex differences in the behaviour and measurements of Corncrakes *Crex crex* in Scotland. *Ringing & Migration* 17, 15–19. doi: https://doi.org/10.1080/03078698.1996.9674115

Van den Bergh, L. (1991). Status, distribution and research on Corncrakes in the Netherlands. *Vogelwelt* 112, 78–83.

Van der Straaten, J. and Meijer, R. (1969). Voorkomen van de Kwartelkoning (*Crex crex*) in het stroombed van Waal en Boven-Merwede. *Limosa* 42 (1), 1–15. http://limosa.nou.nu/limosa_search2.php (In Dutch with English summary).

Van der Straaten, J. and Van den Bergh, L. M. J. (1970). Voorkomen van de Kwartelkoning (*Crex crex*) in Nederland in 1969. [Distribution of the Corncrake *Crex crex* in the Netherlands in 1969]. *Limosa* 43 (3), 138–151. http://limosa.nou.nu/limosa_search2.php (In Dutch with English summary).

Vassen, F. and Ryelandt, P. (1997). Zur Bestandsentwicklung des Wachtelkönigs *Crex crex* in Belgien von 1983 bis 1995 mit Bemerkungen zur Habitatwahl. [Population trends and habitat selection of the Corncrake *Crex crex* in Belgium in 1983–1995]. *Vogelwelt* 118, 242–244.

Venables, L. S. V. and Venables, U. M. (1950). The Corncrake on Shetland. *British Birds* 43 (5), 137–141.

Verbelen, D., Herremans, M., Derouaux, A. and Paquet, J.-Y. (2016). Corncrake *Crex crex* in Belgium: holding on to the verge of extinction. *Vogelwelt* 136, 135–138. https://www.researchgate.net/publication/307507287_Corncrake_Crex_crex_in_Belgium_holding_on_to_the_verge_of_extinction

Voslamber, B. (1989). De Kwartelkoning *Crex crex* in het Oldambt: aantallen en biotoopkeuze. [The Corncrake *Crex crex* in the Oldambt (Groningen) numbers and habitat selection]. *Limosa* 62 (1), 15–24. http://limosa.nou.nu/limosa_samenvatting.php?Language=UK&nr=3123 (In Dutch with English abstract.]

Walther, B. A. (2008). Ringing recoveries of the Corncrake *Crex crex* in Africa and Sinai. *Vogelwelt* 129, 103–108.

Walther, B. A. and Schäffer, N. (2014). Nach Afrika und zurück mit hängenden Beinen: Wachtelkönige im Überwinterungsgebiet. [To Africa and back with hanging legs: Corncrakes in their wintering area]. *Der Falke* 61 (3), 12–15. https://www.falke-journal.de/der-falke-32014

Walther, B. A., Taylor, P. B., Schäffer, N., Robinson, S. and Jiguet, F. (2013a). The African wintering distribution and ecology of the Corncrake *Crex crex*. *Bird Conservation International*, 23, 309–322. doi: http://dx.doi.org/10.1017/S0959270912000159

Walther, B. A., Taylor, P. B., Schäffer, N., Robinson, S. and Jiguet, F. (2013b). The African wintering distribution and ecology of the Corncrake *Crex crex*. Supplementary appendices to the 2013a paper. (Personal correspondence with B. A. Walther).

Wetmore, A. (1931). Two primitive Rails from the Eocene of Colorado and Wyoming. *Condor* 33 (3), 107–109. https://www.jstor.org/stable/1363575

Wetmore, A. (1957). A fossil rail from the Pliocene of Arizona. *Condor* 59, 267–268. https://www.jstor.org/stable/1364657

Wettstein, W. and Szép, T. (2003). Status of the Corncrake *Crex crex* as an indicator of biodiversity in Eastern Hungary. *Ornis Hungarica* 12–13, 143–149.

Wettstein, W., Husi, R. and Schmid, B. (2003). Population structure and dispersal of Corncrakes (*Crex crex*) in Europe revealed by microsatellite markers. In: Wettstein, W. (Ed.) Conservation biology of *Crex crex* L., pp. 53–72. PhD thesis, Berichte aus dem Institut für Umweltwissenschaften der Universität Zurich.

Wettstein, W., Szép, T. and Kéry, M. (2001). Habitat selection of Corncrakes (*Crex crex* L.) In Szatmár-Bereg (Hungary) and implications for further monitoring. *Ornis Hungarica* 11 (1/2), 9–18. http://www.ornis.hu/articles/ornishungarica_vol11_p9–18.pdf

Wilkinson, N. I., Wilson, J. D. and Anderson, G. Q. A. (2012). Agri-environment management for corncrake *Crex crex* delivers higher species richness and abundance across other taxonomic groups. *Agriculture, Ecosystems & Environment* 155, 27–34. doi: https://www.doi.org/10.1016/j.agee.2012.03.007

Willi, G. (1999). The Corncrake (*Crex crex*) in Liechtenstein. In: Schäffer, N. and Mammen, U. (eds.), Proceedings of the International Corncrake Workshop 1998, Hilpoltstein, Germany, pp. 83–84. https://web.archive.org/web/20090105172531/http://www.corncrake.net/Download/liechten.pdf

157

Williams, G., Green, R. E., Casey, C., Deceuninck, B. and Stowe, T. (1997). Halting declines in globally threatened species: the case of the Corncrake. *RSPB Conservation Reviews* 11, 22–31.

Williams, G., Stowe, T. J. and Newton, A. (1991). *Action for Corncrakes. RSPB Conservation Reviews* 5, 47–53.

Winkler, D., Bender, F. and Németh, T. M. (2014). A Haris [*Crex crex* (Linnaeus, 1758)] bioakusztikai vizsgálata a Hanságban. [Bioacoustical study of the Corncrake [*Crex crex* (Linnaeus 1758)] in the Hanság]. *Hungarian Small Game Bulletin* 12, 135–149. doi: https://dx.doi.org/10.17243/mavk.2014.135 (Hungarian with English summary).

Witherby, H. F., Jourdain, F. C. R., Ticehurst, N. F. and Tucker, B. W. (1941). *The Handbook of British Birds*. Vol. 5, pp. 174–180. London: Witherby.

Wojas, L. E., Podkowa, P. W. and Osiejuk, T. S. (2018). A nocturnal rail with a simple territorial call eavesdrops on interactions between rivals. *PLoS ONE* 13 (5), e0197368. doi: https://doi.org/10.1371/journal.pone.0197368

Worthy, T. H. (2004). The fossil rails (Aves: Rallidae) of Fiji with descriptions of a new genus and species. *Journal of the Royal Society of New Zealand* 34 (3), 295–314. doi: https://doi.org/10.1080/03014223.2004.9517768

Wotton, S. R., Eaton, M., Ewing, S. R. and Green, R. E. (2015). The increase in the Corncrake *Crex crex* population of the United Kingdom has slowed. *Bird Study*, 62, 486–497. doi: http://dx.doi.org/10.1080/00063657.2015.108 9837

Yale University (1965). Yale University Prehistoric Expedition to Nubia, 1964–1965; Yale University Peabody Museum – Invertebrate Paleontology collection number VP.053591

Yildirimhan, H. S., Bursey, C. R. and Altunel, F. N. (2011). Helminth parasites of the Balkan green lizard, *Lacerta trilineata* Bedriaga 1886, from Bursa, Turkey. *Turkish Journal of Zoology* 35 (4), 1–17. doi: https://doi.org/10.3906/zoo-0910-1

Zubcov, N. (1999). The Corncrake (*Crex crex*) in Moldova. In: Schäffer, N. and Mammen, U. (eds.), Proceedings of the International Corncrake Workshop, Hilpoltstein, Germany. pp. 63–66. doi: http://citeseerx.ist.psu.edu/viewdoc/download?Doi=10.1.1.519.9307&rep=rep1&type=pdf

CHAPTER 15

FURTHER READING

Ajupov, A. S., Birjukov, V. A. and Pavlov, E. A. (2000). Recent status and numbers of the Corncrake in Tatarstan Republic. In: Mischenko, A. L. (ed.). *Corncrake in European Russia, Collection of Scientific Papers, Series Threatened Birds, Vol. 2*, pp. 141–143. Moscow: RBCU. (In Russian).

Alcorn, S., Donaghy, A. and Moloney, D. (2009). Corncrake fieldwork in North and West Donegal 2009. Unpublished report for the National Parks and Wildlife Service, Department of Arts, Heritage and the Gaeltacht, Ireland.

Anderson, N. (2004). Corncrakes on the SAPPI–WWF birdlife property. *African Birds and Bird* 9, 75.

András, K., Wetstein, W. and Tibor, S. (2000). Haris egyedek felismerése hangelemzés alapján. [Individual recognition of corncrakes (*Crex crex*) by sound analysis. *Ornis Hungarica* 10, 65–70. (Hungarian with English Abstract). Available from: http://www.ornis.hu/articles/ornishungarica_vol10_p65–70.pdf

Anonymous (1979). Last cry from the Corncrake? *Birds* 7, 62.

Anonymous (1986). Corncrake findings. *Birds* 11, 7–9.

Anonymous (1993). *Corncrakes in the Outer Hebrides and Skye 1993*. Sandy: RSPB Conservation Management Advice.

Anscutte, P., Leduc, A. and Tombai, J. C. (1979). Mise au point sur la situation du Râle des genêts (*Crex crex*) dans le Nord et le Pas-de-Calais. Abondance exceptionnelle de l'èspèce en juin et juillet 1979. *Le Héron* 4, 1–13.

Bakka, S. V., Bakka, A. I., Matsyna, A. I., Seduľ, A. S. and Perlova, A. V. (2000). Preliminary results of the Corncrake count in Nizhniy Novgorod region. In: Mischenko, A. L. (ed.). *Corncrake in European Russia, Collection of Scientific Papers, Series Threatened Birds Vol. 2*, pp. 124–127. Moscow: RBCU. (In Russian).

Bakker, M. (2000). Nestwaarnemingen van Kwartelkoningen in de omgeving van Winschoten. *De Grauwe Gors* 28 (3), 95–98. (In Dutch). Http://natuurtijdschriften.nl/download?Type=document;docid=550488

Balčiauskas, L. and Balčiauskienė, L. (1999). Results of Corncrake Survey on the Nemunélis River Valley. *Acta Zoologica Lituanica* 9 (3), 80–85, doi: https://doi.org/10.1080/13921657.1999.10512298

Baldaev, K. (1973). The Corncrake. *Hunting and Hunting Management* 7, 18–19.

Bankovics, A. (1889). The Corncrake. In: Rakonczay, Z. (ed.): *Red Book: Extinct and Threatened Flora and Fauna of Hungary*, pp. 112–114. Budapest: Akadémiai Kiadó.

Barauskas, R., Preikša, Z. Adomaitis. E. and Kirstukas, M. (1998). Estimation of the Corncrake population in Lithuania. *Acta Zoologica Lituanica* 8 (2), 156–158, doi: https://doi.org/10.1080/13921657.1998.10541469

Beaumont, D. J., Bellebaum, J., England, B. J. and Koffijberg, K. (2016). Fifth meeting of the Corncrake Conservation Team 2015. *Vogelwelt* 136, 71–72.

Bekhuis, J. and Erhart, F. (1998). Kwartelkoningen in de uiterwaarden. *Nieuwe Wildernis* 3, 4–7.

Berg, Å. (2008). Standardiserad inventering av kornknarr (*Crex crex*) i Västmanlands och Uppsala län 2006–2007. Rapport 2008:21, Länsstyrelsen in Västmanlands Län (In Swedish).

Berghmans, H., Leysen, K. and Volders, J. (1985). Ontdekking van een belangrijke broedconcentratie van de kwar-telkoning *Crex crex*. *Wielewaal* 51, 36–40.

Bertoli, R. and Leo, R. (2005). Prima indagine sulla distribuzione del re di quaglie (*Crex crex*) in Provincia di Brescia (Lombardia, Italia settentrionale). *Natura Bresciana, Annali di Museo Civico di Storia Naturale di Brescia* 34, 151–154.

Bezzel, E. and Schöpf, H. (1991). Der Wachtelkönig im Murnauer Moos: Artenschutzerfolg durch Ausweisung eines Naturschutzgebietes? [The Corncrake in the Murnauer Moos: Success of conservation by establishing a reserve?] *Vogelwelt* 112, 83–90.

Biodiversity Statistics Team (2020). *Wild Bird Populations in the UK, 1970–2019*. York: Department for Environment and Rural Affairs. Https://www.gov.uk/government/statistics/wild-bird-populations-in-the-uk

BirdLife International Corncrake Conservation Team (2001). Project website. https://web.archive.org/web/20111011222152/http://corncrake.net/

BirdLife International Corncrake Conservation Team (2016). Fifth Meeting of the Corncrake Conservation Team 2015. *Vogelwelt* 136, 71–72.

Boldogh, S. and Szentgyörgyi, P. (2003). A haris (*Crex crex*) állományának vizsgálata az Aggteleki Nemzeti Park Igazgatóság illetékességi területén 1997–2002 között [Research on Corncrake (*Crex crex* L. 1758) in the administrative area of Aggtelek N. P. (N. Hungary) between 1997 and 2002]. *ANP Füzetek* 2, 77–96. (In Hungarian).

Borgo, A., Genero, F. and Favalli, M. (2001). Censimento e preferenze ambientali del re di quaglie *Crex crex* nel Parco Naturale Prealpi Giulie. *Avocetta* 25, 181.

Boswall, J. (1998). Answering the calls of nature: Human mimicry of the avian voice. *Transactions of the Leicester Literary and Philosophical Society* 92, 10–11.

Boyd, J. M. and Boyd, I. L. (1990). *The Hebrides: A natural history*. (The New Naturalist Series) especially pp. 131–134. London: Collins.

Božič, L. (2005c). Raziskava habitata kosca *Crex crex* v Sloveniji. LIFE Project Report LIFE03NAT/SLO/000077. Ljubljana. (In Slovenian). https://www.ptice.si/wp-content/uploads/2014/04/200512_bozic_kmecl_studija_habita-ta_kosca_na_ljubljanskem_barju.pdf

Božič, L. (2005d). Populacija kosca *Crex crex* na Ljubljanskem barju upada zaradi zgodnje košnje in uničevanja ekstenzivnih travnikov. *Acrocephalus* 26 (124), 255–272.

Braaksma, S. and van der Straaten, J. (1973). Wachtelkönig, Wiesenralle [Corncrake] In: Glutz von Blotzheim, U. N., Bauer, K. and Bezzel, E. (eds.), *Handbuch der Vogel Mitteleuropas 5*, pp. 444–468. Frankfurt: Akademische Verlagsgesellschaft.

Brambilla, M. and Rubolini, D. (2009). Intra-seasonal changes in distribution and habitat associations of a multi-brooded bird species: implications for conservation planning. *Animal Conservation* 12, 71–77.

British Trust for Ornithology (2020). Corncrake *Crex crex*. https://app.bto.org/birdfacts/results/bob4210.htm

Broyer, J. (1985). *Le râle de genêt Crex crex en France*. Union Nationale des Associations Ornithologique. Centre Ornithologique Rhône-Alpes.

Broyer, J. (1987a). Répartition du râle de genêts *Crex crex* (L.) en France. *Alauda* 55, 10–29.

Broyer, J. (1987b). L'habitat du Râle de genêts *Crex crex* en France. [The habitat of the Corncrake *Crex crex* in France]. *Alauda* 55, 161–186. (In French with English summary).

Broyer, J. (1991). The situation of the Corncrake in France. *Vogelwelt* 112 (1–2), 71–77. (In German with English and French summary).

Broyer, J. (1994). La régression du râle de genêts *Crex crex* en France et la gestation des milieux prairiaux. *Alauda*, 62, 1–7.

Broyer, J. (1995). Définition d'un calendrier des fenaisons tolérable pour la reproduction du râle de genêts en France. *Alauda* 63, 209–212.

Broyer, J. (1996). Les 'fenaisons centrifuges' une méthode pour réduire la mortalité des jeunes râles de genêts *Crex crex* et cailles des blés Coturnix coturnix. *Revue d'Ecologie* 51 (3), 269–276. ['Outward mowing', as a way of reducing losses of young corncrakes *Crex crex* and quails Coturnix coturnix.]

Broyer, J. (2002). Contribution a une méthodologie pour le suivi des population de Râle des genêts *Crex crex* en période de nidification. [Contribution to the development of a methodology to monitor Corncrake *Crex crex* population during the breeding period]. *Alauda* 70 (1), 195–202.

Broyer, J. and Rocamora, G. (1994). Enquête nationale Râle des genêts 1991–1992. Principaux résultats. *Ornithos* 1, 55–56.

Broyer, J., Rocamora, G., Lang, B. and Metais, M. (1994). *Enquête nationale Râle des genêts 1991–1992*. Synthese Nationale. LPO, Paris.

Burfield, I. and van Bommel, F. (eds.) (2004). *Birds in Europe: Population Estimates, Trends and Conservation Status*. Cambridge: BirdLife International.

Bürger, P. and Pykal, J. (2000). Report on activities of the Corncrake Research Group in the period 1998–1999. *Zpravy CSO* 50, 13–16. (In Czech).

Bürger, P., Pykal, J. and Hora, J. (1995). Dosavadní výsledky výzkumu chřástala polního (*Crex crex*) na Šumavě (1993–1994). [Current results of research on the Corncrake (*Crex crex*) in the Sumava Mountains (1993–1994)]. In: Významná ptačí území v České republice, Sborník referátů, Kostelec nad Černými lesy, pp. 16–20.

Butjev, V. T., Shitikov, D. A., Pavlenkov, V. I. and RED'Kin, Y. A. (2000a). Materials on the Corncrake numbers and distribution in Arkhangelsk region. In: Mischenko, A. L. (ed.). *Corncrake in European Russia, Collection of Scientific Papers, Series Threatened Birds, Vol. 2*, pp. 44–53. Moscow: RBCU. (In Russian).

Butjev, V. T., Shitikov, D. A., Pavlenkov, V. I. and RED'Kin, Y. A. (2000b). Corncrake numbers and distribution in Vologda region. In: Mischenko, A. L. (ed.). *Corncrake in European Russia, Collection of Scientific Papers, Series Threatened Birds, Vol. 2*, pp. 54–64. Moscow: RBCU. (In Russian).

Cadbury, C. J. (1983). Status of the corncrake (*Crex crex*) and corn bunting (*Miliaria calandra*) in the Inner Hebrides. In: Boyd, J. M. and Bowes, D. R. (eds.), *The Natural Environment of the Inner Hebrides. Proceedings of the Royal Society of Edinburgh* 83B, 468–469.

Cadbury, C. J. and O'Meara, M. (1985). The decline of the Corncrake (*Crex crex*) in Europe. *Acta Congr. Int. Orn.* 18, 754–756.

Cadbury, J. (1978). Corncrake Enquiry 1978. *BTO News* No. 92, 1–2.

Casey, C. (1994). (1997). Corncrake Fieldwork in the Shannon Callows 1994. Unpublished report. Dublin: Birdwatch Ireland.

Cempulik, P. (1991). Bestandsentwicklung, Schutzstatus und aktuelle Untersuchungen am Wachtelkönig in Polen. [Population trends, status and conservation of the Corncrake in Poland]. *Vogelwelt* 112 (1–2), 40–45. (In German with English summary).

Chacon, G., Fernandez, J. and Martinez, F. (1987). Descubrimiento de una población nidificante de guión de codornices (*Crex crex*, Linn.) En España. *Alytes* 3, 180–182. (In Spanish).

Christensen, T. and Asbirk, S. (2000). Action plan for the conservation of endangered species of birds: Corncrake *Crex crex*. Copenhagen: Ministry of Environment and Energy, National Forest and Nature Agency.

Clancey, P. A. (1975). Miscellaneous taxonomic notes on African birds XLI. On the probable polytypic status of *Crex crex (Linnaeus)*. *Durban Museum Novitates* 10, 189–191.

Cochard, G., Latraube, F. and Yésou, P. (2011). Evaluation des mesures agri-environnementales sur la faune sauvage. Le cas du râle des genêts dans l'estuaire de la Loire. *Faune Sauvage* 292, 30–36.

Cope, E. D. (1892). A contribution to the vertebrate Paleontology of Texas. *Proceedings of the American Philosophical Society* 30 (137), 123–131.

Copland, A. and Donaghy, A. (2001). A strategy for Corncrake Conservation in Ireland 2001–2010. Unpublished report. Dublin: Bird Watch Ireland.

De Juana, E. (1988). Noticiario Ornitologico. *Ardeola* 35, 297–316.

Deane, C. D. and Sinton, J. A. (1948). Corncrake in exposed positions. *Irish Naturalists' Journal* 9 (8), 216–217. https://www.jstor.org/stable/25533684

Deceuninck, B. (2010). Coordination et mise en oeuvre du plan de restauration du Râle des genêts: enquête nationale de dénombrements des nicheurs. Paris: LPO.

Deceuninck, B. and Broyer, J. (2000). Statut du Râle des genêts en France. Synthèse de l'enquête nationale 1998. [Corncrake *Crex crex* in France, summary of the 1998 national survey]. *Ornithos* 7 (2), 62–69.

Deceuninck, B., Fantin, P., Jolivet, C., Loir, O., HERMANT, D, Morel, F. and Salamolard, M. (1997). Chronologie de la reproduction du râle de genêts *Crex crex* en France. Particularités régionales et évaluation des measures de conservation. [Chronology of the reproduction of Corncrake, *Crex crex* in France - regional particularies and evaluation of conservation]. *Alauda* 65 (1), 91–104.

Delov, V. (1995). Investigations on the Corncrake *Crex crex* L. In the region of Sofia. Annuaire Université Sofia 'St Kliment Ohridski' 88 (4), 25–31.

Dernegi, D. (2006). Baseline survey of breeding Corncrakes at Posof, North-east Turkey, 2006. Final Project Report.

Derwin, J. (1997). Corncrake fieldwork in North Donegal in 1997. Unpublished report. Dublin: Birdwatch Ireland.

Dobrinov, A. V. (2000). About numbers of the Corncrake in western part of city Azov, Rostov region. In: Mischenko, A. L. (ed.). *Corncrake in European Russia, Collection of Scientific Papers, Series Threatened Birds, Vol. 2*, pp. 145–146. Moscow: RBCU. (In Russian).

Dombrowski, A., Hordowski, J., KASPRZYKOWSKI, Z, Golawski, A., Rzepala, M. and Chmielewski, S. (1998). O zmianach liczebności derkacza *Crex crex* we wschodniej Polsce. [Changes in the numbers of corncrake *Crex crex* in eastern Poland]. *Kulon* 3 (2), 205–211.

Donaghy, A. (2007b). Corncrakes: a lot done, more to do. *Wings* 46, 26–27.

Dudás, M., Endes, M., Horváth, R., Molnár, A., Nagy, S., Petrovics, Z. and Szegedi, Z. S. (2003). Haris (*Crex crex*). In: Haraszthy, L. (ed.), *Veszélyeztetett madarak fajvédelmi tervei*, pp. 90–95. Budapest: Birdlife Hungary.

Dumbović, M. V. and Tutiš, V. (2013). Kosac *Crex crex*. In: Tutiš, V., Kralj, J., Radović, D., Ćiković, D. and Barišić, S. (eds.), Crvena knjiga ptica Hrvatske. Ministarstvo zaštite okoliša i prirode, Državni zavod za zaštitu prirode, Zagreb, pp. 193–195.

Editor (1884). An English Corn-Crake in Rhode Island. *Random Notes* 1 (6) p 3.

Enemar, A. (1957). Grasshopper Warbler (*Locustella naevia*) and Corn-Crake (*Crex crex*) in Sweden in 1957. *Vår fågelvärld* 16, 269–287.

Etchécopar, R. D. and Hüe, F. (1967). *The Birds of North Africa*. Edinburgh: Oliver and Boyd.

Feare, C. J. (1975). Further migrant birds in the Seychelles. *Bulletin of the British Ornithologists Club* 95, 48–50.

Flach, E. (2004). Veterinary report for the RSPB/EN corncrake reintroduction project April 2003 to March 2004. In: *Health Surveillance for the Species Recovery Programme*, p. 3. Peterborough: Zoological Society of London and English Nature.

Flade, M. (1991b). Methods for catching Corncrakes. *Vogelwelt* 112 (1–2), 96–102. (In German with English summary).

Flint, V. E. (2000a). Corncrake in the Izmailovsky Park (Moscow). In: Mischenko, A. L. (ed.). *Corncrake in European Russia, Collection of Scientific Papers, Series Threatened Birds, Vol. 2*, pp. 24–28. Moscow: RBCU. (In Russian).

Flint, V. E. (2000b). Results of the Corncrake surveys at clear-cuts in the Tver' region. In: Mischenko, A. L. (ed.). *Corncrake in European Russia, Collection of Scientific Papers, Series Threatened Birds, Vol. 2*, pp. 82–88. Moscow: RBCU. (In Russian).

Florit, F. and Rassati, G. (2005). Il Re di quaglie *Crex crex* in Friuli-Venezia Giulia: 5 anni di monitoraggio (2000–2004). *Avocetta* 29 p 110.

Fokin, S. Y. (2000). Corncrake in the floodplain of Kluaz'ma River. In: Mischenko, A. L. (ed.). *Corncrake in European Russia, Collection of Scientific Papers, Series Threatened Birds, Vol. 2*, pp. 105–110. Moscow: RBCU. (In Russian).

Fox, J. (1993). Corncrake ringing near Dublin 1939–1959. *Irish Birds* 5, 61–66.

Frühauf, J. (2000). Schutz des Wachtelkönigs (*Crex crex*) im Nationalpark Donau-Auen. Wissenschaftliche Reihe Nationalpark Donau-Auen, H. 14/2006.

Frühauf, J. and Zechner, L. (1998). Perspektiven für den Erhalt des Wachtelkönigs (*Crex crex*) im Mittleren Ennstal.- birdlife Österreich, im Auftrag der 'Vogelwarte' (LIFE- Projekt 'Sicherung von Feuchtgebieten und bedrohten Arten im Mittleren Ennstal'), 109.

Fuller, R. J. (1982). *Bird Habitats in Britain*. Calton: Poyser.

Geister, I. (1985). Kosec *Crex crex*. *Acrocephalus* 6 p 48.

Gerritsen, G., Koffijberg, K. and Voskamp, P. (2001). Bescherming van Kwartelkoningen in 2001. Vogelbescherming Nederland/Ministerie van Landbouw, Natuurbeheer en Visserij, Zeist.

Gerritsen, G., Koffijberg, K. and Voskamp, P. (2004). Beschermingsplan Kwartelkoning. Ministerie van LVN/ Directie IFA/ Bedrijfsuitgeverij.

Gibbons, D. W., Avery, M. I., Baillie, S. R., Gregory, R. D., Kirby, J., Porter, R. F., Tucker, G. M. and Williams, G. (1996). Bird species of conservation concern in the United Kingdom, Channel Islands and Isle of Man: revising the Red Data List. *RSPB Conservation Review* 10, 7–18.

Gibbons, D. W., Reid, J. B. and Chapman, R. A. (eds.) (1993). *The New Atlas of Breeding Birds in Britain and Ireland: 1988–1991*. London: Poyser.

Gilbert, G. (2002). The status and habitat of Spotted Crakes *Porzana porzana* in Britain in 1999. *Bird Study* 49, 79–86.

Goodwin, W. (2001). Corncrakes in the Bulawayo area. *Honeyguide* 47, 95.

Gorban, I. M. (1999). Are Corncrakes *Crex crex* numbers increasing in Ukraine? *Vogelwelt* 120 (Suppl.), 329–332.

Gordon, T. (1998). Corncrake fieldwork in Mayo and West Connaught 1998. Unpublished report. Dublin: Birdwatch Ireland.

Grabovsky, V. I. (1983). Akusticheskaya signalizatsiya i kommunikatsiya w lokalnom poselenii korostelev (*Crex crex*). *Zoologicheskii Zhurnal* 62 (2), 314–317.

Green, R. E. (1995b). Diagnosing causes of bird population declines. *Ibis* (Suppl.) 137 pps47–S55.

Green, R. E. (2013). Tracking Scotland's Corncrakes. *Birdwatch*, April, 26–28.

Green, R. E. (2020). Corn Crake conservation. *British Birds* 113 (11), 671–685.

Gregori, J. (1993). Kosec *Crex crex*. [Corncrake – male night singing…] *Acrocephalus* 14, 125–126.

Grishanov, G. V. (2000). Corncrake in Kaliningrad region: distribution by habitats and numbers dynamics. In: Mischenko, A. L. (ed.). *Corncrake in European Russia, Collection of Scientific Papers, Series Threatened Birds, Vol. 2*, pp. 72–77. Moscow: RBCU. (In Russian).

Grobelnik, V. (2000). Oglasănje, ocena številčnosti in izbira mikrohabitata koscev (*Crex crex*, L. 1758) na dveh lokacijah Ljubljanskega barja. Graduation thesis, University of Ljubljana.

Hagemeijer, W. J. M. and Blair, M. J. (eds.) (1997). *The EBCC Atlas of European Breeding Birds, Their Distribution and Abundance*. London: Poyser.

Hagerup, A. T. (1891). Corn Crake. (*Crex crex*) An accidental visitor to South Greenland. In: The birds of Greenland, Chamberlain, M. (ed.), (Translated from Dutch by Arngrimson, F. B.) Boston: Little, Brown and Co.

Hashmi, D. (1991). Bestand und Verbreitung des Wachtelkönigs in der Bundesrepublik Deutschland vor 1990. [Population and distribution of the Corncrake in the Federal Republic of Germany before 1990]. *Vogelwelt* 112, 66–71. (In German with English summary).

Heer, L., Maumary, L., Laesser, J. and Muller, W. (2000). Artenschutzprogramm Wachtelkönig in der Schweiz. [A species action plan for the Corncrake in Switzerland: Status, ecology, state of Corncrake conservation and conservation measures]. Zürich: Schweizer Vogelschutz SVS/Birdlife Switzerland.

Helmecke, A. (2000). Raum- und Habitatnutzung des Wachtelkönigs (*Crex crex* L.) Im Unteren Odertal. MSc thesis, Humboldt-University Berlin.

Helmecke, A., Fischer, S. and Sadlik, J. (2005). Behaviour of a Corncrake (*Crex crex*) female while breeding and rearing young in the Lower Oder Valley. *Otis* 13, 57–62.

Henderson, A. C. B. (1983). Numbers of Corncrakes and habitat use in the Uists, Outer Hebrides, 1983. Unpublished report to RSPB. Sandy

Hoffmann, M. (1997). Rufplatzwahl des Wachtelkönigs *Crex crex* und Verbleib von Individuen nach Verlust des Bruthabitats in Nordostpolen. [Choice of calling place by Corncrakes *Crex crex* and site fidelity of individuals after the loss of their breeding habitat in North-East Poland]. MSc thesis, University of Freiburg, Freiburg. p. 84 (In German).

Horváth, R. (1998). Haris (*Crex crex*). [Corncrake]. In: Haraszthy, L. (ed.), Magyarország madarai. [Birds of Hungary]. Budapest: Mezögazda Kiadó. (In Hungarian).

Hottola, P. (1996). Ruisrääkän biotooppivaatimukset ja perinnemaisemien hoito. [Conservation of Corncrake and management of traditional rural landscapes. Pohjois-Karjalan Ympäristökeskuksen monisteita nro 9. (In Finnish).

Howell, K. M. (1973). A record of the corncrake *Crex crex* from Dar-es-Salaam. *East African Natural History Society Bulletin*, July, 95–96.

Howell, K. M. (1977). Further records of the corncrake *Crex crex* from Dar-es-Salaam. *East African Natural History Society Bulletin*, March/April, 38.

Hoyo, J. Del, Elliott, A. and Sargatal, J. (eds.) (1992). *Handbook of the Birds of the World*. Volume 3. Barcelona: Linx Edicions.

Hudson, J. R. (1973). Corncrake at Kabete. *East African Natural History Society Bulletin*, August, p 112

Irish National Parks and Wildlife Service (2020). The Corncrake Conservation Project. Https://www.npws.ie/agri-ecology-projects/corncrake-conservation-project

Isaksen, K., Eie, K., Folvik, A. and Øien, I. J. (2004). Kartlegging og overvåking av Åkerrikse. Norsk Ornitologisk Forening. Trondheim.

Iviš, D. (2008/09). Gniježdenje kosca (*Crex crex*) na području Gojevića (opština Fojnica). Bilten Mreže posmatrača ptica u Bosni i Hercegovini 4/5 p 121.

Jarukaite, E. (1997). Results of the 'Corncrake – Bird of the year' campaign. *Ciconia* 5, 25–29. (In Lithuanian).

Jonker, M. (1996). De Kwartelkoning in het Oldambt in 1995. *De Grauwe Gors* 24 (1), 46. (In Dutch).

Just, P. (2005). Entwicklung eines statistischen Habitateignungsmodfells zur räumlichen Vorhersage der Vorkommenswahrscheinlichkeit des Wachtelkönigs (*Crex crex* L.) Im Nationalpark Unteres Odertal; Ein landschaftsökologischer Beitrag zum Schutz einer gefährdeten Vogelart. Dissertation zur Erlangung des Doktortitels, angenommen von: Georg-August-Universität Göttingen, Mathematisch-naturwissenschaftliche Fakultäten, 2006–012–25.

Kalotás, Z. S. (2014). Haris (*Crex crex Linnaeus, 1758*). In: Haraszty, L. (ed.), *Natura 2000 fajok és élőhelyek Magyarországon*. Pro Vértes Közalapítvány, Csákvár, pp. 577–580.

Karunaratne, P. B. (1972). The Corncrake or Landrail – *Crex crex* (Linnaeus) – *Ceylon Bird Club News*, Notes for September 197, pp. 41–42.

Keišs, O. (2006). Impact of changes in agriculture on the Corncrake *Crex crex* (L.) Population in Latvia: population dynamics, habitat selection and population structure. PhD dissertation. University of Latvia. (In Latvian with English summary).

Koch, J. C. (1932). Kwartelkoningen en maaimachines. *De Levende Natuur* 36, 323–325. Http://natuurtijdschriften.nl/download?Type=document&docid=490975 (In Dutch).

Koffijberg, K. (1993). Verdwijnt de Kwartelkoning uit Oost-Groningen? *Limosa* 66 p 31.

Koffijberg, K. (1999b). Veel Kwartelkoningen *Crex crex* in Groningen in 1998. *De Grauwe Gors* 27 (3), 188–193.

Koffijberg, K. (2007). Bescherming van Kwartelkoningen in hooiland. *De Levende Natuur* 108, 193–98.

Koffijberg, K. and Boer, P. DE (2004). Bescherming van Kwartelkoningen in het Oldambt (Groningen) in 2003. Groningen: Sovon. (In Dutch). Https://www.sovon.nl/sites/default/files/doc/Bescherming%20Kwartelkoningen%20in%20Oldambt%20Groningen%202003_rap2004_05.pdf

Koffijberg, K. and Schoppers, J. (2009). De Kwartelkoning in Nederland in 2008 en evaluatie van het Beschermingsplan Kwartelkoning. Sovon-informatierapport 2009/02. Sovon Vogelonderzoek Nederland, Beek-Ubbergen.

Koffijberg, K., Prak, B. J. and Jonker, M. (1998). De Kwartelkoning in het Oldambt in 1996 en 1997. *De Grauwe Gors* 26 (2), 40–45.

Koffijberg, K., van Kleunen, A., Majoor, F. and Kurstjens, G. (2007). Evaluatie van effectiviteit van beschermingsmaatregelen voor Kwartelkoningen in Nederland. SOVON-onderzoeksrapport 2007/09. SOVON Vogelonderzoek Nederland, Beek-Ubbergen.

Kotrošan, D., Drocić, N., Trbojević, S., Šimić, E. and Dervović, I. (2012). Program IBA - Međunarodno značajna područja za ptice u Bosni i Hercegovini. Ornitološko društvo 'Naše ptice', unpubl report 'Evaluacija IBA područja u FBIH': Sarajevo.

Lang, B. (1994). Pour un suivi des populations nicheuses de Râles des genêts (*Crex crex*). *Le Cormoran* 8 (40), 275–282.

Larsson, K. (1968). Förekommen av vaktel och kornknarr i Närke. *Var Fagelwärld* 27, 122–135. (In Swedish).

Lastukhi, A. A. (2000). Corncrake in Chuvash Republic. In: Mischenko, A. L. (ed.). *Corncrake in European Russia, Collection of Scientific Papers, Series Threatened Birds*, Vol. 2, pp. 138–141. Moscow: RBCU. (In Russian).

Lawson, W. J. (1961). Corn Crake. *Albatross* 72, 2–3.

Lawton, J. H. (1966). Corncrake pie and prediction in ecology. *Oikos* 76 (1), 3–4. Https://www.jstor.org/stable/3545742

Libois, R. (1995). Sur une halte migratoire du râle des genêts (*Crex crex*) dans le sud du Bénin (Afrique de l'Ouest). *Aves* 32, 67–69.

Libois, R. (1996). Corrigendum: Sur une halte migratoire du râle des genêts (*Crex crex*) dans le sud du Bénin (Afrique de l'Ouest). *Aves* 33 p 63.

Lie-Pettersen, O. J. (1921). Åkerriksen (*Crex crex*). Norsk Ornithol. *Tidsskr.* 1, 96–100.

Liedekerke, R. De (1981). Observations d'un Râle de genêts (*Crex crex*) dans le Condroz. Détails et commentaires. *Aves* 18, 170–172.

Lönnberg, E. (1940). Kornknarrens nuvarande förekomst i Sverige. Kgl. Svenska Vetenskapsakademiens Skrifter i Naturskyddsärenden 37, 1–43.

Ma Ming and Wang Qishan (2000). Rediscovery of Corncrake *Crex crex* in Xinjiang, China. *Zoological Research* 21 (5), 348. (In Chinese).

Mammen, U., Bahner, T., Bellebaum, J., Eikhorst, W., Fischer, S., Geiersberger, I., Helmecke, A., Hoffmann, J., Kempf, G., Kühnast, O., Pfützke, S. and Schoppenhorst, A. (2005). Grundlagen und Maßnahmen für die Erhaltung des Wachtelkönigs und anderer Wiesenvögel in Feuchtgrünlandgebieten. Bfn-Skripten, 141.

Marais, E. and Smith, N. (2004). A plethora of corncrakes. *Bird Numbers* 13, 30–31.

Matauschek, J. M. (2005). The impact of endangered species law on the real estate development process explored with cost-benefit analysis: The case of the corncrake in Hamburg/Germany. German Working Papers in Law and Economics. 2005 (Paper 7) pp. 1–30.

Maumary, L. (1996). La protection du Râle de genêts en Suisse: Rapport du projet pilote 1996. Zürich: Schweizer Vogelschutz SVS/Birdlife Switzerland.

Maurov, I. A. (2000). Corncrake's numbers and features of distribution in the vicinity of Ivanovo City. In: Mischenko, A. L. (ed.). *Corncrake in European Russia, Collection of Scientific Papers, Series Threatened Birds, Vol. 2*, pp. 122–123. Moscow: RBCU. (In Russian).

Mayes, E. and Stowe, T. J. (1989). The status and distribution of the Corncrake in Ireland in 1988. *Irish Birds* 4, 1–12.

Mayr, E. (1949). A second Australian record of the Corncrake. *The Emu* 48, 243–244.

Mellon, C. (1986). The status and distribution of corncrakes *Crex crex* in County Fermanagh in 1986. Unpublished report. Belfast: RSPB.

Mezhnev, A. P. and Zverev, P. A. (2000). Corncrake in Ryazan' region. In: Mischenko, A. L. (ed.). *Corncrake in European Russia, Collection of Scientific Papers, Series Threatened Birds, Vol. 2*, pp. 98–105. Moscow: RBCU. (In Russian).

Mischenko, A. L. (1996). Corncrake survey of Central European Russia. Final report on phase II. Manuscript.

Mischenko, A. L. (2000). Background of the Corncrake counts in European Russia. In: Mischenko, A. L. (ed.). *Corncrake in European Russia, Collection of Scientific Papers, Series Threatened Birds, Vol. 2*, pp. 9–12. Moscow: RBCU. (In Russian).

Mischenko, A. L. (2003). Continuation of Corncrake Monitoring in European Russia. Russian Bird Conservation Union, Moscow.

Mischenko, A. L. and Butjev, V. T. (2000). Weather features in 1995 and 1996 and their influence to the Corncrake breeding. In: Mischenko, A. L. (ed.). *Corncrake in European Russia, Collection of Scientific Papers, Series Threatened Birds, Vol. 2*, pp. 41–44. Moscow: RBCU. (In Russian).

Mischenko, A. L. and Sukhanova, O. V. (1999b). Corncrake *Crex crex* in European Russia: Methods and results of a large-scale census. *Vogelwelt* 120 (Suppl.), 323–327.

Mischenko, A. L. and Sukhanova, O. V. (2000a). Results of the two-year project 'Corncrake survey in European Russia'. In: Mischenko, A. L. (ed.). *Corncrake in European Russia, Collection of Scientific Papers, Series Threatened Birds, Vol. 2*, pp. 147–169. Moscow: RBCU. (In Russian with English summary).

Mischenko, A. L. and Sukhanova, O. V. (2000b). Corncrake in Novgorod and Pskov regions. In: Mischenko, A. L. (ed.). *Corncrake in European Russia, Collection of Scientific Papers, Series Threatened Birds, Vol. 2*, pp. 64–72. Moscow: RBCU. (In Russian).

Mischenko, A. L. and Sukhanova, O. V. (2006). Corncrake monitoring in European Russia. *Bird Census News* 19, 63–68.

Mischenko, A. L., Sukhanova, O. V., Butjev, V. T. and Mezhnev, A. P. (2000). Corncrake survey and monitoring in the Central European Russia 1994. In: Mischenko, A. L. (ed.). *Corncrake in European Russia, Collection of Scientific Papers, Series Threatened Birds, Vol. 2*, pp. 13–24. Moscow: RBCU. (In Russian).

MME Birdlife Hungary (2016). Magyarorszag madarai: Haris. [Birds of Hungary: Corncrake]. http://www.mme.hu/magyarorszagmadarai/madaradatbazis-crecre (In Hungarian).

Mosalov, A. A., Ganitsky, I. V. and Efremov, A. A. (2000). Distribution and numbers of the Corncrake in Lipetsk, Orel and Kursk regions. In: Mischenko, A. L. (ed.). *Corncrake in European Russia, Collection of Scientific Papers, Series Threatened Birds, Vol. 2*, pp. 129–135. Moscow: RBCU. (In Russian).

Müller, A. and Illner, H. (2001). Erfassung des Wachtelkönigs in Nordrhein-Westfalen 1998–2000. Bestand und langfristige Bestandsentwicklung einer vom Aussterben bedrohten Brutvogelart. LÖBF-Mitteilungen 2/01, 36–51.

Myrberget, S. (1963). Åkerriksa i Norge. [The Corncrake (*Crex crex*) in Norway]. *Sterna* 5, 289–305.

Nash, J. K. (1929). The scarcity of the Corn-crake in the Lothians. *Scottish Naturalist* 1929, 5–7.

National Parks and Wildlife Service (NPWS) (2014). *A Framework for Corncrake Conservation to 2022*. Dublin: Department of Arts, Heritage and the Gaeltacht.

Neill, P. (1806). *Tour through Some of the Islands of Orkney and Shetland 1806*. Edinburgh: Constable.

Németh, T. M. (2012a). A haris (*Crex crex* Linnaeus, 1758) habitatválasztása az Őrségi Nemzeti Park területen. MSc thesis, University of Western Hungary, Sopron.

Németh, T. M. (2012b). A haris (*Crex crex*) állományvizsgálata az Őrségben. *Magyar Apróvad Közlemények* 11, 49–58.

Newbery, P. (2006). The Corncrake reintroduction project in the UK. *Reintroduction News* 43–44.

Niehuis, M. and Hoffmann, D. (1999). Ungewöhnlich starkes Auftreten des Wachtelkönigs (*Crex crex*) in der Pfalz 1998. *Fauna Flora Rheinland-Pfalz* 9, 351–353.

Nikolaev, V. I. (2000). Corncrake on the border of Tver' and Moscow regions. In: Mischenko, A. L. (ed.). *Corncrake in European Russia, Collection of Scientific Papers, Series Threatened Birds, Vol. 2*, pp. 78–82. Moscow: RBCU. (In Russian).

Noël, F. (2003). The decline of Corncrake is worsening in France. *Ornithos* 10, 136.

Noël, F., Deceuninck, B., Mourgaud, G. and Broyer, J. (2004). Plan national de restauration du Râle des genêts. Rochefort: Ligue pour la Protection des Oiseaux (LPO).

O'Connor, R. J. and Shrubb, M. J. (1986). *Farming and Birds*. Cambridge: Cambridge University Press.

O'Meara, M. (1979). Distribution and numbers of Corncrakes in Ireland in 1978. *Irish Birds* 1, 381–405.

O'Meara, M. (1986). Corncrake declines in seven areas, 1978–1985. *Irish Birds* 3, 237–244.

Ogilvie-Grant, W. R. (1913). Carolina Crake in the Outer Hebrides. *British Birds* 7, 202–203.

Øien, I. J. and Folvik, A. (1995). Åkerriksa - røsten som forstummer. *Vår fugelfauna* 18 (2), 105–111.

Olech, B., Osiejuk, T. S. and Ratynska, K. (2002). Individual and contextual properties of Corncrake *Crex crex* territorial call. In: Abstracts 23rd International Ornithological Congress, Beijing, China, 11–17 August 2002, pp. 238–239.

Olech, B., Osiejuk, T. S. and Ratynska, K. (2002). Individual and contextual properties of Corncrake *Crex crex* territorial calls. Abstracts 23rd International Ornithological Congress. Beijing, China, 11–17 August 2002, pp. 238–239.

Olson, S. L. and Wingate, D. B. (2000). Two new species of flightless rails (Aves: Rallidae) from the Middle Pleistocene 'crane fauna' of Bermuda. *Proceedings of the Biological Society of Washington* 113, 356–368.

Osiejuk, T. S., Olech, B. and Ratyńska, K. (2003). Effect of season time, plasma testosterone level and body size on call rhythm of corncrake *Crex crex*. In: Abstract 4th Conference of the European Ornithologists' Union, Chemnitz, Germany, 16–21 August 2003. *Vogelwelt* 42, 123–124.

Owsiński, A. (2002). Acoustic communication and territorial behaviour of Corncrake *Crex crex*. Department of Ecology, Warsaw University. Unpublished MSc thesis. (In Polish).

Pedrini, P., Rizzolli, F., Cavallaro, V., Marchesi, L. and Odasso, M. (2002). Status e distribuzione del Re di quaglie (*Crex crex*) in provincia di Trento (Alpi centro-orientali, Italia). *Studi Trentini di Scienze Naturali, Acta Biologica* 78 (2000), 55–60.

Peet, N. B. and Gallo-Orsi, U. (2000). *Action Plan for the Corncrake*. Cambridge: BirdLife International.

Pettersson, J. (1992). Kornknarren – en av fågelvärldens doldisar. *Calidris* 21, 55–58.

Pettersson, J. (1994). Kornknarren på Öland 1994. *Calidris* 23, 123–127.

Pettersson, J. (1995). Kornknarren - riksinventeringsart 1994. *Vår fågelvärld* 54 (2), 23–26.

Pettersson, T. (2007). *Åtgärdsprogram för kornknarr 2007–2010.* Stockholm: Naturvårdsverket.

Pinechot, J. (2017). Suivi bioacoustique du Râle des genêts en MVO-ANNEE 2016 Rapport 12/09/2017 - B.E.C.

Potapov, R. L. and Flint, V. E. (eds.) (1989). Handbuch der Vögel der Sowjetunion. Volume 4: Galliformes, Gruiformes. Wittenberg Lutherstadt: A. Ziemsen Verlag.

Pritchard, D. E., Housden, S. D., Mudge, G. P., Galbraith, C. A. and Pienkowski, M. W. (eds.) (1992). *Important Birds Areas in the United Kingdom including the Channel Islands and the Isle of Man.* Sandy: RSPB/JNCC.

Prünte, W. and Raus, T. (1970). Uber das Vorkommen des Wachtelkönigs *Crex crex* in Mittelwestfalen. *Anthus* 7, 1–6.

Rassati, G. (2001). Il Re di quaglie *Crex crex* durante l'anno 2000 in due aree campione in Carnia (Alpi Orientali, Friuli-Venezia Giulia). [The Corncrake *Crex crex* during the year 2000 in two sample areas in Carnia (Eastern Alps, Friuli-Venezia Giulia)]. *Avocetta* 25 p 239.

Rassati, G. (2004). Evoluzione faunistica nelle aree rurali abbandonate. La presenza del Re di quaglie (*Crex crex*) e della Lepre comune (*Lepus europaeus*). [Wildlife evolution in abandoned rural areas. The presence of the Corncrake (*Crex crex*) and the Brown hare (Lepus europaeus)]. *Agribusiness Paesaggio & Ambiente* 7, 41–48.

Rassati, G. (2006). The development of industrial estates as a threat to Corncrake *Crex crex* in the mountain areas of Friuli (Eastern Alps, North-eastern Italy). *Gli Uccelli d'Italia* 31, 109–111.

Rassati, G. (2009). The spring and summer censuses of Corncrake *Crex crex* in three sample areas of Carnia (Eastern Alps, Friuli-Venezia Giulia, North-eastern Italy) (Years 2000–2005). *Gli Uccelli d'Italia* 34, 50–57.

Rassati, G. and Rodaro, P. (2003). Aspetti stazionali caratteristiche vegetazionali e gestionali di alcuni siti riproduttivi del Re de quaglie *Crex crex* in Carnia (Alpi Orientali, Friuli-Venezia Giulia). *Avocetta* 27, 175.

Rassati, G. and Rodaro, P. (2007). Habitat, vegetation and land management of Corncrake *Crex crex* breeding sites in Carnia (Friuli-Venezia Giulia, NE Italy). *Acrocephalus* 28 (133), 61–68. http://www.dlib.si/stream/ URN:NBN:SI:DOC-PFW55E7N/0cb94435–50e1–4c20-ac06-cd1ced597bdb/PDF

Ravkin, Y. S. (1997). Number and distribution of Corncrake in West Siberian Plain. *Siberian Ecology Journal* 6, 631–634.

Read, R. H. (1916). Land-rail on St Kilda. *British Birds* 9, 255.

Red'kin, Y. A. (2000). Numbers and distribution of the Corncrake in Ivanovo region (under the counts of 1995–1996). In: Mischenko, A. L. (ed.). *Corncrake in European Russia, Collection of Scientific Papers, Series Threatened Birds*, Vol. 2, pp. 113–121. Moscow: RBCU. (In Russian).

Reichholf, J. H. (1991). Der Wachtelkönig *Crex crex*: eine kurze biologische Charakterisierung. [The Corncrake *Crex crex*: A short biological sketch]. *Vogelwelt* 112, 6–9.

Ripley, S. D. (1977). *Rails of the World: A Monograph of the Family Rallidae*. Boston, MA: David R. Godine Publishers.

Ripley, S. D. and Beehler, B. M. (1985). Rails of the world a compilation of new information, 1975–1983 (Aves: Rallidae). *Smithsonian Contributions to Zoology*. 417, 1–28.

Roalkvam, R. (1984). Åkerrikse *Crex crex* i Rogaland og Norge. *Vår fuglefauna* 7, 87–90.

RSPB (1994–97). *Locations of Corncrakes in the Inner Hebrides*. (Produced annually). Glasgow: RSPB.

RSPB (1995). *Habitat Management for Corncrakes*. RSPB: Edinburgh.

Ryelandt, P. (1990). Statut du Râle de genêts (*Crex crex*) en Fagne et Famenne. *Aves* 27, 244–261.

Ryelandt, P. (2010). Râle des genêts *Crex crex*. In: Jacob, J.-P., Dehem, C., Brunel, A., Dambiermont, J. -L., Fasol, M., Kinet, T., van der Elst, D. and Paquet, J.-Y. (eds.), *Atlas des oiseaux nicheurs de Wallonie 2001–2007*, pp. 198–199.

Sadlik, J. (2005). Untersuchungen am Wachtelkönig (*Crex crex*) im Nationalpark Unteres Odertal. *Otis* 13, 49–56.

Salamolard, M., Egreteau, C., Rocamora, G. and Blanchon, J. (1995). Programme LIFE- Râle des Genêts. Bilan etudes et conservation 1994. LPO report to BirdLife International, Rochefort: LPO.

Salathe, T. (1991). Möglichkeiten und Probleme eines internationalen Schutzprogrammes für den Wachtelkönig. [Opportunities and problems for an international management programme for the Corncrake]. *Vogelwelt* 112 (1–2), 108–16. (In German with English summary).

Schäffer, N. (1994). Methoden zum Nachweis von Bruten des Wachtelkönigs *Crex crex*. *Vogelwelt* 115, 69–73.

Schäffer, N. (1995a). Rufverhalten und funktion des rufens beim wachtelkönig *Crex crex*. [Calling behaviour and functions of calls in the Corncrake *Crex crex*]. *Vogelwelt* 116, 141–151.

Schäffer, N. (1995b). Corncrake *Crex crex* investigation in Northeast Poland in 1994. Cambridge: BirdLife International.

Schäffer, N. and Green, R. E. (1997). Etappen des Wachtelkonigschutzes. *Vogelwelt* 118, 115–117.

Schäffer, N. and Lanz, U. (1997). Aufruf zur Erfassung von Wachtelkönig - Vorkommen in Deutschland. [Call for survey of Corncrakes in Germany]. *Vogelwelt* 118, 248–250.

Schäffer, N. and Weisser, W. W. (1996). Modell für den Schutz des Wachtelkönigs *Crex crex*. [A strategy for the conservation of the corncrake *Crex crex*]. *Journal of Ornithology* 137, 53–75. doi: https://doi.org/10.1007/BF01651499 (In German with English summary).

Schlemmer, R. (2001). Wachtelkönig - Schutzkonzept für den Inneren Bayerischen Wald. 23pp. Gutachten im Auftrag des Naturparks Bayerischer Wald e. V,. Regensburg.

Schmid, H. and Maumary, L. (1996). Die Situation des Wachtelkönigs *Crex crex* in der Schweiz und im Fürstentum Liechtenstein 1970–1994. [The status of the corncrake *Crex crex* in Switzerland and Liechtenstein 1970–1994]. *Der Ornithologische Beobachter* 93, 169–175.

Schneider-Jacoby, M. (1991). Verbreitung und Bestand des Wachtelkönigs in Jugoslawien. [Distribution and size of the Corncrake population in Yugoslavia]. *Vogelwelt* 112, 48–57. (In German with English summary).

Schneider-Jacoby, M. (2010). Dabarsko polje, značajno područje za kosca (*Crex crex*) u Bosni i Hercegovini. *Bilten Mreže posmatrača ptica u Bosni i Hercegovini* 6, 61–62.

Schröder, K., Schikore, T., Eikhorst, W., Koffijberg, K. and Richter, M. (2007). Verbreitung, Bestand und Habitatwahl des Wachtelkönigs (*Crex crex*) in Niedersachsen und Bremen - Ergebnisse einer landesweiten Erfassung im Jahr 2004 sowie Aufarbeitung und Analyse der Bestandsentwicklung und Schutzsituation. Vogelkdl. Ber. Niedersachs. 39, 1–38.

Searle, R. F. C. (1970). Corn Crake (R198). WBC News, 70 p 10.

Sekulic, G. (2011). Corncrake *Crex crex* in Serbia. *Ciconia* 20, 28–45. (In Serbian).

Šere, D. (1994). Kosec *Crex crex*. *Acrocephalus* 15 p 55.

Sheppard, R. and Green, R. E. (1994). Status of the Corncrake in Ireland in 1993. *Irish Birds* 5 (2), 125–138.

Shvets, O. V. and Brysgalina, E. A. (2000). Some data on the Corncrake in Tula region. In: Mischenko, A. L. (ed.).

Corncrake in European Russia, Collection of Scientific Papers, Series Threatened Birds, Vol. 2, pp. 127–128. Moscow: RBCU. (In Russian).

Skulov, N. I. (2000). Project 'Watching to corncrace'. [sic]. In: Mischenko, A. L. (ed.). *Corncrake in European Russia, Collection of Scientific Papers, Series Threatened Birds, Vol. 2*, pp. 110–112. Moscow: RBCU. (In Russian).

Sothmann, L. (1991). Biologie, Status und Schutz des Wachtelkönigs. [Biology, status and conservation of Corncrakes]. *Vogelwelt* 112, 2–6.

Stattersfield, A. J. and Capper, D. R. (eds.) (2000). *Threatened Birds of the World*. Barcelona: BirdLife International, Lynx Edicions.

Stiefel, A. (1991). Situation des Wachtelkönigs in Ostdeutschland (vormalige DDR). [Situation of the Corncrake in East Germany (former DDR)]. *Vogelwelt* 112, 57–66.

Stowe, T. J. and Hudson, A. V. (1991b). Corncrakes outside the breeding grounds, and ideas for a conservation strategy. *Vogelwelt* 112, 103–107.

Stowe, T. J. and Tonkin, J. M. (1985). Conservation requirements of Corncrakes in South Uist, Western Isles. Unpublished report to Nature Conservancy Council. Sandy: RSPB

Streesse, U. P. (1972). Der Wachtelkönig (*Crex crex*) im Hamburger Raum. Hamburger Avifaunistische Beiträge, Band 10. Hamburg.

Stroud, J. (1986). The status and conservation of the Corncrake on Islay 1985. In: Galbraith, C. A. (ed.), *The Third Argyll Report*, pp. 89–92. Argyll Bird Club.

Stutchbury, B. J. M., Tarof, S. A., Done, T., Gow, E., Kramer, P. M., Tautin, J., Fox, J. W. and Afanasyev, V. (2009). Tracking long-distance songbirds migration by using geolocators. *Science* 323 p 896. Https://jstor.org/stable/20403063

Sukhanova, O. V. (1997). Determination of agricultural and grazing influence to Corncrake key areas in Central Russia. Report Manuscript.

Sukhanova, O. V. (2000). Survey methods on the Corncrake Project in 1995–1996. In: Mischenko, A. L. (ed.). *Corncrake in European Russia, Collection of Scientific Papers, Series Threatened Birds, Vol. 2*, pp. 29–40. Moscow: RBCU. (In Russian).

Sukhanova, O. V. and Mischenko, A. L. (2000). Corncrake in Moscow, Vladimir and Smolensk regions. In: Mischenko, A. L. (ed.). *Corncrake in European Russia, Collection of Scientific Papers, Series Threatened Birds, Vol. 2*, pp. 88–97. Moscow: RBCU. (In Russian).

Sundberg, J. (1989). Kornknarr med avvikande läte. *Vår fågelvärld* 48 p 91.

Sutherland, W. J. (1994). How to help the Corncrake. *Nature* 372 p 223.

Szabó, D. Z. and Demeter, L. (2004). Corncrake in the Gheorgheni and Ciuc Basins in Romania. *Migrans* 6, 4.

Tatai, S. (2009). A haris (*Crex crex*) védelme Györ-Moson-Sopron megyében. Szélkiáltó. 14 p. 25.

Taylor, P. B. (1996). Family Rallidae (rails, gallinules and coots). In: del Hoyo, J., Elliott, A. and Sargatal, J. (eds.), *Handbook of the Birds of the World: Vol. 3 Hoatzin to Auks*, pp. 108–209. Barcelona: Lynx Edicions.

Taylor, P. B. (2000a). The distribution, status and habitat requirements of the corncrake *Crex crex* in Central and Southern Africa: Report on a study visit to Zimbabwe and Zambia, December 1999-January 2000. Pietermaritzburg: University of Natal. (Unpublished report for the RSPB).

Taylor, P. B. (2000b). The status and conservation of globally threatened rails in wetland and grassland habitats of Zambia and Zimbabwe: Report on a study visit to Zimbabwe and Zambia, December 1999-January 2000. Pietermaritzburg: University of Natal. (Unpublished report for the RSPB).

Thom, V. M. (1986). *Birds in Scotland*. Calton, UK: Poyser.

Thorup, O. (1999b). Engsnarrens *Crex crex* yngleforhold I kulturlandskabet, og artens fortid, nutid og eventuelle fremtid I Denmark. Dansk. Orn. Foren. Tidsskr. 93, 71–81.

Tkachenko, A. A. (2000). K ekologii korostelja (*Crex crex* L.) Na Charkovschtschine. Ptizi basseina Sewerskogo Donza 6–7, 59–60.

Tomialojc, L. (1994). Corncrake *Crex crex*. pp. 228–229. In: Tucker, G. M. and Heath, M. F. *Birds in Europe: Their Conservation Status*. BirdLife Conservation Series No. 3. Cambridge, UK: BirdLife International.

Tout, P. (1995). The status and distribution of Corncrakes (*Crex crex*) during 1995 in Friuli-Venezia Giulia (Northeast Italy). Unpublished report for the Osservatorio Faunistico, Province of Udine.

Trontelj, P. (1997a). Distribution and habitat of the Corn Crake (*Crex crex*) at the Upper Soča basin (Julian Alps, Slovakia). *Annales* 11, 65–72.

Uhl, H. and Engleder, T. (2011). Artenschutzprogramm Wachtelkönig in Oberösterreich. Projektbericht 2011. Unpublished. Bericht im Auftrag des Landes Oberösterreich, Linz, Österreich.

Van der Straaten, J. (1968). Kwartelkoningen (*Crex crex*) langs de grote rivieren. *Limosa* 41 (3) p 150. Http://limosa.nou.nu/limosa_search2.php (In Dutch).

Van Dijk, A. J. (1998a). De Kwartelkoning *Crex crex* in Drenthe: terug van weggeweest. *Drentse Vogels* 11, 11–20.

Van Dijk, A. J. (1998b). Kwartelkoning *Crex crex* onder mijn raam: over trefkansen van roepende mannetjes. *Drentse Vogels* 11, 21–23.

Van Weperen, M. (2009). Habitat selection of the Corncrake (*Crex crex*) in floodplains along the Dutch Rhine river branches, MSc thesis, Radboud Universiteit, Nijmegen.

Vaurie, C. (1965). *The Birds of the Palaearctic Fauna: Non-passeriformes*. London: Witherby.

Végvári, Z. (2008). Corn Crake. In: Hadarics, T. and Zalai, T. (eds.), *Nomenclator Avium Hungariae,* p. 97. Budapest: Birdlife Hungary.

Vlček, J. and Peške, L. (2017). Prostorová aktivita mláděte chřástala polního (*Crex crex*) na hnízdišti na Šumavě. [Spatial activity of a juvenile Corncrake (*Crex crex*) at the breeding site in the Šumava Mts]. Sylvia 53, 58–64. Https://www.birdlife.cz/wp-content/uploads/2017/12/Sylvia53_4Vlcek.pdf (In Czech with English abstract and summary).

Von Transehe, N. (1965). Die Schnarrwachtel *Crex crex* [C. Pratensis]. In: von Transehe, N. (ed.), *Die Vögelwelt Lettlands,* pp. 158–159. Hannover-Döhren: Verlag Harro von Hirschheydt.

Wahlin, B. J. O. (1944). Kornknarren (*Crex crex* L.) Pa Gotland. *Fauna och Flora* 39, 69–73.

Wamiti, W. and Muigai, F. (2005). Corncrake records from Mpala Ranch and South Kinangop. *Nature Africa* 35, 19–21.

Weid, R. (1991). The Corncrake in intensively used meadows in Franconia. *Vogelwelt* 112 (1–2), 90–96. (In German with English summary).

Wernham, C. V., Toms, M. P., Marchant, J. H., Clarck, J. A., Siriwardena, G. M. and Baillie, S. R. (eds.) (2002). *The Migration Atlas: Movements of the Birds of Britain and Ireland*. London: Poyser.

Wettstein, W. (1999). Conservation status of the Corncrake (*Crex crex*) in Szatmár-Bereg (Eastern Hungary). Proceedings of the Second International Wildlife Management Congress 1999. Gödöllö, University of Agricultural Sciences, Hungary and the Wildlife Society, USA, p. 107.

Wettstein, W. (2002). *Population Structure, Dispersal and Migration of Corncrakes (Crex crex) in Europe*. Progress report, November 2002, Zurich University.

Wettstein, W. (2003). Conservation biology, population structure and large-scale spatial behaviour of corncrakes (*Crex crex* L.) In Europe. (Doctoral dissertation) University of Zurich, Switzerland.

Wettstein, W., Hobson, K. and Schmid, B. (2003). Tracing a vagabond: potential and limitations of indirect methods to estimate philopatry and migratory connectivity of Corncrakes *Crex crex*. In: Wettstein, W. (ed.), *Conservation Biology of Crex crex L.* PhD thesis, Berichte aus dem Institut für Umweltwissenschaften der Universität Zurich 6, pp. 87–105.

Whilde, A. (1977). A note on the Storm Petrel and Corncrake. *Irish University Review* 7 (1), 70–72. https://www.jstor.org/stable/25477155

Williams, J. G. (1977). *A Field Guide to the Birds of East Africa*. London: Collins.

Winden, P. De and Kurstjens, G. (1998). Recente broedgevallen van de Kwartelkoning in het Maasdal: de definitieve terugkeer in Limburg? *Limburgse Vogels* 9, 60–62.

Yudkin, A. M., Adam, A. M., Toropov, K. V., Shukov, V. S., Fomin, B. N., Pokrovskaja, I. V., Zybulin, S. M., Ananin, A. A., Panteleyev, P. A., Solovyev, S. A., Polushkin, D. M., Shor, E. L., Anufriev, V. M., Koslenko, A. B., Tertitzkij, G. M., Vachrushev, A. A. and Blinova, T. K. (1997). Number and distribution of corncrake and Aquatic Warbler in West Siberian Plain. *Siberian Ecology Journal* 4 (6), 631–634. (In Russian).

Zabelin, M. M. (2000). Corncrake in Tambov region. In: Mischenko, A. L. (ed.). *Corncrake in European Russia, Collection of Scientific Papers, Series Threatened Birds, Vol. 2*, pp. 136–138. Moscow: RBCU. (In Russian).

Zavjylov, E. B. and Tabachishin, B. G. (2000). Current status of the Corncrake population in Saratov region. In: Mischenko, A. L. (ed.). *Corncrake in European Russia, Collection of Scientific Papers, Series Threatened Birds, Vol. 2*, pp. 143–145. Moscow: RBCU. (In Russian).

Appendix 1: Scientific names of animals and plants mentioned in the book

Birds

African Crake	*Crex egregia* (or *Crecopsis egregia* in some texts)
African Hawk-eagle	*Aquila spilogaster*
Ash-throated Crake	*Porzana albicollis*
Barn Owl	*Tyto alba*
Black-shouldered Kite	*Elanus caeruleus*
Black Sparrowhawk	*Accipiter melanoleucus*
Black-headed Heron	*Ardea melanocephala*
Chough	*Pyrrhocorax pyrrhocorax*
Clapper Rail	*Rallus crepitans*
Corncrake	*Crex crex*
Common Cuckoo	*Cuculus canorus*
Common Quail	*Coturnix coturnix*
Crows	*Corvus* spp
Cuckoo	*Cuculus canorus*
Buzzard	*Buteo buteo*
Dark Chanting Goshawk	*Melierax metabates*
Grasshopper Warbler	*Locustella naevia*
Harrier	*Circus* spp
Hooded Crow	*Corvus corone*
Magpie	*Pica pica*
Eagle Owl	*Bubo bubo*
Extinct Rail	*Belgirallus minutus*
Extinct Rail	*Belgirallus oligocaenus*
Extinct Rail	*Creccoides osbornii*
Extinct Rail	*Eocrex primus*
Extinct Rail	*Palaeorallus troxelli*
Extinct Rail	*Rallicrex kolozsvarensis*
Extinct Rail	*Rallus phillipsi*,
Gull	*Larus* spp
Marsh Harrier	*Circus aeruginosus*
Montagu's Harrier	*Circus pygargus*
Nkulengu Rail	*Himantornis haematopus*
Raven	*Corvus corax*
Red Kite	*Milvus milvus*
River Warbler	*Locustella fluviatilis*
Spotted Crake	*Porzana porzana*
Tree Pipit	*Anthus trivialis*
Wahlberg's Eagle	*Hieraaetus wahlbergi*
Water Rail	*Rallus aquaticus*
White Stork	*Ciconia ciconia*
Wren	*Troglodytes troglodytes*

Mammals

American Mink	*Neovison vison*
Cat	*Felis catus*
Dog	*Canis familiaris*
European Polecat	*Mustela putorius*
Fennec Fox	*Vulpes zerda*
Ferret	*Mustela putorius furo*
Fox	*Vulpes vulpes*
Hedgehog	*Erinaceus europaeus*
Leopard	*Panthera pardus*
Otter	*Lutra lutra*
Racoon Dog	*Nyctereutes procyonoides*
Serval	*Leptailurus serval*
Stoat	*Mustela erminea*
Weasel	*Mustela nivalis*
Wild Boar	*Sus scrofa*

REPTILES

Boomslang	*Dispholidus typus*
Desert Monitor	*Varanus griseus*

AMPHIBIANS

Frog	*Anura* spp

INVERTEBRATES

Ant *Formicidae*	
Bacteria	*Campylobacter coli*
Bacteria	*Campylobacter jejuni*
Cockroach	*Blattodea*
Cranefly	*Tipulidae family*
Cricket	*Orthoptera*
Dragonfly	*Odonata*
Dung beetle	*Scarabaeoidea*
Earwig	*Dermaptera*
Eimeria	*Eimeria crecis*
Eimeria	*Eimeria nenei*
Flukeworm	*Prosthogonimus ovatus*
Grasshoppers and Crickets	*Orthoptera* spp
Hoverfly	*Syrphidae*
Leatherjacket	(see Cranefly)
Helminth species	*Brachylaima fuscata*
	Cardiofilaria pavlovskyi
	Dilepsis undulata
	Echinostoma revolutum
	Leucochloridium holostomum
	Prosthogonimus cuneatus
	Prosthogonimus ovatus
	Rallitaenia pyriformis
	Rallitaenia rallida
Parasitic fly	*Ornithomyia avicularia*
Termite	*Isoptera*
Weevil	*Sitona* spp

PLANTS

Alder	*Alnus glutinosa*
Acacia	*Acacia* spp
Alfalfa	*Medicago sativa*
Barberry	*Berberis* spp
Beard-grass	*Bothriochloa* spp
Birch	*Betula* spp
Bird Vetch	*Vicia cracca*
Black Pine	*Pinus nigra*
Borage	*Anchusa* spp
Broad-leaved Cottongrass	*Eriophorum latifolium*
Brown Bent grass	*Agrostis tenuis*
Butterbur	*Petasites hybridus*
Caraway	*Carum carvi*
Cock's-foot grass	*Dactylis glomerata*
Common Beech	*Fagus sylvatica*
Common Cat's-tail	*Phleum pratense*
Common Comfrey	*Symphytum officinale*
Common Cottongrass	*Eriophorum angustifolium*
Common Couch grass	*Agropyron repens*
Common Dogwood	*Cornus sanguinea*
Common Hawthorn	*Crataegus monogyna*
Common Hazel	*Corylus avellana*
Common Nettle	*Urtica dioica*
Common Reed	*Phragmites australis*
Compact Rush	*Juncus conglomeratus*
Cow Parsley	*Anthriscus sylvestris*
Creeping Bent	*Agrostis stolonifera*
Curly Dock	*Rumex crispus*
Elder	*Sambucus nigra*
European Hop-Hornbeam	*Ostrya carpinifolia*
European Spindle	*Euonymus europaeus*
False Oat-grass	*Arrhenatherum elatius*
Fescues	*Festuca* spp.
Goldenrod	*Solidago* spp
Gorse	*Ulex europaeus*
Great Mannagrass	*Glyceria maxima*
Hair Grass	*Setaria* spp
Hawthorn	*Crataegus* spp
Hogweed	*Heracleum sphondylium*
Honeysuckle	*Lonicera* spp
Jointgrass	*Hemarthria* spp
Lemongrass	*Cymbopogon* spp
Lovegrass	*Eragrostis* spp
Meadow Buttercup	*Ranunculus acris*
Meadow Fescue	*Festuca pratensis*
Meadow Foxtail	*Alopecurus pratensis*
Meadow-sweet	*Filipendula ulmaria*
Miombo	*Brachystegia* spp
Perennial Rye-grass	*Lolium perenne*
Poplar	*Populus* spp
Red Clover	*Trifolium pratense*
Reed	*Phragmites australis*
Reed Canary-grass	*Phalaris arundinacea*
Scots Pine	*Pinus sylvestris*
Sedges	*Carex* spp.
Seed-thrower Grass	*Sporobolus* spp
Sesame	*Sesamum indicum*
Signal Grass	*Urochloa* spp
Soft Rush	*Juncus effusus*

Scientific names of animals and plants mentioned in the book

Sorrel	*Rumex acetosa*	Wild Privet	*Ligustrum vulgare*
Thatching Grass	*Hyparrhenia* spp	Willow	*Salix* spp
Verbena	*Lantana* spp	Woodruff	*Galium odoratum*
Weeping Fig	*Ficus* spp	Yellow Iris	*Iris pseudacorus*
Whin	*Ulex europaeus*	Yellow Oat-grass	*Trisetum flavescens*
White Bedstraw	*Galium album*	Yellow-rattle	*Rhinanthus minor*
White Clover	*Trifolium repens*	Yorkshire-fog	*Holcus lanatus*

APPENDIX 2: NAMES FOR *CREX CREX*

VERNACULAR NAMES (ENGLISH-LANGUAGE) (GREENOAK, 1997)

Bean Cracker (South Pembroke); Bean Crake (South Pembroke); Corn Drake (North Riding); Corn Rake (Yorkshire); Corncrake; Crake Gallinule; Cracker (North Shropshire); Craker (North Shropshire); Creck (North Shropshire); Daker (Surrey); Daker-hen (Westmorland); Gadwell Drake; Gallinule Crake; Gorse Duck; Grass Drake (West Riding); Grass Quail (Cheshire); Hay Crake (Yorkshire); Land Drake (Shropshire); Land Hen (Shropshire); Land Rail; Meadow Crake; Meadow Drake (Nottinghamshire); Rape-scrape (West Country).

VERNACULAR NAMES (SCOTS GAELIC) (DWELLY, 1973)

Cearrsach; Cleabhar caoch; Eun rap; Garra gart; Traghna; Traineach; Troghnadh; Traon; Traona; Traonach; Traonachan; Trean-ri-trean; Treanaire; Treona; Treubhna; Treun-ri-treun; Treunna.

VERNACULAR NAMES (SCOTS) (ROBINSON, 1985; HULL, 2001)

Corn Scrack; Corncraik; Corncrake; Cornecrake; Craik; Craker; Daker; King of the Quail; Land Rail; Quailzie; Skirlcraik; Skirlcrake; Skirlie.

SELECTED NAMES IN SELECTED OTHER LANGUAGES (ROBINSON, 2005; TAYLOR AND KIRWAN, 2020)

Albanian:	Mbreti i shkurtës	**Danish:**	Engsnarre
Asturian:	Guiyu de Parpayueles	**Dutch:**	Kwartelkoning
Basque:	Giloi	**English:**	Corncrake
Catalan:	Guàtlera maresa	**Estonian:**	Rukkirääk
Chinese:	长脚秧鸡	**Faroese:**	Akurskritt
Cornish:	Crekyar	**French:**	Râle des genêts
Croatian:	Kosac	**Finnish:**	Ruisrääkkä
Czech:	Chřástal polní	**German:**	Wachtelkönig

Hungarian:	Haris	**Portuguese:**	Codornizão
Icelandic:	Engirella	**Romanian:**	Cristel de câmp
Irish:	Traonach	**Russian:**	Коростель
Italian:	Re di quaglie	**Scots Gaelic:**	Traon
Japanese:	Uzurakuina ウズラクイナ	**Serbian:**	Prdavac
Latvian:	Grieze	**Slovak:**	Chrapkáč poľný
Lithuanian:	Bręslė, Paprastoji griežle	**Slovenian:**	Kosec
Luxembourgish:	Wuechtelkinnek	**Spanish:**	Guión de Codornices
Maltese:	Gàllozz Ahmar	**Swahili:**	Kiluwiri wa Ulaya
Manx:	Eean Raip	**Swedish:**	Kornknarr
Moldavian:	Cristel de câmp	**Turkish:**	Bildircin Kılavuzu
Montenegrin:	Kosac	**Ukrainian:**	Деркач лучний
Norwegian:	Åkerrikse	**Welsh:**	Rhegen yr Yd
Polish:	Derkacz		

Appendix 3: Numbers of calling males Corncrakes in Britain and Isle of Man 1978–2014

Region	Area	1978–79	1988	1993	1994	1995	1996	1997	1998	1999	2000
Shetland	Total	3–5	1	3	–	–	–	–	4	–	–
Orkney	Total	102–105	29–36	6	20	39	43	21	13	15	11
Outer Hebrides	Lewis	31–38	66–76	106	89	96	104	114	77	50	55
	Harris	7	5	4	7	8	5	5	3	4	3
	Berneray	5	1–2	2	0	0	1	4	2	2	1
	North Uist	75	56–59	66	51	53	66	78	73	66	66
	Benbec-ula	33	22–23	17	19	23	27	45	41	36	31
	South Uist	83	91–100	50	49	58	81	62	65	101	98
	Barra & Vatersay	26–28	59	26	40	44	58	74	47	46	56
	Pabbay & Mingulay	–	–	0–	–	–	–	–	0	–	–
Inner Hebrides	Skye	31–34	26–28	8	9	9	21	23	12	16	23
	Canna	9	1–2	3	2	0	0	0	2	0	0
	Rum	1–2	0	1	0	0	0	0	0	0	0
	Eigg	4–6	0	1	2	0	0	0	0	0	0
	Muck	4	0	1	1	0	0	0	0	0	3
	Coll	28	20	20	25	37	40	42	40	48	53
	Tiree	85	99–103	111	126	140	117	136	136	144	153
	Mull	1	2–3	1	1	0	0	0	2	2	0
	Iona	25	3	4	3	4	5	8	12	13	9
	Treshnish Isles & Lunga	1	0	2	–	–	–	–	3	–	–
	Colonsay & Oron-say	22	14–18	10	6	9–12	8	8	14	21	21
	Islay	22–24	19	9	13	14	7	17	4	7	8
	Jura	1	1	0	–	–	–	–	0	–	–
	Gigha	1	4	0	–	–	–	–	0	–	–
	McCor-maig Isles	0	0	1	–	–	–	–	0	–	–